Children and Pensions

Children and Pensions

Alessandro Cigno and Martin Werding

CESifo Book Series

The MIT Press
Cambridge, Massachusetts
London, England

For information about special quantity discounts, please email special_sales@mitpress.mit.edu

This book was set in Palatino on 3B2 by Asco Typesetters, Hong Kong.
Printed and bound in the United States of America.

Library of Congress Cataloging-in-Publication Data

Cigno, Alessandro.
Children and pensions / Alessandro Cigno and Martin Werding.
    p.   cm. — (CESifo book series)
Includes bibliographical references and index.
ISBN 978-0-262-03369-5 (hardcover : alk. paper)
1. Family allowances. 2. Social security. 3. Family demography—Economic aspects.
4. Child welfare. I. Werding, Martin. II. Title.
HD4925.C55   2007
331.25′2—dc22   2007001910

10 9 8 7 6 5 4 3 2 1

Contents

List of Figures

List of Tables

CESifo Book Series in Economic Policy

This volume is part of the CESifo Book Series in Economic Policy. Each book in the series aims to cover a topical policy issue in economics. The monographs reflect the research agenda of the Ifo Institute for Economic Research and they are typically "tandem projects" where internationally renowned economists from the CESifo network cooperate with Ifo researchers. The monographs have been anonymously refereed and revised after being presented and discussed at several workshops hosted by the Ifo Institute.

Hans-Werner Sinn

Acknowledgments

This book has benefited from comments by Massimo Livi-Bacci, Junsen Zhang, participants in two CESifo workshops held in Munich in May 2002 and May 2003, and four anonymous referees. Responsibility for any remaining errors and infelicities rests with the authors.

The authors gratefully acknowledge the support of CESifo—the joint international platform of the University of Munich's Center for Economic Studies (CES) and the Ifo Institute for Economic Research—and of Hans-Werner Sinn, who first suggested the project to us.

Introduction

This book bears the same title as the presidential address that the first author gave to the 1991 meeting of the European Society of Population Economics. That lecture sparked off a number of independent investigations by a number of authors including the present ones—what might be loosely called an uncoordinated research program. The results are summarized in the present book. The focus of the lecture was a North–South divide:

> ...the population of the world can be divided into...those who starve and those who diet. To this one could add that...where there are people who starve there is also a population explosion problem,...where there are people who worry about their waistline the problem is population ageing. (Cigno 1992)

That divide has not disappeared. If anything, it has become deeper. But a new one has appeared, or become more apparent, within the ranks of developed countries. While some of these countries, notably the United States of America, have well-balanced age structures and relatively stable populations, others, notably Japan and most of the countries that form the European Union, are aging rapidly (the same can be said about several developing countries, including China). Were it not for immigration, the populations of this second group of countries would now be shrinking, or doing so faster than they are already. In older days, that would have worried their national governments for its defense implications. Nowadays, it worries them more for what it does to public pensions. Aging does reduce the number of those who make pension contributions relative to those who draw pension benefits. But relative numbers are only part of the problem.

What ultimately matters for a pay-as-you-go pension scheme, as all public ones essentially are, is the total contributive capacity of future generations, hence total income growth. Now there is an obvious connection between age structure and population growth. Is there also one between youthfulness and per-capita income growth? *The Economist* does not appear to have doubts. Its August 2002 front cover shows a heavily pregnant Statue of Liberty look-alike busily knitting stars-and-stripes socks, and a flat-capped old man, easily identifiable as Europe, warily turning his back on the young lady. The lead article breezily associates age structure with productivity, and talks of the severe problems that "Old Europe" is having in keeping pace with "Young America." But why? The fact that two phenomena occur in the same place at more or less the same time does not mean that one is the cause of the other. Indeed, since both demographic and economic growth are the result of individual actions, one should look upstream for the factors that lead individuals to behave in that way.

Cigno (1992) put forward the hypothesis that the very high fertility typical of developing countries could in some measure be ascribed to the absence of well-developed financial markets and public pension systems. That hypothesis seemed justified in the light of evidence available at the time, and has been amply vindicated by subsequent empirical findings concerning both developed and developing countries. The present book takes the argument further by postulating that differences in fertility, and productivity growth, between the United States, on the one hand, and the European Union and Japan, on the other, can be ascribed in some measure to differences not only in public pension coverage but also in the design of pension and other age-related transfers. This is not to say that there are no other important reasons for the different demographic and economic performances of these countries. Given, however, that there is great public concern about the consequences of low fertility and slow productivity growth for the financial viability of public pension systems, it is particularly interesting to look at the way pension policy affects fertility decisions and productivity growth.

In the present book, we present theoretical arguments to the effect that public pension coverage per se (i.e., apart from any forced intergenerational transfer that might be associated with it) can reduce aggregate fertility and raise aggregate household saving. We also argue theoretically that public pensions and other age-related transfers, as they are currently designed, discourage private investment in the human capital of future adults and hence hamper productivity growth. There is firm evidence that public pension coverage does reduce the fertility rate and increase the household saving rate. By contrast, the evidence regarding the effect on productivity growth is limited and contradictory. Whether this possibly negative effect is large enough to outweigh the positive one via increased saving is an empirical question to which we do not yet have a conclusive answer.

A reason why the United States has a relatively young population, we argue, is that they have always had a "light" public pension system, and took action to make it even lighter the moment growth begun to falter. Does it follow that Europe and Japan should do the same? To some extent they are doing it already—albeit less promptly, and starting from a much higher point than the United States—and this is beginning to help pension finances. But cutting pension systems back is neither the only, nor necessarily the best, way to make them viable. Furthermore the financial health of existing institutions cannot be the ultimate object of policy. The latter should be judged by what it does for social welfare, not for whether it allows existing institutions to survive. This brings us to the question, Why have a public pension system in the first place?

If the number and earning ability of the members of each generation were independent of the actions taken by the members of the previous generation, the justification for having a public pension system would be essentially public compassion in the face of moral hazard. A compassionate society cannot avoid helping the old and destitute who cannot help themselves. Knowing that, however, working-age persons close to the poverty line have no interest in saving because this would not bring them any appreciable return in terms of old age consumption. A possible remedy to the problem is a compulsory pension system designed to provide everyone with a safety net (a flat-rate benefit) in old age financed by a levy on the income of all working-age individuals. That scheme is what has come to be known as a *Beveridgean* pension system, after William Beveridge, the British scholar who was influential in the design and introduction of such a system in the United Kingdom at the end of the Second World War.

Fertility and earning ability of a generation are not exogenous, however. They depend on actions taken by members of the previous generation, which were in turn influenced by government policy. Although individual fertility is subject to many random influences, there is evidence that aggregate fertility changes are explained by changes in the structure of the incentives that condition individual behavior. By reducing the weight of unwanted pregnancies in realized fertility, the diffusion of modern contraceptive technology since the late 1960s has strengthened the argument for treating the fertility rate as the outcome of deliberate choice. There is indeed evidence that the contraceptive revolution has made fertility more responsive to policy. A person's earning ability also is subject to many random factors. There too the probability of a favorable outcome increases with education. The outcome thus depends in part on decisions taken by that person's parents.

If the benefits of having an extra child or investing in the human capital of existing children accrued entirely to the parents, the endogeneity of the size and earning ability of each generation would not justify public intervention other than for equitative purposes. But suppose that the benefit of an extra child, or of an increase in the future earning ability of existing children, does not go entirely to the parents, not even through the pleasure that they derive from seeing their children do well. There is then an argument for transferring these "external" benefits to the parents so that they can be induced to produce the socially desirable number of children, and to undertake the efficient level of educational investment. Conventional child benefits can be seen as a way of internalizing the external effect of fertility, educational subsidies as a means of internalizing that of educational investment. Conventional pension benefits do not serve either of these purposes.

The problem is that age-related benefits, in particular, pensions, were originally designed without a full understanding of their incentive effects. Although recent research has dealt quite extensively with that, the public debate about pension reform is still largely concerned with other issues. Low fertility still tends to be regarded pretty much in the same fashion as global warming—something to be deprecated but about which there is precious little governments are able or willing to do. Parental investment in their children's human capital does not come into the picture at all. There is more. In addition to taking demographic trends as essentially exogenous ("the demographics are known"), and overlooking any possible link between pensions and parental investment in their children's human capital, much of the current debate appears to assume that individual actions are coordinated only by the market, and that public pensions are invariably of the Beveridgean type. What is wrong with making these two additional assumptions?

Let us start with the first one. In a Beveridge-style scheme there is either no link, or a very weak one, between what a person puts in and what she gets out. Even if individuals pay something called a pension contribution, it is an income tax in all but name. Such a tax introduces a wedge between the marginal product of labor and the take-home wage rate. As this reduces the opportunity-cost of leisure, and of any other activity alternative to making money, the existence of a Beveridgean pension scheme reduces the supply of labor, hence per-capita income. That is not necessarily true, however, of what is called a Bismarckian pension scheme (after Chancellor Otto von Bismarck, who first introduced it in newly united Germany in the second half of the nineteenth century), where individual pension entitlements are closely related to individual pension contributions. If such a scheme is actuarially fair (i.e., if the expected value of lifetime pension benefits is equal, at the date of retirement, to the capitalized value of pension contributions), the money that an individual is obliged to pay into his personal pension account is not a tax, but delayed wages. Unless the individual is credit rationed, there is then no pension-induced tax wedge, and no distortion of the work–leisure decision.

Bismarckian pensions distort labor decisions only insofar and inasmuch as the scheme is not actuarially fair. Suppose, for example, that the expected value of a person's pension benefits is lower than the value of the contributions made, capitalized at the relevant market interest rates. Obliging anyone to participate in such a scheme is equivalent to imposing a tax on him. If contributions increase with earnings, this tax discourages labor. But only the difference between capitalized contributions and expected benefits, not the whole of the contributions paid, is a tax on labor. Conversely, if a person gets out of the system more than she puts in, the difference between benefits and contributions is a subsidy rather than a tax, and the distortion is then in the sense of too much rather than too little labor. It is thus curious that politicians, industrialists, and practical economists talk so much of the "disincentive to work" effect of public pensions, even where their country has an essentially Bismarckian system, and the latter is close to being actuarially fair to the average citizen.

Let us now look at the second assumption, namely that the market is the only spontaneous coordination mechanism. This is patently false. Families play a major role in the coordination of individual decisions regarding reproduction and private intergenerational transfers. Informal intrafamily arrangements have disadvantages in comparison with nationwide schemes but also advantages. One advantage is information. Individuals face a lower cost of acquiring information regarding the actions and characteristics of other members of the same family than the market or any public authority does. This means that moral hazard and adverse selection problems are less severe in a family than in a state- or market-based scheme. Furthermore intrafamily arrangements can deliver personal services for which neither the market nor the public sector can provide perfect substitutes. The disadvantages have to do with risk-spreading and risk-pooling, and with contract enforcement. Weighing advantages and disadvantages, the optimal (second-best) policy is likely to leave space for informal intrafamily arrangements.

Another subject of heated political debate, at least in Europe, is the statutory age of retirement. Since all public pension schemes are essentially pay-as-you-go, it is quite obvious that if a man is expected to live 78 years, rather than 68 like his father, but both retire at the age of 63, the former will likely have to be supported by others for three times as many years as the latter. Therefore, given a fixed age of retirement, rising life expectancy affects the balance sheet of a public pension scheme in much the same way as falling fertility. But longevity is a "problem" only because there is a statutory age of retirement. If people were not obliged (or permitted) to retire at an age when they could still be producing income, a rise in life expectancy could only increase social welfare.

There is another consideration to be made. Life expectancy is influenced by individual choice (eating habits, life-style, recourse to medical care, etc.) as well as government policy. In a general sense, mortality is as endogenous as fertility. In developed countries, however, the policy measures that directly or indirectly affect mortality are primarily those related to public health. Only an unrealistically large cut in pensions or child-related transfers would have a noticeable effect on mortality. As this book is primarily about age-related transfers in developed economies, we will treat life expectancy as exogenous to the policy decision. This does not imply that life expectancy is less important than fertility, only that it goes its own way.

The first four chapters of this book are essentially description, an orderly exposition of facts through a variety of statistical artifacts. Although the book is not intended to be country specific, the factual information provided regards essentially the three so far more important economic areas of the world: the European Union, Japan, and the United States of America. Of the European Union, we only look in detail at the four larger countries—France, Germany, Italy, and the United Kingdom—plus Sweden, which has interesting features of its own. The subsequent three chapters are of analysis, theoretical and empirical, positive and normative. Their purpose is not to present new findings, but to use the results of frontier research to inform the public debate. Technicality is kept to a minimum, and the limited mathematical analysis is always illustrated verbally and diagrammatically. The final chapter uses recent econometric estimates of the effects of pensions and child benefits on savings and fertility behavior in Germany as a laboratory for simulating the consequences of the policies under discussion. The Conclusion pulls together the different threads and advances a reform proposal. Chapters 5 through 7 are directed essentially at economists, but the rest of the book should be accessible to a wider public.

1   Demography

Demography accounts for a good deal of the looming public pension crisis. To illustrate the pressure that demographic trends are placing on current systems of old-age provision we first look at the past development of birth rates, and then at the population structure that is expected to arise from these developments in the United States, the European Union, and Japan.

1.1   Fertility

Most industrialized countries have experienced a fertility decline since the late nineteenth or early twentieth century. This secular trend was interrupted by a short-lived upswing, the so-called baby boom, in the aftermath of World War II, followed by an accelerated decline during the late 1960s or early 1970s. Very recently fertility has recovered to a limited extent in some countries but not in others. The few exceptions are given by the relatively small countries of northern Europe (where, however, it is still not clear whether the new pattern will persist), but most notably by the United States, which is today the world's most obvious demographic outlier.

Figure 1.1 shows the postwar pattern of fertility in the countries considered in this book.[1] The fertility measure adopted is the *total fertility rate* (the total number of children a woman would have if, in each year between age 15 and 44, she had as many children as all women of the same age have had in a given calendar year). Unlike the crude birth-rate (live births per head of population in a given year), the total fertility rate is independent of population age and sex structure, so the latter is appropriate for making comparisons across different countries as well as over time. The variable that the theoretical economist mostly has in mind is completed fertility (the number of children that a

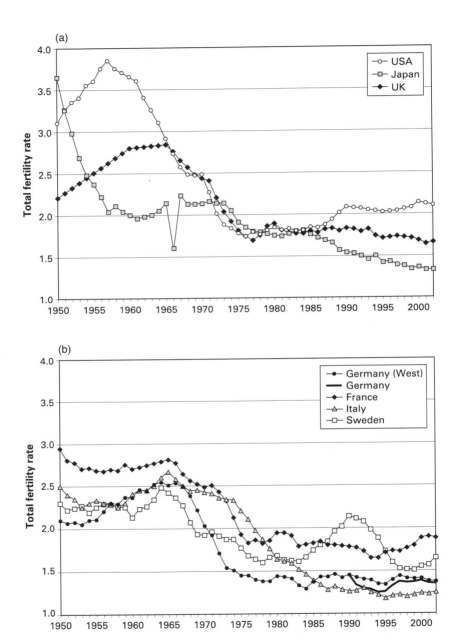

Figure 1.1
Total fertility rates in major industrialized countries.

woman actually has over her entire reproductive cycle), but completed cohort fertility can be calculated only ex post, which means it is available only for older cohorts. If cohort fertility is changing, or if the timing of births is shifting over time, total fertility rates can deviate from the series of relevant completed fertility rates in one way or another. In steady state, however, the total fertility rate coincides with completed cohort fertility. Over a long period of time, total fertility thus tends to behave like cohort fertility.

The pattern of variation in fertility rates turns out to be the same everywhere, but the precise timing and size of upswings and downswings varies from country to country. In the United States the baby boom occurred a little earlier, and peaked at a much higher level (3.85 births per woman in 1957) than in Europe (where fertility reached a maximum in the mid-1960s at between 2.3 and 2.8 births per woman). The fertility decline has been sharpest in Japan, where the total fertility rate has fallen from more than 4.5 births per woman in the late 1940s, to the current 1.3.[2] On the other hand, there are countries where the decline has not been so sharp, but the current fertility level (1.2 in Italy) is even lower than in Japan.

Over the past decade total fertility rates have been largely stable at levels ranging between more than 2.0 (United States) and less than 1.4 (Germany, Japan, and Italy). The only exception among the countries considered is Sweden, where the fertility rate fluctuated between a remarkable 2.1 in 1990, and 1.6 at the time of writing.

It is worth keeping in mind that in industrialized countries a total fertility rate of about 2.1 is needed to keep the population size and age structure unchanged over time. This "replacement level" of fertility provides us with a useful benchmark because it tells us how many births are required to maintain a certain population constant in the long run by means other than migration. This benchmark does not have any particular appeal from a normative point of view. It is nonetheless interesting to note that even during the baby boom, fertility in many European countries never went above its replacement level by as much as it has now fallen short of it. If current fertility trends continue, European populations will consequently tend to shrink, and the average citizen to grow older and older.

By contrast, if the past fertility trend persists, aging will affect the US population only temporarily, when the large cohort of the baby boomers finally enters retirement. Japan faces two problems at once: large age cohorts approaching retirement as in the United States,[3] and long-term fertility decline as in most of Europe. This country is thus likely to be the most severely affected by changes in age structure.

1.2   Population Projections

What will happen to population structures 25 or 50 years from now is conditioned by what has happened to fertility rates since World War II. But, if we want to predict future age structures, we must take into account also a number of other demographic phenomena. First, it is clear that immigration can offset fertility decline. That is very much the case in the United States and, to a lesser extent, Germany. Second, life expectancy has gone up particularly sharply in Japan, and is expected to do so also in the other countries considered. This too will affect future age structures. Third, age structures over the next 25 (or even 50) years will be affected by the number of children born from now on, and these numbers are sensitive to current policy.

1.2.1   Projected Age Structures

The long-term projections that demographers provide are built on a small set of assumptions, covering trends in fertility, mortality, and net migration.[4] As a rule, it is assumed either that the past trend of a variable will continue or its present level will remain unchanged.[5] Migration is usually seen as the main source of uncertainty, and dealt with by imagining alternative scenarios. Where life expectancy at birth over the next 25 to 50 years is concerned, the usual assumption is that it will continue to increase in the countries under consideration at modest speed (by about one year per decade in most "baseline" or "middle" scenarios). Fertility rates are now generally assumed to stay constant even in countries where they are particularly low.

The problem with making predictions on the basis of this kind of assumptions is that, in reality, fertility, migration, and even mortality are either a direct result of or conditioned by a multiplicity of human actions. Since the latter respond to changes in the economic environment, including changes in economic policies, assuming no change or extrapolating past trends is equivalent to assuming that the environment will either not change or continue to develop the way it has done in the past. Be that as it may, we proceed now to present projections of population age structures over the next 50 years based on the very assumptions we have just questioned. These demographer's projections should be interpreted as predictions of what would happen *if* the economic environment—in particular, the policies that can be expected to have a more direct impact on reproductive behavior—were to remain unchanged for the next 50 years. Subsequent chapters of this book are dedicated to a discussion of how those policies should be changed, if we wanted those projections to look different.

A standard way of representing the sex and age structure of a population at a given point in time is to display the data in the form of a so-called population pyramid. That expression is actually a little outdated. A pyramid—with many young people at the bottom, fewer and fewer people as we go up the age scale—is what one would get if the population had been growing for several decades without ever encountering shocks such as wars, epidemics, or periods of extreme economic hardship or uncertainty. For industrialized countries one would have to go back to before World War I to find something like a true population pyramid. After a century that included the Great Depression, several periods of hyperinflation, two periods of global war, and last, but not least, a strong fertility swing, the age structure of the countries we are considering now looks more like a fir tree. Structures projected for the future look like pineapples, or even mushrooms.

Figure 1.2 compares the outcome of official population projections for the year 2050 with the population structures observed in the year 2000 for the seven countries under consideration. To improve comparability with the United States in terms of population size, we also provide information regarding the whole of the pre-2004 fifteen-country European Union (EU-15). The data are taken from US Bureau of Census (2000, "middle series"), Japanese National Institute of Population and Social Security Research (2002, "medium variant"), and Eurostat (2000, "baseline scenario").[6]

Starting from a current level of about 275 million people, US population is predicted to grow across all age brackets over the next five decades, reaching a total of 404 million in 2050. In the course of this development, the signs of fertility decline (the "trunk" of the current tree-like structure) will disappear, but growth will be much stronger for older age cohorts. The reason is simply that the baby boomers, now in their 40s and 50s, will become older in the course of the projection period. Since, all over the world, women tend to live longer than men, upper bars representing numbers in the year 2050 pop out of the left of the figure, indicating a substantial surplus of females over males in the "90+" group. Despite this detail the center of gravity of the diagram is

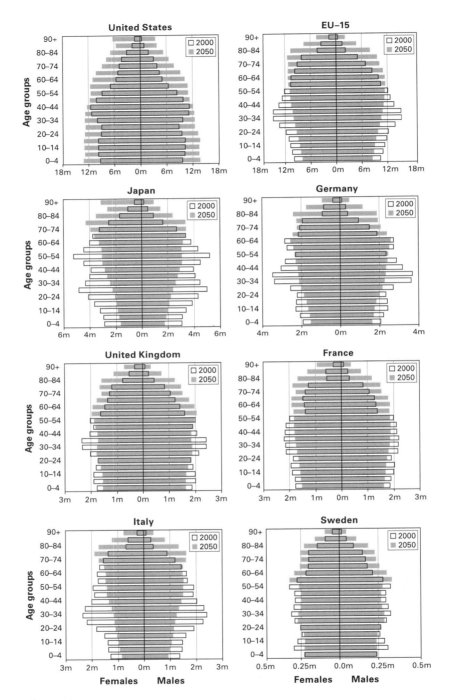

Figure 1.2
Population pyramids, 2000 and 2050.

much closer to the bottom in 2050 than in 2000, or at either date in any of the other countries. The median age is predicted to be 38 in the year 2050, as against 35 in the year 2000.

By contrast, the total EU-15 population, now 376 million people, is projected to shrink to 363 millions by the year 2050. Here too Europe's baby boomers will swell the ranks of those aged 80 and over, while the number of people under 55 years of age will be lower than it is today. As a consequence the median age will go up from a current 38 to no less than 47 years. As was to be expected, things are even more dramatic in Japan, where total population is projected to decline from 127 to 101 million persons, and the median age to increase from 41 to 53 years. In the case of Japan, a second wave of large cohorts—the descendants of those born in the early postwar period—will contribute to the emergence of a population structure, in 2050, shaped almost like an inverted pyramid. Demographic prospects for individual European countries are somewhere between the Japanese and US extremes—closer to the former in Germany and Italy, closer to the latter in France, Sweden, and the United Kingdom.

1.2.2   Old-Age and Total Dependency Ratios

Another widely used way of condensing the information provided by population data and demographic projections is given by demographic "dependency ratios." The total dependency ratio expresses the number of presumably inactive individuals (generally defined to consist of those aged 0 to 14, and those aged 65 or more) as a proportion of the number of presumably active ones (those aged 15 to 64). This ratio is supposed to measure the burden imposed on the latter by the need to support the former. Although the young and the old are equally central to the theme of this book, the latter loom larger in current debates over the future of public pensions. It is also clear from figure 1.2 that in most cases the projected burden represented by elderly people is heavier than that created by children and youths. Indeed the projected reduction in the number of children and youths is generally regarded as something that will partly compensate for, rather than add to, the problems created by the projected increase in the number of old people.

The total dependency ratio can be split into an old-age and a youth dependency ratio. The former is usually defined as the proportion of the population aged 65 and over to that aged 15 to 64.[7] This ratio is

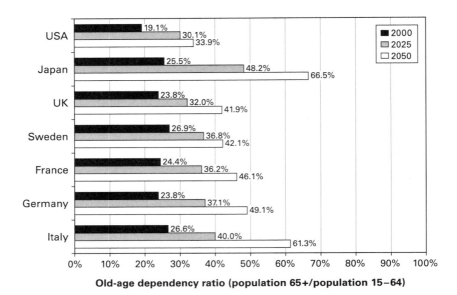

Figure 1.3
Old-age dependency ratios, 2000, 2025, and 2050.

now about 1:4 in most developed countries (see figure 1.3).[8] With the exception of Sweden, it will increase by more than 50 percent, and in some cases by more than 100 percent, between the years 2000 and 2050 in all the countries examined here. At least, this is what the "middle" or "baseline" scenarios of existing population projections are indicating on the assumption of next-to-constant fertility rates, constant flows of net immigration, and a mild further rise in life expectancy. Once again, the projected increase in old-age dependency is particularly strong in Japan (and Italy), where it will approach a ratio of 2:3 by 2050. Old-age dependency in 2050 is predicted to be remarkably low in the United States, where it should barely exceed a 1:3 ratio.

The youth dependency ratio is defined as the proportion of the population aged 0 to 14 in that aged 15 to 64. The value of this ratio ranges between about 1:5 (Japan and Italy) and slightly under 1:3 (United States). Over the next 50 years, projected changes in this ratio are limited to a maximum of 6 percentage points (only 3 in the case of France, Sweden, and the United Kingdom).

As a consequence, the change in the total dependency ratio is much smaller than that in old-age dependency alone (see figure 1.4).[9] Total dependency is expected to go up from a current 1:2 to more than 2:3

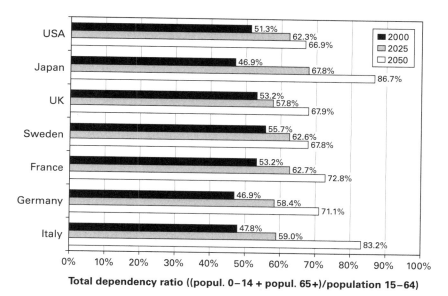

Figure 1.4
Total dependency ratios, 2000, 2025, and 2050.

in all the countries considered. In Japan and Italy it is projected to become higher than 4 : 5.

1.3   Implications for Public Expenditure

The term *dependency* has economic connotations. We do not go into the intricate, and largely unresearched, relationship between changes in population structure and economic growth.[10] Suffice it to say that changes in the ratio between the number of persons of working age and that of persons who are either too young or too old to work, of the order of magnitude projected for most industrialized countries, will give rise to strongly competing demands for output. Indeed changes in the overall dependency ratio underestimate the problem, because the demands made by children and youths are not interchangeable with those coming from the old, and the same level of total dependency will have very different implications if the underlying youth and old-age dependency ratios are of equal size, as in the case of the United States, or a third and two-thirds, as in the case of Sweden or the United Kingdom. Therefore a reduction in the youth dependency ratio does not compensate on a one-for-one basis for an increase in the

Table 1.1
Age-related public expenditure and demographic change

	Age-related public expenditure on...		Taxes and non-tax receipts (2000)	Change[b] against baseline when...	
	Youths[a] (2000)	Old-age pensions (2000)		YDR −1%	OADR +1%
	Percentage of GDP			*Percentage points*	
United States	4.3	4.4	31.6	−0.14	+0.23
Japan	3.4	7.9	29.4	−0.15	+0.31
Germany	5.4	11.8	44.4	−0.10	+0.51
France	7.5	12.1	47.4	−0.11	+0.50
United Kingdom	6.0	4.3	38.7	−0.09	+0.18
Italy	4.6	14.2	44.2	−0.17	+0.54
Sweden	8.5	9.2	56.3	−0.08	+0.34

Source: OECD (2001a, 2002a, 2003a, 2004); own calculations.
Note: YDR = youth dependency ratio; OADR = old-age dependency ratio (changes in percentage points).
a. Expenditure on child benefits, family services, and (pre-primary, primary, and secondary) education.
b. Assuming that age-related expenditure per head of the relevant age group are constant in proportion to GDP per individual at working age.

old-age dependency ratio. Furthermore resources expended on young people have the characteristics of an investment, while support for the old goes essentially into consumption.

Concentrating on a narrow selection of age-related public expenditures, we will now provide rough estimates of what the projected changes in demographic dependency ratios will do to the fiscal systems of the countries affected, given the policies currently pursued. As expenditure related to the young, we identify public funds spent on the provision of cash benefits for families with young children, services to families, and (pre-primary, primary, and secondary) education. With respect to expenditure for the old, we confine our attention to public old-age pensions. Table 1.1 gives the current GDP shares of all these expenditure categories, together with the current GDP ratios of tax revenues and non-tax government receipts.

We have pointed out that the population projections imply a continuation of current policies to the year 2050. Interpret this as meaning that all types of age-related expenditure per head of the relevant age group will remain constant as a percentage of GDP per person of working age. A one percent change in old-age (youth) dependency then implies that the GDP share of old-age (youth) related public expenditure will change between now and 2050 in the way indicated in the right-hand panel of table 1.1. The projected changes in old-age dependency would thus raise public expenditure by between 0.2 and 0.5 percent of GDP. The projected changes in youth dependency have a smaller effect, ranging from about 0.1 to 0.2 percent of GDP.

If we further assume that a constant share of GDP will be spent on all other budget items, the projected changes in age-related expenditure will have to be financed by an equivalent increase in the tax-to-GDP ratio (or, alternatively, in the primary deficit ratio). It then follows that taxes and other public revenues will have to grow between now and 2050 by around 3 percent of GDP in the United Kingdom and United States, more than 12 percent in Japan and Germany, and close to 20 percent in Italy. Of course, these are very rough estimates. Furthermore current policies often entail measures that are expected to reduce pension benefits over the long run (precisely to avoid scenarios as extreme as those sketched here). More careful calculations will be presented in the next chapter.[11]

In chapters 5 and 6 we will argue that demographic variables respond to economic policy. Not everybody agrees with this, and even those who do are sometimes heard saying that it is irrelevant for practical policy purposes anyway, because the demographic scene is already set for the next 20 or even 50 years. That is an exaggeration to say the least. The number of persons who will be aged 0 to 14 in 2050, or even in 2025, in any particular country is not known because they are not yet born. The number of those who will be 15 to 64 is also uncertain, not only because many of them are not yet born but also because net migration and, to less an extent, life expectancy are uncertain. All we know for certain is how many of today's residents will be old in the year 2050, if they live that long. But we are again uncertain about migration and life expectancy.[12]

Therefore neither the youth nor the old-age dependency ratios are known. We can estimate the number of people who will have more than 65 years in 2025 or 2050, but that is not enough to calculate an old-age dependency ratio because the denominator depends on a number of factors, including policy. Educated guesses of future old-age dependency ratios like those reported in figure 1.3 may be valuable nonetheless, if these ratios are not too sensitive to changes in the only variable that can be affected by the instruments of public policy we

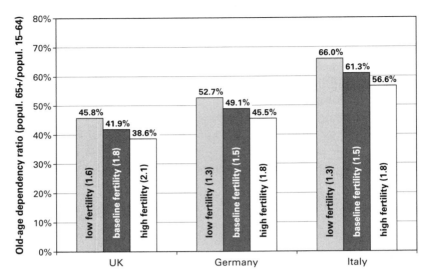

Figure 1.5
Old-age dependency projected to 2050 using alternative fertility assumptions.

want to address here, namely fertility. To ascertain that, we now look at the old-age dependency implications of making alternative fertility assumptions for three countries with very different aging patterns—Germany, Italy, and the United Kingdom—holding constant the baseline assumptions on mortality and migration suggested by Eurostat (2000).

Eurostat assumes that over the next 50 years completed cohort fertility will stay largely constant in the "baseline" scenario,[13] drop by another 10 to 15 percent in the "low-fertility" scenario, go up by 15 to 20 percent in the "high-fertility" scenario. Figure 1.5 illustrates the implications of these changes for the projected 2050 old-age dependency ratio in the countries in question.[14] The effects are indeed not too strong. For substantial changes in old-age dependency to obtain, one would have to induce much larger changes in fertility behavior. What this means, in practice, is that where old people are concerned, the effects of more than three decades of low birth rates cannot be easily undone by fertility incentives over the projection horizon. Yet there is some room for maneuver, and induced fertility changes would, in any case, make a difference to what will happen toward the end of the twenty-first century.

The reason we focus on induced changes in fertility rather than life expectancy is not that we attach little importance to the latter. On the contrary, we are aware of arguments to the effect that the strength of the upward trend in life expectancy is badly underestimated in current population projections.[15] The reason is rather that this book is about public support for the young and the old. In less developed countries, these policies affect mortality as well as fertility. In the rich countries with which we are concerned, however, they essentially affect only fertility. Mortality is affected by health policy, and by the international research effort, but is largely exogenous with respect to the policies examined here.

2

Public Support for the Old

Public support for the aged plays an important role in the fiscal systems of virtually all industrialized countries. In most of them it includes compulsory participation in some pension scheme.[1] This prompts two questions. One is why, the other is how. We will deal with the first question in chapter 7. Here we touch briefly on the second. Suppose it has been decided that every person over a certain age should get a pension. One way to implement this decision is to give the state the monopoly of supplying the service. Another is to oblige everyone to buy an annuity from a private institution of their choice (in much the same way as motorists are obliged, in many countries, to buy third-party insurance), and leave it for the tax-benefit system to redistribute consumption from the rich to the poor in the usual way. An argument in favor of the former is that it saves on advertising.[2] An argument in favor of the latter is that competition improves the quality of management. Some countries have gone for the former and others for the latter. Many have, Solomonically, decided to have the service provided partly by the public and partly by the private sector. In this chapter we examine the different arrangements.

2.1 Public Pension Schemes

Public support for the old may include not only money transfers but also direct provision of, or price subsidies on, goods and services exclusively or predominantly consumed by that age group. Here we focus on money transfers, pensions of one kind or another. Actual pension schemes may differ in several respects. One is the *extent of coverage*, that is to say, the categories of individuals covered (all citizens, all employees, or a subset of the latter), and the types of risk insured (the usual package includes disability, longevity, and survivors). Another is the *level of coverage*, that is to say, the amount of pension benefits that a person receives in a lifetime. The latter depends on three factors: age of retirement, pension benefits in the first year of retirement, and indexation of benefits over subsequent years. Yet another difference is between systems that commit to a particular benefit schedule (*defined-benefit* pension systems) and adjust contributions to keep financial balance, and systems that commit to a certain contribution schedule (*defined-contribution* pension systems) and adjust benefits. But the two key features of a public pension scheme are the way in which it is financed, and the link between individual benefits and individual contributions.[3]

Most important for its incentive effects is the distinction between schemes characterized by a strong link between individual contributions and individual benefits, and schemes where the link is weak or inexistent. Schemes of the first type are referred to as "social insurance" or *Bismarckian* (after the German Chancellor Otto von Bismarck), schemes of the second type as "social security" or *Beveridgean* (after William Beveridge, a British scholar influential in having it introduced in the United Kingdom). Bismarckian schemes need individual accounts to keep track of individual contributions; Beveridgean ones do not. If individual benefits bear no relation whatsoever to contributions made, the latter are effectively earmarked taxes. If, as is generally the case, contributions increase with income, they are a tax on labor. Although the case where there is no relation between benefits and contributions is only a limiting case,[4] it is customary in the English language literature to refer to pension contributions as social security *taxes* even if the scheme happens to be Bismarckian. That is misleading, particularly if it is taken to imply that pensions must necessarily discourage labor. We will see in chapter 5 that the opposite may indeed be true.

The relationship (or lack of it) between individual benefits and contributions is mirrored, to some extent, in the relationship between the contributions collectively made by a generation of workers, and the benefits that will collectively accrue to that same generation. If the contributions made by a generation are invested, and their capitalized value used exclusively to pay benefits to that same generation (*prefunded* pensions), there is no intergenerational transfer. If the contributions made by the currently active generations are used to pay benefits to currently retired generations (*pay-as-you-go* pension systems), an intergenerational transfer is generally possible. Notice that a pension scheme can be run on a pay-as-you-go basis only if participation is mandatory. If it is voluntary, it must be fully pre-funded because no organization can credibly commit to paying benefits out of contributions that may or may not be forthcoming. Indeed financial market regulations in developed countries generally prevent private organizations from offering inadequately funded schemes. By contrast, a public pension scheme can rely partly or totally on current contributions to pay current pensioners, since the government has the power to coerce present and future workers to contribute to it.

A pension scheme is said to be *fully funded* if, at any one moment, the value of its reserves is equal to the expected present value of the benefits it is committed to pay.[5] This definition suggests that such a scheme does not rely on payments by currently active persons. In the case of a government scheme, however, that is not necessarily true if its reserves are invested in (domestic) government bonds. In the absence of a rule making sure that the balance of the overall government budget balance is increased by the amount of the bonds added to the reserves of the pension fund, drawing on reserves to pay for current pensions is equivalent to drawing on current contributions, since the government will then have to use its tax revenue to honor the debt. The only difference reserves make in such a case is that pensions are financed out of general taxation, rather than earmarked contributions, but the system is effectively pay-as-you-go.

It is often taken for granted that pay-as-you-go pension schemes transfer resources from younger to older generations. Strictly speaking, the only intergenerational transfer *necessarily* implied by a pay-as-you-go pension scheme is that in favor of the very first generation. Even if the scheme is phased-in gradually, so as not to give full benefits to the generations who have not paid full contributions, it is unavoidable that the very first cohort of pensioners gets something for nothing (this point is further developed in section 2.4). Apart from this inevitable transfer, a pay-as-you-go pension scheme makes it *easier* for a government to surreptitiously make transfers in favor of current workers and pensioners at the expense of future ones. If pensions are fully funded, such transfers can still be made, but only by more overt means. In any case the decision to favor a generation at the expense of another is political. A government may take such a decision for electoral reasons, or for more noble ones, such as helping a generation affected by a severe calamity (war, deep economic recession, natural disaster). If this kind of intergenerational redistribution is done systematically, the pay-as-you-go scheme provides mutual *intergenerational insurance*. That is in fact one of the arguments in favor of pay-as-you-go.

In the absence of deliberate intergenerational redistribution, the allocation of risk between adjoining generations depends on whether the pension scheme is committed to a predefined benefit schedule (DB), or to a predefined contribution schedule (DC). Until about 20 years ago the majority of pension schemes—whether public or private—was DB. As DB implies that individuals know in advance how much they will get in old age, such a scheme is obliged to adjust contribution rates, or accumulate reserves, in order to honor its commitments. The risk of a fall in the number or contributive capacity of new entrants, or of a low return to the assets held as reserves, is thus born by the generations currently making contributions (those of working age). More recently DC schemes have become more widespread. Subject to minimum pension guarantees, risks in a DC scheme are borne by the generations currently receiving benefits (those of retirement age).

Initially, the move toward DC-type pensions was made only by funded, employer-based or fully private, pension plans. There the risks to be re-allocated concern only the return to the assets held in reserve (hence interest rates and stock prices). More recently the reforms enacted in a limited number of countries have demonstrated that the same logic can be applied to unfunded public schemes. If individual benefits are based on individual contributions—which implies that the pension fund administration keeps individual accounts—traditional DB arrangements can be replaced by a system of notionally defined contributions (NDC) that "earn" a notional rate of return. The risks borne by retired members of an NDC scheme are then those associated with this notional rate of return, usually equal to the rate of payroll growth, or to the aggregate growth rate of the economy. We will see examples of that in section 2.3.

It is not obvious that a switch from DB to DC or NDC raises welfare. In principle, the change from DB to DC should reduce transaction costs because the latter does not require precautionary arrangements to back the guarantees given.[6] The same cannot be said, however, in favor of NDC. Nor can it be argued that a switch to NDC removes the government's ability to arbitrarily make intergenerational transfers, since this can still be done by changing the basis on which the notional rate of return on contributions is calculated. The argument must then be that NDC is more transparent than a conventional DB system, as it rests on a single parameter, the rate of return to contributions. Changes of policy are thus more visible. It should also be said that NDC has been used as a vehicle for bringing about other desirable adjustments (e.g., in Italy, to eliminate unfair disparities in the treatment of different categories of persons).

A scheme is said to be *actuarially fair* if, at the date when a person retires, the expected value of his future benefits is equal to the capitalized value of his past contributions.[7] Private pension schemes are necessarily less than actuarially fair, not only because their administrative and advertising costs can be substantial but also because the insurer makes its profit by charging its risk-averse clients an insurance premium.[8] In a large public scheme, by contrast, administrative costs per person covered can be assumed to be negligible. There are no advertising costs, since participation is mandatory[9] and the pension fund does not have to show a profit, so a public scheme can then be actuarially fair. If it is less (or, indeed, more) than actuarially fair, that is a political choice. If the return on the contributions made is lower than that offered by financial markets, participants in the scheme pay an *implicit tax*. Conversely, if the scheme pays better than the market, participants receive an *implicit subsidy*. Sample calculations will be presented in section 2.4.

Differences between national pension systems reflect differences in national attitudes toward the appropriate degree of compulsion (regarding participation and level of coverage), and toward the appropriate degree of public administration involvement in the running of the various schemes. Industrialized countries nowadays appear to be converging toward a common pattern of pension coverage based on three parallel schemes, or "pillars," but the relative importance of each pillar varies a great deal from country to country. The *first pillar* is run directly by the government. The *second pillar* is based on the employment relationship. The *third pillar* is provided by the insurance or other financial markets. While participation in the first of these schemes is generally compulsory for all citizens, and often provides a very basic level of coverage, participation in the other two is mandatory in some countries, and optional in others (if the latter, there are usually fiscal incentives to participate).

2.2 Simple Pension Algebra

To keep the algebra simple, we will do a little violence to reality. We will reason *as if* each generation enters working age at the very time the earlier generation reaches retirement.[10] This way at any moment in time all workers are the same age and all pensioners are the same age. The only relevant dates are those when one generation replaces another generation in the market place.

Suppose that the pension scheme is *fully funded* (*ff*). Consider a person who reaches working age at date t and retirement age at date $t + 1$. Let θ^t denote the present value at t of the contributions made by this person between dates t and $t + 1$. Let η^{t+1} denote the expected value at $t + 1$ of the benefits accruing to the same person from that date onward. This expectation reflects uncertainty about the date of death of the participant, as well as about future interest rates. Let r^t denote the value of a money unit invested at the date t, and continuously capitalized at the market rates of interest until date $t + 1$. Abstracting from administrative costs, we say that the scheme is *actuarially fair* if

$$\theta^t r^t \equiv \eta^{t+1}. \tag{2.1}$$

The internal rate of return to contributions (i.e., the interest rate that converts θ^t into η^{t+1}) is thus $i^t_{ff} = r^t - 1$.[11]

In a pure *pay-as-you-go* (*payg*) scheme, the money paid in by current contributors is not invested, but distributed to current beneficiaries. Such a scheme can be sustained only if participation is compulsory. Let N^{t+1} be the number of persons who reach working age, and N^t the number of persons who retire, at date $t + 1$. If the scheme is obliged to break even at each date, it must then be true (abstracting again from administrative costs) that

$$\theta^{t+1} N^{t+1} \equiv \eta^{t+1} N^t, \tag{2.2}$$

where η^{t+1} and θ^{t+1} are now to be interpreted as generational averages. In contrast with (2.1), (2.2) is sensitive to changes in the demographic profile (N^t, N^{t+1}). If the scheme is allowed to make surpluses or deficits, the left-hand side of (2.2) need not be equal to the right-hand side. If it is obliged to break even "on average," the scheme will accumulate reserves in good times and run them down in bad ones. The scheme is then actually a hybrid of full funding (because reserves are invested) and pay as you go.

The contribution required of a participant in a public pension scheme is generally an increasing function of his income, or just earnings. We may thus rewrite (2.2) as

$$\theta'^{t+1} y^{t+1} N^{t+1} \equiv \eta^{t+1} N^t, \tag{2.2'}$$

where θ'^{t+1} is the average contribution rate. Given (N^t, N^{t+1}, y^{t+1}), equation (2.2') can be used to determine either the average contribution rate that is needed to pay for a predefined level of pension benefits, or the average level of pension benefits compatible with a predefined contribution rate.

A series of (2.2) budget constraints implies that those who started their working life at date t will have collectively paid $\theta'^t y^t N^t$ into the pension scheme by the time they retire at date $t+1$. For the average member of this generation the internal rate of return is given by

$$i^t_{payg} = \frac{\theta'^{t+1} y^{t+1} N^{t+1}}{\theta'^t y^t N^t} - 1 \equiv \frac{\theta'^{t+1}}{\theta'^t} g^t n^t - 1, \tag{2.3}$$

where $g^t \equiv (y^{t+1}/y^t)$ is the growth factor of per-capita income (or earnings), and $n^t \equiv (N^{t+1}/N^t)$ the growth factor of the active population. This makes it clear that the profitability of a pay-as-you-go scheme does not depend just on the age-dependency ratio (see chapter 1). With constant contribution rates, $\theta'^{t+1} = \theta'^t = \theta'$, the internal rate of return for the average participant is equal to the growth rate of total income (or earnings), $gn - 1$ (Aaron 1966).

If we take a look at any long time series of data on industrialized countries, we notice that apart from irregularities associated with post–World War II reconstruction, the growth rate of total income (or earnings) tends to be lower than the long-term interest rate,[12]

$$g^t n^t < r^t. \tag{2.4}$$

In the literature this inequality is known as the *Aaron condition*,[13] and it implies that once the system has been fully phased in, the average rate of return is lower in an unfunded than in a funded pension scheme.

In a Bismarckian ("social insurance") type of scheme, the same (2.3) applies to all members of the same cohort of pensioners because the rule used for converting individual contributions into individual benefits is the same for everyone. Social insurance schemes may thus fail to be actuarially fair $(i^t_{payg} \neq i^t_{ff})$ but may still be intragenerationally fair in the sense that all members of the same generation get the same return. By contrast, in a (Beveridgean) social security scheme, (2.3) applies only to the average participant. If everyone pays contributions at the same rate θ' but gets the same η, the internal rate of return is then lower than average for the rich and higher than average for the poor. The same is true if there is a weak link—rather than no link at all—between individual benefits and individual contributions.[14] Thus, even if the Aaron condition applies, i^t_{payg} can be negative for those at the top end of the income distribution, and it can easily exceed $r^t - 1$ for those at the bottom end. But this pattern of intragenerational redistribution will emerge only if the scheme is designed to take from the rich and give to the poor.[15] In real life, pension schemes often reflect the political bargaining power of different categories, as well as equity considerations.

Let us now look at the intergenerational redistribution that takes place in an unfunded scheme. At an early stage in the history of the scheme, current pensioners may not have paid contributions over their entire working life, yet they receive full-fledged pension benefits based on the simple pay-as-you-go mechanics. They thus enjoy *inaugural gains*. Because pensions are being financed by contributions that give rise to benefit entitlements for subsequent generations, these gains create an implicit form of public debt. Once the system is mature, the implicit debt is rolled onto the indefinite future. If contributions remain constant over time, every generation that contributes to the scheme throughout its entire active life finds itself paying for part of the debt service. Compared with a situation where each generation has to provide for its own old age through a fully funded scheme, the difference between i^t_{ff} and i^t_{payg} is then reflected in a loss of lifetime income for each generation that did not benefit from inaugural gains. We will return to this issue in section 2.4, where we show how population aging affects these income losses.

In practice, contribution rates vary over time, and a pension fund may be financed by debt. If contribution rates increase, there are new inaugural gains, a new rise in the implicit public debt, and so on. If there is debt-financing, the pension fund deficit raises the explicit public debt. In either case the (average) rate of return of unfunded systems may reach or exceed $r^t - 1$ even if the Aaron condition is satisfied. However, since θ' must be less than unity, policies of this type cannot be pursued forever. In other words, with unfunded pensions, it is possible to have arbitrary levels of return for some of the generations involved. Over the long run the actual rate of return to participating in an unfunded scheme cannot be above the level that equates the expected present value of contributions to the expected present value of benefits.

Our discussion so far has implicitly assumed that pay-as-you-go schemes are invariably of the DC type. Indeed, as pointed out in the last subsection, that is increasingly the case. But what happens if the system is DB? If that is the case, the contribution rate must be adjusted, period by period, to balance the pension fund budget. The internal rate of return for those who entered working life at t is then $g^t n^{t-1} - 1$.[16] As n^{t-1} is used instead of n^t, cohort t is effectively insured against low fertility (because θ'^{t+1} is adjusted to compensate for that). In the presence of protracted demographic aging, however, the repeated increases in contribution rates required to keep the system DB may be politically unsustainable (that is indeed a reason for the switch to DC).

2.3   Public Pension Schemes in Selected Countries

A prototypical social insurance scheme is the German *Rentenversicherung* introduced by Chancellor Otto von Bismarck in 1889. This scheme is generally regarded as the earliest system of public old-age provision in the world. In later years the model spread to most of continental Europe, and to many other parts of the industrialized world. The prototypical social security scheme is generally thought to be the State Basic Pension scheme, introduced in the United Kingdom in the late 1940s,[17] and later imitated by most Commonwealth countries. Although social security schemes are said to be an Anglo-Saxon tradition, the idea came originally (like the Anglo-Saxons themselves) from Denmark, where a public pension scheme of that type was first established in 1891. Since then, most Scandinavian countries have moved toward multi-pillar pension systems that combine the features of the two competing models. Also the US Social Security scheme is a compromise between the two traditions. By contrast, the United Kingdom has always stuck by a flat-rate pension scheme. For a while the United Kingdom had also an earnings-related tier (SERPS), but this was later removed. Other European pension systems (those of Italy, Sweden, and of the majority of central and eastern European countries) have recently moved further in the opposite direction by tightening the link between individual contributions and individual benefits. In the rest of this section we briefly describe the public pension schemes of our selection of countries as under their year 2003 legal framework.[18]

Among the public pension systems considered, those of United Kingdom and United States redistribute most between rich and poor members of the same generation. As pointed out in section 2.1, this implies that the net taxes falling on individuals in different earnings brackets can be substantially higher or lower than the average. In order to assess the overall generosity of different pension systems, it is common to compare the "replacement rates" implied by those systems. As they only relate benefits in the first year after retirement to end-of-career earnings, however, these rates are not too instructive. An alternative is to compare "benefit levels" (or "quasi-replacement rates") relating current pension benefits to the average earnings of those who are still active. These benefit levels can vary substantially across individuals with different wage rates, or different employment records. Depending on how they are indexed, benefit levels for a given individual can also change with time, from the date of retirement onward. In the following, we will refer to estimates of benefit levels for individuals who have earned average wages during a complete work career. In each case we relate net income in the retirement period to net income in the active period of life.[19]

2.3.1   US Social Security

As already mentioned, the US Social Security scheme is situated halfway between the Bismarckian and the Beveridgean extremes.[20] Membership is compulsory for all gainfully occupied individuals, including the self-employed. Only a fraction of public-sector employees at the federal, state and local level, and a minuscule number of others, are outside the scheme.[21] Those covered by US Social Security now have to pay 12.4 percent of gross wage income as contributions. The rate has remained stable since 1990. Old-age pensions are assessed on the basis of the "best 35" years of contributions. Earnings in each of these years are indexed by wage growth. Average indexed earnings are then converted into benefit entitlements at differing rates, decreasing from 90 to 15 percent as one moves from low to high wages. For an average earner with a full lifetime work record, benefits are around 40 percent of current average wages in the first year in retirement. The benefit level decreases in later years, as pensions after the first year of retirement are only indexed by consumer price inflation. In any case, public pensions in the United States leave substantial room for supplementary provision on an occupational or fully private basis in order to maintain earlier living standards during old age.

Starting in 1983, annual contribution rates were increased above the level of current "cost rates" (defined as the fraction of taxable income that would be needed to balance a pure pay-as-you-go budget). Surpluses are accumulated in Social Security Trust Funds to meet the increase in pension expenditure that is expected to occur when baby boomers start to retire after 2010. The US authorities have thus pioneered the introduction of "demographic buffer funds" in pay-as-you-go pension schemes, a strategy that has since been adopted in quite a number of other countries. Another major reform, enacted in 1983, is the gradual increase of the age limit for claiming full benefits from 65 to 67 for both males and females.

Despite relatively favorable demographic prospects (see chapter 1) the debate on US Social Security reform has never really abated during the last two decades. Most recently a new President's Commission to Strengthen Social Security (2002) has come up with a number of proposals. The common theme behind all the alternatives considered by the commission is how—and if so, to what an extent—old-age provision in the US could be privatized even further than it is already. So far, however, no final conclusion about the future of US Social Security has been reached.

2.3.2   UK National Insurance

UK National Insurance provides benefits of various kinds. The most important type of old-age benefits are those deriving from the State Basic Pension scheme.[22] As the name suggests, the scheme pays benefits at a uniform flat rate, meant to provide a minimum level of retirement income to everybody. A scheme providing supplementary, earnings-related pension benefits (SERPS) was introduced in 1978. In the mid-1980s, however, compulsory membership in this scheme was abolished, and individuals were allowed to opt in favor of employer- or market-based provision. Today two-thirds of the British labor force have used this option. Only a small minority, about 5 percent, has no cover other than the Basic Pension (Blake 2002).

Participation in the Basic Pension scheme is mandatory for all dependent workers. In general, these have to pay National Insurance contributions at the rate of 21.9 percent of gross earnings, of which about 2 percentage points are allocated to the National Health Service, and the rest to the public pension scheme. A rebate of between 2.2 and 4.6 percentage points (depending on the type of contracting-out arrangement) is granted to those who opt out of SERPS, so that the effective rate of contribution to the State Basic Pension scheme is in the range of 15 to 18 percent.[23] Individual benefit entitlements depend only on the number of years of contributions, up to a maximum of 45 years. For shorter periods of contribution, several rules (e.g., related to number of years in education, or to home responsibilities) allow a person to receive full benefits nonetheless. Where these rules do not apply, and provided that the person has paid contributions for at least ten "qualifying years," benefits are paid on a pro rata basis.

Currently full State Basic Pension benefits are about 25 percent of current average wages for a single-earner couple (16 percent for individuals). One of the reasons for this low level of benefits is that over the last twenty years the British have pursued a very restrictive approach to indexing pension benefits (at, and after, award) and all relevant earnings thresholds to consumer prices only. If this policy were maintained into the future, Basic Pensions would be virtually phased out over the next fifty years, thereby reducing the projected fiscal cost of public pensions despite the expected adverse demographic change.[24] For the fiscal year 2002 to 2003, however, the British government has returned to a form of pension indexation that is very close to a full earnings uprating (of all relevant amounts except the "upper earnings limit," which restricts contributions to be paid by high-wage earners).[25] It may be too early to judge whether this is a major policy change. In any case, the financial burden of paying for future pension benefits in the United Kingdom may increase.

2.3.3   *The German* Gesetzliche Rentenversicherung

Germany has a long tradition of social insurance schemes providing earnings-related pension benefits at a relatively generous level.[26] Through mandatory participation, *Rentenversicherung* covers the vast majority of individuals in employment. The exceptions are civil servants (a subgroup of public-sector employees) and many, but not all, the self-employed. The current contribution rate is 19.5 percent of gross wages.[27] The amount of contributions made—hence wages earned—in any single year of employment is relevant when assessing individual benefit entitlements. The benefit formula translates differences between individual and average wages into differences between individual and average pension benefits.

Up until now the *Rentenversicherung* has basically offered a predefined level of benefits. For any given work biography, an individual's benefit entitlements are a fixed percentage (about 70 percent for an average earner with 45 years in employment) of current average wages. Contribution rates are adjusted annually to collect the funds needed to cover total pension expenditure. In order to maintain this strategy, contribution rates had to be increased many times until the early 1990s. Two major reforms have taken place since then. One is that, starting from 1998, injections into the pension budget financed from general government revenues have been increased above the level required to pay for a number of noncontributory benefits, thus effectively relaxing the pay-as-you-go budget constraint.[28] The other is that German authorities have now redefined the mechanism for indexing public pensions, with a view to reducing the level of future pension benefits.

In fact indexation has been addressed by a longer series of reforms. Before 1992, pension benefits (both at and after award) were indexed by gross wages. In view of population aging, this could not be maintained for much longer.[29] Net-wage indexation was introduced in 1992. The most recent reform, enacted in 2001, established that pension benefits should be indexed by current wages net of pension contributions, making changes in other charges irrelevant. In addition the indexation formula was manipulated in such a way that the benefit level will be reduced by about 10 percent over the next thirty years. As a result of this reform the "replacement rate" for an average earner with a full work record is projected to go down to about 63 percent of average wages. As a compensatory measure the government has introduced subsidies for what are called "precautionary savings" (private pension contributions) in order to encourage the growth of a third pillar of old-age provision. So far, however, the take-up of the subsidy has been very limited.[30]

2.3.4   *The French* Régime Général

In France the *Régime Général*, administered by Caisse Nationale d'Assurance Vieillesse (CNAV), is the most important scheme of public old-age provision. Participation is mandatory for all dependent workers outside the public sector and large national firms.[31] Although the link between individual contributions and individual benefits is less strict than in the German case, this "general regime" offers another example of a continental European social insurance scheme. Contributions are currently levied at a rate of 16.45 percent of gross wages. Provided that the individual has a work record covering 40 years or more, benefits are assessed on the basis of the best 10 to 25 years of contributions (the reference period will rise to 25 years by 2012). With shorter periods of labor force participation, benefits are reduced on a pro rata basis. For an average earner, the full benefit at award is about 50 percent of current average wages. Additional cover is provided by large, unfunded, occupational pension programs where participation is also mandatory.

The latest reform of the *Régime Général* worth mentioning here dates back to 1993. In that year the extension of the reference period was approved. Additional measures taken at the same time were an increase (from 37.5 to 40) in the number of years necessary to qualify for a full pension, and a switch from wage to price indexation of pensions after the first year of retirement. The latter appears to be the most effective in reducing future levels of pension expenditure. Meanwhile discussion as to new rounds of reform has become very lively. An increase of the statutory retirement age—currently an unusually low 60 years for both males and females—is said to be on the agenda together with measures directly aimed at further reducing the level of public pension benefits at award. For quite a while French governments have tended to postpone decisions on these politically sensitive issues. At least in 2003 an amendment was passed to increase the number of years qualifying for a full benefit to 42, which will gradually become effective until 2020.

2.3.5   *The Italian* Fondo Pensioni Lavoratori Dipendenti

In contrast with France and Germany, Italy offers a remarkable example of fundamental pension reform in continental Europe. The most important branch of the Italian public pension system[32] is the *Fondo Pensioni Lavoratori Dipendenti*, run by Istituto Nazionale della Previdenza Sociale (INPS). Participation in this scheme is compulsory for all dependent workers in the private sector. Before the reforms, public pension benefits in Italy were extremely generous,[33] which has driven up the contribution rate to the current level of 32.7 percent of gross wages; that rate has been stable since 1996. Before the reforms took effect, contributions were actually about 5 percentage points lower than they are now, but that was only because of (largely debt-financed) government subsidies.

Driven both by the need for fiscal consolidation in preparation for entering the European monetary union, and by a particularly unfavorable demographic outlook (see chapter 1), the Italians were quicker than others in restructuring their pension scheme. Pension reform came about in two major steps, one taken in 1992 (the "Amato reform") and the other in 1995 (the "Dini reform"). Before 1992, benefits accruing to an average earner with a full work record were based on wages earned in just the last five years before retirement. They amounted to no less than 80 percent of current average wages. Furthermore "seniority" pensions (*pensioni di anzianità*), based on the number of years in work, were granted at a full rate to individuals with only 35 years of contributions regardless of age at the point of retirement.

In line with reforms made in other countries, the 1992 reform package extended the reference period over which benefits are assessed to virtually the whole working life. It also switched from wage to consumer price indexation of benefits after the first year of retirement. The 1995 reform established a new philosophy for operating a public pay-as-you-go pension scheme based on "notionally defined contributions" (NDC).[34] The Italians themselves prefer to call this method "contributions-related" (*sistema contributivo*) to stress the difference with the old *sistema retributivo* where entitlements were calculated on the basis of income earned rather than contributions made.

In the post-1995 scheme, individual contributions are treated "as if" they were paid into individual accounts and attracted interest. In actuality individual contributions are capitalized at the rate of GDP growth. In the long run this is expected to reduce the benefit level by more than 30 percent compared with the pre-reform method. Additional steps are being taken to discourage early retirement. Benefit entitlements for early retirees are being reduced in a way that is close to actuarially fair. An important limitation of these reforms is that their phase in is extremely gradual. The 1995 reform package is not scheduled to become fully effective until 2050.[35] Contribution rates will consequently remain high for the next thirty years, and will come down to a level of about 26 percent only around the middle of the century. Nonetheless, the reform will have a notable impact on the financial viability of the Italian public pension scheme, and curb intergenerational redistribution from future to present generations.

Italy has also something approximating a second (employer-based) pillar of old-age provision, *Trattamento di Fine Rapporto* (TFR). Under TFR, employers retain a fraction of the wages due to their employees, and pay it back (with interests) in a lump sum when the person leaves their employment. If this happens at retirement, rather than for a job change or a layoff (both unlikely in the Italian situation), this money constitutes another form of old-age provision. There is talk of developing also a third (market-based) pillar, possibly drawing on TFR reserves to get a number of nongovernment pension funds started. But the latter is resisted by employers, who use TFR as a cheap form of corporate finance.

2.3.6   The Swedish Public Pension Scheme

The Swedish also enacted a major pension reform—not unlike the Italian one, but with a faster pace of implementation—in the late 1990s.[36] This reform, effective since the year 2000, has wiped out their traditional two-tier system, consisting of a universal flat-rate entitlement (the *Folkpension*), and an earnings-related benefit for all employed individuals, the *Allmän Tilläggspension* (ATP), assessed on the basis of the "best 15 years" in employment.

Under the old system the benefits accruing to a single-earner couple with average wages and a full lifetime work career for the active spouse amounted to about 70 percent of current average wages. The basic pension component was financed mostly by general tax revenue, while ATP was financed by contributions paid mostly by employers, and by the self-employed. In the mid-1990s the total contribution rate attributable to old-age pensions was about 16 percent. One should add that, over the years, the ATP scheme accumulated reserves sufficient to cover pension expenditure for three and a half years. Worried, however, by the prospect that, at present contribution rates, these funds would have been depleted by the year 2012, and that contribution rates would have then had to increase to about 23 percent, or even higher, the Swedish decided to switch to an entirely new public pension system.

The new system has again two tiers. Since 2001 total contribution rates are fixed at 18.5 percent of gross wages. Sixteen percent are used to finance a new scheme of earnings-related pensions (*Inkomstpension*), which is run on a pay-as-you-go basis and, like the new Italian system, modeled on the idea of an NDC-type arrangement. Another 2.5 percent are channeled into a new *Premiepension* scheme, a form of mandatory savings that is based on a rather strict, but at the same time flexible, regulatory framework ensuring that all employed individuals participate and can invest their funds in a large variety of financial products.[37]

The NDC logic of the *Inkomstpension* scheme implies that contributions made in any year of employment now matter for the level of individual pension benefits. Again, the internal rate of return that is used for converting contributions into benefit entitlements is based on the aggregate growth rate, adjusted for expected duration of the benefit period following individual decisions to retire. In Sweden, benefits paid to each age cohort are also adjusted to changes in prospective life expectancy, implying an even higher degree of actuarial fairness than in Italy. Furthermore transition to the new regime is rather quick in this case, the reform becoming fully effective until 2020. As a result the new system is expected to go along with constant contribution rates, while over the long term the benefit level is expected to decrease by up to 50 percent. Of course, this is where increasing entitlements to receive supplementary *Premiepension* benefits are meant to come in as an important element of the overall reform package.

2.3.7   The Japanese Public Pension Scheme

Up to a point the Japanese public pension system resembles the Swedish pre-reform package, or UK National Insurance before the opt-out clause was introduced.[38] It is a two-tier system providing universal flat-rate benefits through the National Pension (*Kokumin Nenkin*) scheme and "supplementary," earnings-related pensions through the Employees' Pension Insurance (*Kôsei Nenkin Hoken*) scheme. The latter represents the most important form of old-age provision for most private-sector employees. There is also an employer-based second pillar, and a fully private third pillar. The Employees' Pension Insurance scheme is pay-as-you-go. Unlike public pension schemes in most other industrialized countries, this fund holds substantial reserves. As a result authorities enjoy more flexibility in determining current contribution rates and benefit levels than if they were bound by a strict pay-as-you-go constraint. However, like the "demographic buffer funds" introduced in the United States and elsewhere, these reserves are mainly invested in domestic government bonds. Therefore they do not fully insulate public budgets from the fiscal consequences of demographic aging (see the discussion in section 2.1).

Currently total contributions to both public schemes amount to 17.35 percent of regular gross wages (plus 1 percent of annual "bonuses" representing about a fourth of total wage income in Japan). At award, total benefits accruing to a single-earner couple where the active partner earned average wages in a full lifetime career amount to roughly 65 percent of current average wages. Since the Japanese have switched to CPI indexation since 2000, the individual benefit level decreases in the years following the award.

As we saw in chapter 1, Japan expects to be hit harder by demographic aging than any of the other countries considered. Thus pension reform is very much on the Japanese political agenda. On the other hand, the latest changes enacted in 2000 were incremental in nature. In addition to the change in indexation rules, the benefit level provided by the Employees' Pension Insurance scheme was immediately curtailed by 5 percent. A further 10 percent reduction will be phased in over the next twenty years. Also the share of National Pension benefits funded by general tax revenues (rather than earmarked contributions) has increased from zero to about one-third. According to current forecasts, this will do something to limit the expected increase in contribution rates (to about 28 rather than 34 percent) in 2050. More radical reforms under consideration range from a freeze on contribution rates to a long-term phase-out of the earnings-related Employees' Pension scheme.

2.4   Aging and the Tax Implied in Public Pensions

To the extent that the return offered by a public pension scheme is lower than that offered by the market, compelling people to participate in the former is equivalent to imposing a tax on them. Conversely, if the return offered the public scheme is higher than that offered by the market (as was the case for a period in Italy), we should be talking of a subsidy. Perhaps no one should claim originality for putting things in these terms. By introducing the notion of an *implicit tax*, however, Lüdeke (1988) and Sinn (1990) paved the way for a more thorough understanding of the implications of pay-as-you-go financing.[39] We will return to this idea in chapter 5. Here we use the information presented in the preceding sections to measure the implicit tax befalling the generations covered by existing public pension schemes.

We start by calculating the net present value of the contributions paid, and the present value of the benefits received at the time of retirement—both as fractions of lifetime earnings—by various generations of pensioners. The implicit tax rate faced by the average member of the generation that entered working life at date t is

$$\vartheta^{\prime t} = \frac{\theta^t - (\eta^{t+1}/r^t)}{y^t}. \tag{2.5}$$

By definition, this rate is zero for every participant if the scheme is actuarially fair, for the average participant if it is fully funded. We will develop the argument for the case of a pure pay-as-you-go scheme. Replacing θ^t with $\theta'^t y^t$, and using (2.2') to substitute for η^{t+1} in (2.5), we get

$$\vartheta'^t = \frac{\theta'^t y^t - (\eta^{t+1}/r^t)}{y^t} = \theta'^t \frac{r^t - (\theta'^{t+1}/\theta'^t)g^t n^t}{r^t}$$

$$\equiv \vartheta'(\underset{+}{\theta'^t}, \underset{-}{\theta'^{t+1}}, \underset{+}{r^t}, \underset{-}{g^t}, \underset{-}{n^t}). \tag{2.5'}$$

Essentially, ϑ' reflects the interests forgone through compulsory membership in a pay-as-you-go scheme. Since $\vartheta'(.)$ is decreasing in n^t, the implicit tax rate increases with population aging.[40] This rate is positive so long as the Aaron condition is met, and the contribution rate payable by the next generation does not rise. An increase in θ'^{t+1} would reduce ϑ'^t, and perhaps even change its sign (i.e., convert it into a *subsidy*). Keep in mind that ϑ' will be roughly uniform across members of the same age cohort in a social insurance scheme, but it will vary a great deal between higher and lower than average earners in a social security one.

Strictly speaking, all of this applies only to the generations that participate in a mature pay-as-you-go pension scheme. Even if a scheme is phased in gradually, there will be a generation 0 for which the implicit tax, $\vartheta^0 \equiv \vartheta'^0 y^0$, is negative because its members will have received pension benefits (not necessarily at the full rate) in period 1 without paying contributions. Generations $1, 2, 3, \ldots$ also may receive benefits without paying contributions through their entire working life. In section 2.2 we argued that these inaugural gains will give rise to an implicit debt, ID^t, with

$$ID^0 \equiv -\vartheta'^0 y^0 N^0 \equiv -\vartheta^0 N^0. \tag{2.6}$$

Thus the debt implicitly issued by introducing a pay-as-you-go pension scheme is the sum of the implicit subsidies enjoyed by the early generations. For all t greater than 0, ID^t can be reduced by increasing ϑ'^t.

At each t the present value of the implicit public debt is equal to the present value of the implicit taxes that will be collected from those who are currently young, and from all generations yet to be born. In particular,[41]

$$ID^0 = \sum_{t=1}^{\infty} \left(\vartheta^t y^t N^t \prod_{s=0}^{t-1} r^{-s} \right).$$

Among other things, this makes the point that the presence of implicit taxes in an unfunded pension scheme is not necessarily a sign of inefficiency (a deadweight cost). It could just be a reflection of intergenerational redistribution. If unfunded schemes were Pareto optimal, reforms aimed at reducing the burden imposed by the pension system on one generation would necessarily result in higher burdens for other generations. Unfunded pensions would then be a kind of zero-sum game, and the only reason for being concerned about demographic ageing would then be intergenerational fairness. In subsequent chapters, however, we will argue that existing schemes are not Pareto optimal, and that it is thus possible to reduce the burden on one generation without necessarily increasing it on future ones.

A host of studies uses a variety of indicators to measure the effects of population aging on different cohorts in specific national pension schemes. Fenge and Werding (2004) were the first to calculate the implicit lifetime tax rate profiles imposed by public pension schemes on the generations born between 1940 and 2000 for a large sample of countries.[42] This comparative study highlights the impact of population aging on public pension schemes, and the effectiveness of different sets of countermeasures. We now report their results regarding the countries examined in section 2.3. In interpreting these simulations, it should be kept in mind that they calculate effect of a policy under the assumption that the policy does not affect behavior (labor supply, fertility, voluntary transfers). In other words, these are accounting exercises. The same applies to the other simulations that will be presented in chapters 3 and 4. Only in chapter 8 will we carry out simulations based on an estimated econometric model, that account for behavioral changes.

The main ingredients of the calculation are (1) historical time series of average earnings, contribution rates, and benefit levels; (2) financial projections for each of the pension schemes covered, based on recent population forecasts and the current legal framework; and (3) stylized biographies for a representative "one-earner" couple in each of the age cohorts considered. The financial projections are carried out using the CESifo Pension Model, a simple simulation tool suited for calculations of this kind.[43] The model offers a rough, but flexible, accounting framework within which to forecast the long-term financial prospects of unfunded pension schemes. Like many simulation models of its kind, it largely abstracts from individual responses to changes in the key parameters of the public pension system.

The calculations include all branches of conventional "old-age, survivors, and disability insurance" schemes whenever these elements are combined in a comprehensive scheme.[44] The assumptions made about the future development of important economic variables are largely the same for all the countries considered. Wages are assumed to grow at a real rate of 1.75 percent a year. Annual real interest rates are set at 4 percent.[45] Here we focus on "current policy" scenarios incorporating recent changes in pension law.

The stylized biographies on which the estimates of ϑ' are based include a period of active labor force participation of the household's head between the ages of 20 and 64. Earnings in that period are subject to pension contributions. Between 54 and 64, the head becomes inactive and receives a disability pension with some positive probability. From age 65 the household receives an old-age pension, inclusive of spouse benefits (in some countries) and survivor pensions, for another 10 to 20 years. The length of the retirement period is based on conditional life expectancies of males and females at retirement. The probability of becoming disabled, and life expectancy, are adjusted according to national averages. The results of the simulations are presented in figure 2.1.

As the figure shows, there is a general upward trend in the implicit lifetime taxes imposed on individuals who participate in public pension schemes throughout the industrialized world. This is largely due to the change in demographic fundamentals highlighted in chapter 1. But there is also considerable variation across countries, regarding both the level and the trend of the tax profiles, that cannot be attributed to demography. In light of the definition of ϑ', part of the difference in levels may be explained by differences in the gap between real interest rates, and real rates of payroll growth. In addition to these economic factors, differences in the level of ϑ' reflect also different political attitudes toward public pensions relative to other forms of old-age provision. This can be inferred from the level of benefits and contribution rates in first-pillar schemes, indicating how much room is left for the second and third pillars.[46]

In some cases an upward drift of the implicit tax profiles indicates that the system is still on its way to maturing. For the generations born before the 1970s, this is the case in France, Italy, and, to less an extent, the United States, where public schemes were expanded during the 1960s and 1970s. In Japan one can see clear signs of *inaugural gains* (negative values of ϑ'). By contrast, the upward trends of implicit taxes

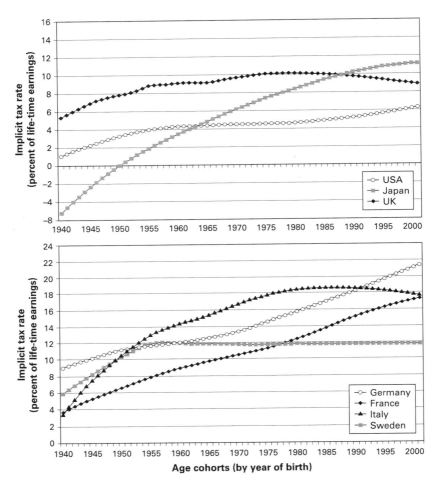

Figure 2.1
Implicit taxes involved in public pension schemes.

imposed on those born in the 1970s or 1980s is mainly due to demographic aging.

Take, for example, Germany. The German statutory pension scheme has always been generous toward average earners with a full lifetime work career. Not surprisingly, the level of implicit taxes generated by the German pension system is one of the highest among the countries considered here. Furthermore, since the latest reforms imply only minor corrections to benefit levels and contribution rates, the upward trend that arises from the current demographic prospects is predicted to continue to the end of the simulation period.

Things are not very different in France. Implicit tax rates are lower than in Germany simply because public pension coverage is lower. The story is slightly different for Japan. There too benefit levels are less generous than in Germany. Furthermore, following a massive expansion in the early part of the simulation period, the Japanese public pension scheme is slowly moving away from pre-funding. Combined with the extreme demographic scenarios expected for this country, this is resulting in a rapid rise in implicit tax rates—from strongly negative for the oldest cohorts considered in the simulation, to European-style rates for those born today.

Because of a historical peak in benefit levels, and to a very high level of implicit debt inherited from past policies, the implicit tax rates that the Italian public pension scheme imposes on an intermediate range of age cohorts are even higher than in Germany. The reforms enacted in 1992 and 1995 are expected to halt, or even reverse, the upward trend in these implicit taxes in time to help today's young, and the future generations. Given the long transition period, however, the rates remain very high for those born in the mid-1980s, and also for those born soon after that. The Swedish case resembles the Italian one except in that the reforms are phased in much faster. Also Sweden is not hit by demographic aging as severely as Italy and other European countries. As a consequence implicit tax rates in Sweden level off for those born in the late 1950s, and are virtually the same for younger generations.

Compared with continental Europe, the United Kingdom and United States stand out for their low levels of, and small increases in, the implicit taxes created by their public pension schemes.[47] The main reason is that the public pensions provided by Anglo-Saxon countries are very low. If the United Kingdom continues with the extreme form of CPI indexation applied in the past, there is virtually no increase in implicit tax rates over their present level. As indicated in the last section, however, this form of indexation may now be abandoned. Still, the United Kingdom's outlook will remain favorable by European standards.[48] Demography plays an important role in the extremely low level of implicit tax rates estimated for the United States. As mentioned in the last section, that country has also started to accumulate reserves (in Social Security Trust Funds) well ahead of the expected retirement of the

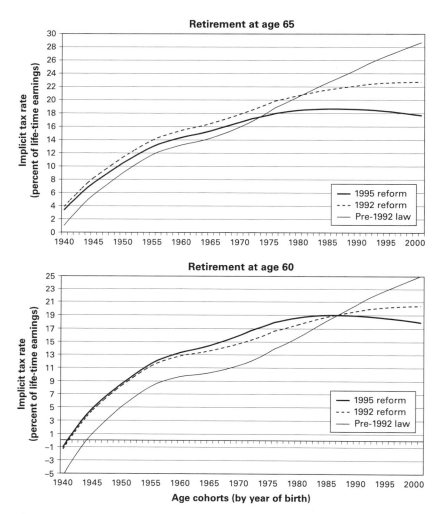

Figure 2.2
Implicit taxes—The case of Italy.

baby-boom generation. This will help spread the burden across several generations.

The implicit taxes that we have calculated are an upper bound on the implicit taxes actually borne by individual pensioners. For the sake of comparability, we have assumed that everybody retires at the age of 65. In actual fact many retire earlier than that. The implicit tax paid by the average participant is thus lower than indicated in figure 2.1. For some participants, the tax is clearly negative. Figure 2.2 illustrates the point for the case of Italy. We choose this country because, until the recent reforms, the legal age of retirement in that country was only 60 for men and 55 for women. It is clear from the two panels included in the figure, that the generations already retired at the time of writing enjoy an implicit subsidy. The average member of these generations fares even better because, as mentioned in the last section, it was (and still is, until the reforms become fully operative) possible for a person to retire at any age, provided only that she has paid contributions for a specified number of years. Additionally, in Italy as in the other countries considered, people have been allowed to take early retirement for a variety of contingent reasons (a sudden surge of unemployment at the national level, exceptionally high unemployment in particular geographical areas, etc.).

Therefore not everyone who participates in a mandatory pension system will actually suffer an implicit tax. What is rather true is that disparities of treatment, within as well as between generations, not fully captured by figure 2.1, may give rise to intragenerational and intergenerational transfers, distortions in the allocation of resources, and possibly also iniquities.

3   Public Support for
Families and Children

Public support for children, and families with children, exists in most developed countries. It may include cash payments, tax allowances, price subsidies, and benefits in kind. In some countries cash benefits are paid at a flat rate, so much per child. But this does not make them a lump-sum transfer because the *total* amount of benefits to which a family is entitled depends on the number of children, and that is in turn affected by parental decisions. In general, the child benefit rate may vary with number of children, birth order, family income, and other circumstances.

Cash benefits may be partially or totally replaced by tax allowances. If the latter take the form of deductions from the final tax bill, they are equivalent to a cash payment (except for non-tax payers, who have to be taken care of in some other way). If they take the form of deductions from taxable income, by contrast, the benefit is larger for higher earners. Tax allowances are in that case "regressive," in the sense that the rich get more than the poor. On the other hand, tax allowances provide a better approximation of the true opportunity cost of parental time spent with children.

Transfers in kind are another important alternative to cash transfers. Day and health care, schooling, school meals, and educational material are obvious examples. These goods and services may be provided free of charge or at subsidized rates. To ensure that redistribution goes from the rich to the poor, the amount of the subsidy is in some countries directly related to family income. In general, the take-up of these subsidies depends on demand for the good or service to which they apply. Only where fruition is compulsory—as in the case of certain forms of health care, or in that of primary and secondary schooling—can the value of the benefits received by each child be expected to be the same for all families.

All these subsidies are supposed to benefit children, not the other members of the family. In the case of cash benefits and tax allowances, however, they constitute additional resources for the family as a whole. Whether and to what extent they are actually spent on children depends on decisions taken by parents. By contrast, benefits in kind can only be used for the children themselves. But even these can substitute for expenditure that the children's parents would have carried out anyway, and are thus a subsidy for the family as a whole. Where the three types of benefits differ is in their effect on parental behavior. We postpone the discussion of these issues to chapters 5 and 7. Here we limit ourselves to surveying the policies adopted in the countries under consideration.

3.1   Cash Benefits

Child-related cash benefits are surveyed from time to time at an international level, in particular for EU member countries. Some of these comparative studies are now out of date.[1] Others are restricted to certain subsets of policy measures[2] or to relatively small subsets of countries.[3] A recent research project conducted for the UK Department of Work and Pensions (Bradshaw and Finch 2002) has collected up-to-date information on broadly defined packages of child-related benefits, both monetary and in kind, for a large number of industrialized countries. We draw from this report the information that relates to France, Germany, Italy, Japan, Sweden, United Kingdom, and United States.

3.1.1   Monetary Benefits for Families with Children

Monetary benefits can be broadly classified as cash transfers and tax allowances. In the countries considered, they are contingent on one or more of the following:

1. Type of family (couple or single parent)

2. Number of children (economically dependent and living in the household or still being educated and away at school.)

3. Family income

4. Parents' labor force status (mother employed, unemployed and seeking employment, or stay-at-home).

As a major distinction, child-related cash transfers are either independent of family income or means-tested to restrict their allocation to those who are considered needy. They are unrelated to family income in Sweden and the United Kingdom. On a more limited scale, flat-rate cash benefits also exist in Japan and France (there becoming more significant for families with two or more children). In some countries cash support is given only within the context of "social assistance" programs aimed at families with next to no income of their own. Such programs are in place virtually everywhere, but eligibility rules and the level of support provided vary a great deal from country to country. In Italy, Japan, and, to a lesser extent, France, means-tested child support reaches a broad range of low-income families.

Albeit with differing implications, tax allowances are particularly important in France, Germany, the United Kingdom, and the United States. The German system of child-related tax allowances,[4] and the French method of taxation based on "family splitting," tend to neutralize the effects of strongly progressive income tax schedules.[5] In the United States and the United Kingdom, the tax system is now designed so as to effectively subsidize labor force participation by low-wage earners in an attempt to move them "from welfare to work." In these cases tax credits with a major child component for low earners lead to substantial tax reductions for those at the lower end of the income scale.

Most national systems of child-related cash benefits are a combination of different elements, reflecting different traditions, and different ideas as to why families with children should receive public support. This makes it hard to predict the total entitlements of families in different situations. In the following, we simply look at the outcomes that the different systems generate for the "model families" identified by Bradshaw and Finch (2002). Outcomes are measured as the increase in disposable household income that can be attributed to child-related benefits. The rules taken into account are those existing in 2001, the year for which Bradshaw and Finch provide the relevant information. The representativeness of these "model families" is clearly open to question. But the approach does at least ensure that like is compared with like, and highlights how families in a similar situation are treated by the tax-benefit systems of different countries.

We start by looking at a narrower range of "baseline" cases, covering just a few of the many potential sources of variation. In most existing child benefit systems, two aspects are really important for determining the outcome, namely the type of family (single parent vs. couple) and the number of children living in the household. We will initially confine our attention to the cases of single parents with one child, and couples with one or two children. Gross household income in these baseline cases is fixed at the relevant national average: average female earnings in the case of single parents, average male earnings plus half of average female earnings in the case of couples. The idea is that the vast majority of single parents are single mothers and that, with national variations, single as well as married women now very often maintain some degree of labor force participation even when they have young children.[6] Since child benefits can vary with the child's age, we specify that the child is aged 7 in the case of one-child families. For families with two children, we assume that one child is aged 7 and the other 14.

Figure 3.1 shows the total amounts, and the structure of, child-related cash benefits on a monthly basis for our three "baseline" cases.[7] The benchmark is the net disposable household income of a single adult for the case of single parents, of a childless couple for the case of couples with children. All nominal amounts are expressed in euros. Amounts relating to non-eurozone countries are converted into euros using OECD purchasing power parities (PPPs).

The figure confirms the points we have made about the size and structure of national child benefit packages. It also shows that total monetary benefits for one child (in primary education) varies a great deal across countries. It can be as low as 11 euros (Italy, couple with one child) or as high as 213 euros (Germany, single mother with one child) per month. In the majority of cases, however, child-related monetary benefits are worth between 85 and 150 euros a month for families with just one child.[8]

Note that in the United Kingdom and in Sweden the amount of benefits is the same for single parents and couples with one child each. In all other countries, the entitlements of single mothers can be substantially higher for several reasons. The most important is that compared with cohabiting parents, single parents may enjoy additional tax allowances and/or be eligible for additional benefit components. This is clearly the case in Germany, France, Italy, and Japan.

Not surprisingly, total amounts of benefits are always higher for a couple with two children than for a one-child family. In Germany, Sweden, and Japan benefit entitlements double when a couple has two children instead of just one child. The increase is less than proportional

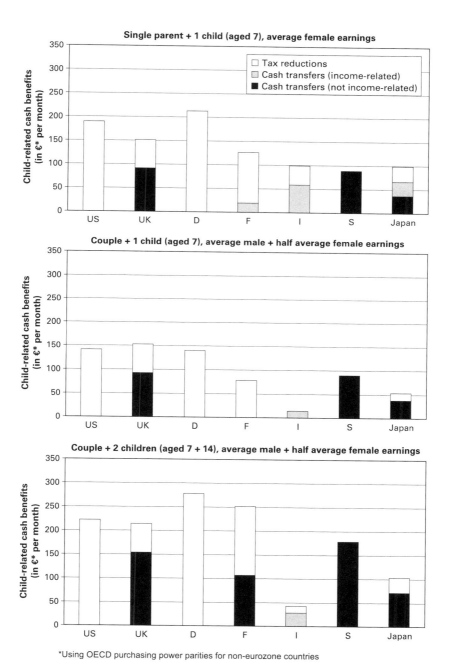

Figure 3.1
Child-related monetary benefits—Baseline cases.

in the United States and the United Kingdom. It is much more than proportional in Italy and France where, again, additional benefit components enter the picture as the family gets larger.

Let us now look at additional model families. We will introduce more variation in terms of family size, household income, and patterns of labor force participation of the parents. We will not consider additional sources of differentiation of benefits by children's age,[9] and will mention special rules applicable to children of pre-school age only when we talk of child-care facilities (in section 3.2). For ease of presentation, we now focus on totals, dropping any information on the composition of the benefit packages.

3.1.2 Parents with Different Numbers of Children

In figure 3.2 the set of baseline family types is extended to include only two more cases—single parents with two children (aged 7 and 14) and couples with three children (aged 7, 14, and 17).[10] Assumptions regarding household income remain unchanged: regardless of how many children they have, single mothers are assumed to live on average female earnings, and couples are assumed to live on average male earnings plus half the average female earnings.

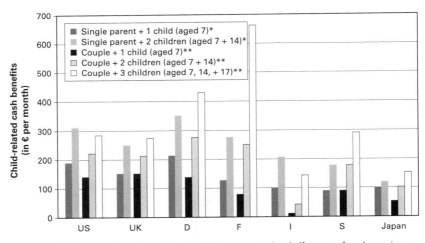

* With average female earnings. ** With average male + half average female earnings.

Figure 3.2
Child-related monetary benefits—Number of children.

The figure basically confirms our earlier inferences. Benefits are generally higher for single parents than couples with the same number of children. The exceptions are Sweden and the United Kingdom for one-child families and Sweden for two-children families.

For single parents, total benefits increase less than in proportion to the number of children in the United States, United Kingdom, Germany, and Japan, in proportion—or just a little more than proportionally—in France, Italy, and Sweden. For couples with children, the increase is less than proportional in the United States and United Kingdom, proportional in Germany and Japan, more than proportional in France, Italy, and Sweden. This slight divergence seems to indicate that as the number of children gets larger, the special rules applicable to single parents are handled a little more restrictively than the general rules applicable to all family types. Furthermore the French system apparently encourages fertility much more than any of the others do.

We have stated that the amount of benefits related to rearing just one child tends to be between 85 and 150 euros a month (4 to 6 percent of national average earnings). Consequently benefits for families with two children (couples with three children) tend to fall between 170 and 300 (270 and 400) euros a month, equivalent to between 8 and 12 (10 and 16) percent of average earnings. The outliers are Italy and Japan, where child-related cash benefits are much less generous than elsewhere, and France, which pays much higher benefits to families with three or more children.[11] By the construction, all these numbers relate to the uniform income levels that we have specified.

3.1.3 Parents with Different Earnings

We now return to our three baseline family types to spell out the consequences of differences in earnings for the entitlement to receive child-related cash benefits. At the household level, the range of feasible earnings is certainly different for single parents and couples with children. For a single mother, the effect on household income of staying at home or working part-time while her children are very young is much stronger than for a married, second-earner woman. Furthermore even single mothers with higher than average qualifications may find it difficult to devote enough time to a job to earn much in excess of average earnings for full-time employment until the children are in all-day schooling or day care, or become self-reliant. Couples, on the other

hand, can engage in several forms of a division of labor. In the following, we will therefore consider some variations on the baseline cases:[12]

1. Single parent, with one child aged 7
· Living on social assistance (no earnings)
· Earning the minimum wage rate for 16 hours of regular work per
week
· With half the average female earnings
· With average female earnings
· With average male earnings

2. Couples, with one child aged 7, or with two children aged 7 and 14,
· Living on social assistance (no earnings)
· Earning the minimum wage rate for 16 hours of regular work per
week
· With half the average male earnings
· With average male earnings
· With average male, plus half average female, earnings
· With average male plus average female earnings

We include social assistance (plus housing benefits accruing in this
case), though this takes us into a different policy area. It is unusual for
(child-related) welfare benefits reserved for households with no income
of their own to be integrated in the same mechanism that provides
child benefits for households on average earnings. This lack of integra-
tion can create problems, notably in reducing work incentives for those
on the margin of the welfare system. That is precisely what led the
United States and the United Kingdom to redesign their national welfare systems over the last ten years. Both countries have now a grad-
uated benefit scheme aimed at households with low earnings, which
reflects the policy trade-off between ensuring a decent living standard
for and providing work incentives to persons with only low-earning
ability. The effects of these policy changes can be seen in figure 3.3.[13]
As the figure shows, for persons only capable of earning the minimum
wage rate, the step from social assistance to employment is harder to
take in other countries where sizable child-related welfare benefits are
forgone by gaining employment.

The numbers shown in figure 3.3 are again based on a comparison
between net disposable income in families with children, on the one
hand, and net disposable income of single adults and childless couples
in the same earnings category, on the other hand. The patterns that
arise are very diverse.

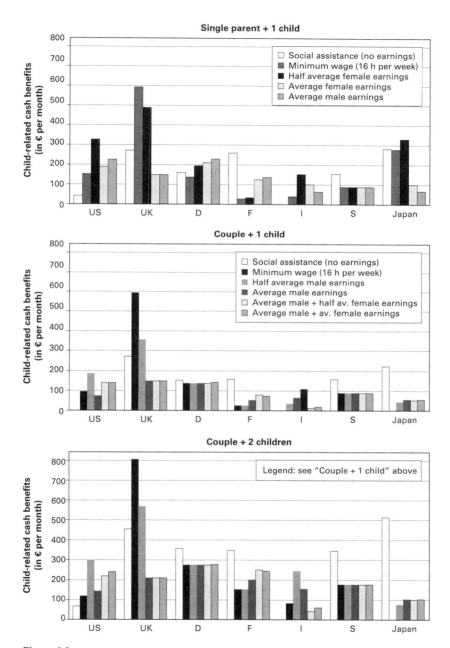

Figure 3.3
Child-related monetary benefits—Levels of earnings.

In the United Kingdom, the United States, and, with much lower benefits, Italy, the relationship between child-related cash benefits and income has an inverse-U shape: the welfare benefits increase up to a certain level of income and then decrease. This is because of the low welfare benefits for persons not working, and higher benefits for those who take employment at low wages, which is typical of the welfare-to-work policies enacted in those countries.[14] Even the main difference between the US earned income tax credit (EITC) and the UK working families tax credit (WFTC)[15] shows in the graphs. In the United States, the tax-based wage subsidy is first phased in over a small range of very low wages and then phased out. In the United Kingdom, the phase-out of benefits starts immediately from a lower limit of 16 hours worked per week, which is one of the eligibility rules.

Different countries have different strategies also with regard to households that have passed the income threshold where these special programs cease to be applicable. In the United States and in Italy, child-related cash benefits start rising with income again. In the United Kingdom, benefits become independent of income. In Germany, Sweden, and Japan, monetary benefits related to number of children are also largely independent of income, at least over the income categories covered here, and for households out of social assistance. In all three countries, however, child-related benefits are higher for households with no earnings than for households that include wage earners.

A peculiarity of Germany is that child benefits for single parents appear to rise strongly with income. The reason is that special tax allowances play an important role in this family type. This does not apply to couples with children because, since 1996, the general child tax allowance is applied only if it leads to tax reductions higher than the per-child cash benefit offered as an alternative.[16] The French, by contrast, appear to be less afraid of child benefits increasing with parental income. However, over the income range covered in figure 3.3, the effect of income is not strong. As we saw in the last subsection, the effect of the number of children is much more important.

For families with one child (two children), child-related cash benefits are again mostly in the range of 85 to 150 (170 to 300) euros per month, or between 4 and 6 (8 and 12) percent of average earnings. For families on lower incomes, the corresponding amounts of benefits can be substantially larger or smaller than that. In the United Kingdom, for example, child benefits can reach 600 (800) euro a month, more than 20 (30) percent of average earnings. In Italy and Japan, they go down to zero. There is thus a great deal of variation across countries with respect to child benefits for families in different earnings brackets.

3.2 Benefits In-Kind

Most industrialized countries provide benefits in-kind, some of which are very clearly earmarked for families and children. Here we survey only the main types of in-kind benefits: child-care provision for children of pre-school age, public schooling at primary and secondary levels, and health care for children economically dependent on their parents. This selection leaves out some other areas where children are the designated recepients of government support.

For instance, eligibility for low-cost public housing and rent subsidies is often related to the presence of children. But measures in this area are so diverse across countries that we decided to simply include their financial consequences (i.e., differences in effective housing costs between households with and without children) for social assistance recipients in our computation of cash benefits, and ignore everything else.[17]

In many countries there is also a deep involvement of the public sector in education at the tertiary level in the form of free or subsidized university tuition, student loans or scholarships, for example. As the amount of subsidy that a family receives under this rubric depends on many factors—not least their children's intelligence—other than those considered so far, it makes little sense to provide estimates for our model families.[18]

3.2.1 Child Care

Day care for pre-school aged children is important for several reasons. First, children are given an opportunity to mingle with their peers under professional supervision, and thus they learn to socialize. Second, children receive some basic ("pre-primary") education. Third, children are being looked after by an adult, thus enabling parents to combine child-rearing with employment. Day-care facilities are publicly provided or, at least, heavily subsidized in many countries. At the same time, whether they are publicly or privately owned, day-care institutions are often subject to a good number of regulations to ensure quality of service.

Table 3.1
Day care for children at pre-school age

| Country | Fraction of children in day care (%)[a] | | Forms and costs of day care for children aged < 3 | | | |
	Aged ≤ 3	Aged 3–4	Standard form	Fees charged[b]	Special transfers[b]	Net costs[b]
United States	16	54	Child-minder	882.30	0.00	882.30
United Kingdom	15	42	Family day care or child-minder	527.53	0.00	527.53
Germany	9	54	Day nursery	327.23	0.00	327.23
France	39	100	Child-minder	274.26	96.09	178.17
Italy	9	71	Day nursery	232.41	10.33	222.08
Sweden	40	82	Municipal day care center	205.99	0.00	205.99
Japan	27	85	Public day nursery	315.53	0.00	315.53

Source: Bradshaw and Finch (2002, ch. 5).
a. Year 1999 to 2000 data.
b. Year 2001 figures, in euro–PPPs per month (2001); computed for a couple with one child on average male earnings plus half the average female earnings.

The fraction of children in a given age group that has access to these institutions greatly differs from country to country, and also region to region. There is further variation across the narrowly defined pre-school age group: aged less than 3, 3 to 4, or 5 to 6. The variations may reflect differences in demand, but also different norms and policy choices.

Table 3.1 gives an overview of the prevalent day-care forms for children aged less than three years old. Beyond age three the patterns of day care are more uniform internationally. Additionally the table lists the fraction of pre-school children younger or older than 3 that is in day care, the fees charged for the predominant type of service, the effects of special benefits not covered in section 3.1, and the net cost per child that the parents have to face as a result.

In most of the countries surveyed, the fees charged to parents are lower than the total cost of these services. Because subsidies are paid directly to the supplier of the service, the figures given in table 3.1 do not fully reflect the actual amount of transfers involved in provision of pre-school care. The accounting procedures applied by the public sector in many countries are not even capable of producing the kind of information needed to estimate the true resource cost of publicly provided day care. We may nonetheless get some idea of the value of these benefits if we look at the high fees charged for day care in the United Kingdom and the United States. The range is from 500 to 900 euros a month per child. This may reflect differences in the type of service provided (i.e., the "technology"), the prices of the inputs, and the quality of services provided. The lower fees charged to parents in the other countries considered does, however, suggest that substantial child-related benefits are tied to the utilization of day-care services.

Additionally several countries allow for special tax reductions—for instance, by making child-care fees deductible from the parents' income tax base—or offer specific direct transfers targeted at families with very young children. These additional benefits are also included in table 3.1. Assuming that the actual cost of pre-school services is around 700 euros per child on average, we can conclude that if special tax allowances are taken into account, the total value of benefits (monetary and in kind) associated with a child in day care is between zero (in the United States, and perhaps the United Kingdom) and 520 euros (in France) a month in the case of a couple, between 330 (in Germany) and 650 euros (again in France) a month in the case of a single parent.[19]

3.2.2 Schooling

As with day care, there is no reliable micro-level data on public policy for education at a primary and secondary level that can help us calculate the value of benefits in-kind with similar accuracy as in the case of cash benefits. In all the countries surveyed here, public school education is basically free of charge and open to all children, at least for as long as schooling is compulsory (Bradshaw and Finch 2002, p. 90). In most countries, parents face additional costs for textbooks and other learning materials, school meals, uniforms, transportation, extracurricular activities, and outings. For these expenditures parents may receive additional tax allowances or direct transfers. According to data reported in Bradshaw and Finch (2002, ch. 5), the monthly net cost to parents of a child aged 7 attending school ranges between 56 euros in Japan and −29 euros (a net benefit!) in Sweden. But most of the benefits associated with free public schooling are clearly not included in such data.

Again, part of the problem is that accounting standards in the public sector simply do not offer the kind of data that is needed to determine the full value of these benefits, not to mention their differentiation by school type, age of children, final educational attainments, and other sources of cost variation. The OECD regularly collects information regarding the aggregate proportion of GDP spent on public education at a primary and secondary level in member countries (e.g., see OECD 2003a). Combining these data with information regarding the level of GDP, and the number of school-age children in each country, we can at least calculate the per-student value of public expenditure on education.[20] Two assumptions implicit in our procedure are that compliance with compulsory school attendance by children aged 6 to 15 or 16 is next to universal, and that the share of fully private schools in primary and secondary education is negligible (which is not quite true in the United Kingdom, and clearly not the case in the United States).[21] The results are presented in table 3.2. Note that the estimates in the table are only rough estimates; they leave out a considerable number of cost components and ignore public involvement in tertiary education.

Although there is some variation across countries in the GDP ratio of the relevant categories of public spending, monthly amounts of expenditure per child are surprisingly uniform. Besides the United Kingdom, where the final result is about 480 euros a month per child, our esti-

Table 3.2
Public expenditure on primary and secondary education

	Expenditure per GDP (%)[a]	Aggregate Expenditure[b]	Number of children aged 6 to 15/16[c]	Expenditure per student and month[b]
United States	3.49	344.2	39,429,841	711.39
United Kingdom	3.36	49.6	8,451,951	478.48
Germany	2.89	59.5	8,222,800	603.34
France	4.03	58.2	7,641,407	634.23
Italy	3.21	38.2	5,146,765	618.27
Sweden	4.35	10.1	1,138,403	722.89
Japan	2.67	88.8	11,364,268	637.07

Sources: OECD (2003a, c) for expenditure ratios and GDP; US Bureau of Census (2000), the Japanese National Institute of Population and Social Security Research (2002), and Eurostat (2000) for population data.
a. Year 2000 figures.
b. Year 2000 in euro–PPPs (billions of euros for aggregate expenditure, euro for per-student amounts).
c. Statutory school age ends at age 15 in Germany, Italy, and Japan; at age 16 in the United States, the United Kingdom, France, and Sweden.

mates range from about 600 euros for Germany to about 720 euros for Sweden. While there are important differences in input prices (primarily, teachers' salaries), the difference in the amount spent by the government in the different countries is thus rather small. Nevertheless, there are important differences in the structures of national school systems (comprehensive or streamed systems, teacher–student ratios, hours of classes per day, etc.), and possibly also in the quality of educational services provided, so the effective value of public schooling can be much more heterogeneous across countries than it appears from these figures.

3.2.3   Health

We conclude our survey on child-related benefits with a look at the public provision of health care for children who are economically dependent on their parents in the usual set of countries. Apart from the United States, all the countries considered have a national health, or health insurance, system where no additional contributions are required for the cover to be extended to children. Still there can be charges in some areas of medical treatment meant to limit utilization, but these charges are generally lower for children than for adults.

Health services provided by hospitals, general practitioners, and dentists are entirely free for children in the United Kingdom, Germany, and Sweden.[22] In France, Italy, and Japan, minor charges are imposed uniformly on children and adults. With the exception of children of households with no, or very low, income who are eligible for the public Medicaid program, parents in the United States have to pay the full cost of their children's health care, or health insurance.

In their comparative study of child benefits, Bradshaw and Finch (2002) define a "standard health package" for children and calculate the total amount that parents are required to pay as contributions, premiums, or fees for the services available in different countries. As already mentioned, charges are zero in the United Kingdom, Germany, and Sweden. They range from 2 to 4 euros a month per child in France, Italy, and Japan, but amount to no less than 125 euros in the United States. Since health services in the United States are by far the most expensive in the world,[23] it is difficult to argue that the high health cost of a child in that country can be used as a measure of the full cost of health services received by children in the other countries considered. Nonetheless, the various pieces of evidence available on the issue indicate that the value of the net health-related transfer arising from existing arrangements in countries other than the United States can amount to up to about 100 euros a month per child.

Summing Up

Attaching a single figure to the entire package of child benefits offered by each country is no easy task. Given the many sources of differentiation, both across families and across countries, and the limited evidence available on the full range of benefits provided by the public sector, we could easily be way off the mark. On the other hand, not trying to tie things together would leave us without a term of comparison for other age-related public expenditures.

We have seen that monetary benefits range from 85 to 150 euros a month per child aged 17 or less, often regardless of family type (single parent vs. couple) and number of children in the household.[24] Day care for small children is worth 300 to 500 euros a month more per child. For children at school age, free schooling is worth about 600 euros a month per child. Finally, public health care may be worth another 100 euros a month per child. This adds up to between 485 and 850 euros a month per child receiving day care or attending school.

Having come this far down this road, we could go even further. If a child born today is expected to receive public day care between the ages of 2 and 6, and public education from 6 to 17, the present value of the benefits (considered in this chapter) that the family will receive before the child reaches the age of 18 is between 111,000 and 129,000 euros. For parents with average wages, that amounts to between 25 and 30 percent of the present value of their earnings in the same period, or between 10 and 12 percent of their lifetime earnings. But calculations of this kind involve a host of assumptions. We will thus refrain from going any further.

4

Child-Related Elements in
Public Pension Schemes

In chapter 3, we examined various types of subsidies to families with children. There is, however, another way in which childbearing can be subsidized, and this is through the pension benefits to which their parents will be entitled. In chapter 2, we examined other, more conventional, aspects of public pension schemes. The present chapter is devoted to the largely unexplored question of how childbearing affects pension entitlements.[1] In many cases these effects are either unintended or the result of measures brought in as an afterthought to compensate women with children for the supposedly adverse effect of a reform that has nothing to do with childbearing. Such child-related policies are more recent than most of the other policy instruments examined so far. Our findings will prove relevant for the theoretical arguments that we develop in chapters 5 and 7, and for our policy discussion in chapter 8.

4.1 Rules Applied in Selected Countries

In this section we attempt a comparative quantitative assessment of the rules applied in the different countries under consideration under the year 2003 legal framework by simulating their implications for a balance sheet of different categories of persons. We begin with a discussion of the prima facie basis for child-related pension benefits.

The argument generally advanced in connection with "social insurance" is that in the absence of corrective measures, the strong link between pension benefits and contributions that characterizes such schemes translates any withdrawal from the labor market, or reduction in the amount of labor supplied, into lower pension benefits. This does not occur in a pure "social security" scheme, and does not matter so much even in a social insurance type of scheme if individual benefits are assessed based on income earned in a relatively small number of years, those in which the pensioner earned the most; "spouse" or "survivor" benefits have broadly the same effect. One way to justify the introduction of child-related pension benefits in a social insurance type of scheme might then be to say that this policy will allow mothers to make up for the pension benefits forgone while rearing children. These are indeed the terms in which the policy has been discussed and justified in the countries that have adopted it. But, is it really true that withdrawing from a social insurance scheme constitutes a disadvantage?

All the public pension systems considered in this book impose an implicit tax on the average member born 1955 or later. The reason, as we saw in section 2.4, is that the actuarial value of the benefits expected by those generations falls short of the capitalized value of their (expected) contributions. It might then be argued that the average person would be better off staying out of such a system (but remember that persons on lower than average earnings can gain from the system thanks to the redistribution that takes place in virtually all real-life public pension schemes). Without going into the intricacies of membership rules, the obvious counterargument is that the only way of staying out of the system is to stay out of the labor market. Therefore the money saved by not contributing to a public pension scheme is not available for alternative uses, it is simply not there.[2] Does this apply also to the case of a woman who leaves her job to look after a child?

Assuming that fertility is a result of choice, a woman has children if either the money or the money-equivalent of the utility that she expects to receive from her children compensates her for the cost. (Saying that fertility cannot be perfectly controlled is an argument for subsidizing parents with too few, as well as parents with too many, children.) As the loss of earnings and pension benefits consequential on having a child is part of this cost, the counterargument is thus not applicable to a woman who leaves her job to look after a child. If a woman receives public transfers for having children, she may in fact be doubly subsidized: she is allowed to escape the tax implied in a less than actuarially fair pension system, and additionally she receives fertility-related transfers. Like conventional child benefits, fertility-related pension benefits should thus be regarded as an incentive to have children and be justified in those terms. By contrast, subsidies or tax exemptions on education and other goods consumed by young children may be seen as an inducement to spend more for each child. We will deal with both issues in chapter 7.

4.1.1   United States

The United States provides a good example of an unintended relationship between pension benefits and childbearing. Apart from benefit entitlements designed to meet specific contingencies—orphans' pensions, survivor benefits for surviving parents with small children, or child benefits for pensioners with dependent children—that exist also elsewhere, US Social Security does not provide any extra benefits for workers who have reared children. As in some other countries, however, pension benefits are calculated on the basis of money earned in the best 35 out of a maximum of 40 years. This leaves room for offsetting short periods of reduced labor force participation (e.g., due to care for small children) or reduced wages (e.g., due to low earning capacity following a period of parental leave). But the rule is not designed to compensate parents for the opportunity cost of rearing children, and offers limited scope for using it to that end.

The same can be said of the weights used in the social security benefits formula. Indexed monthly earnings are effectively divided into three earnings brackets and then converted into pension benefits at differing rates (decreasing from 90 to 15 percent as one moves from low to high wages). The benefit formula can help reduce the opportunity cost of child rearing by containing the loss of potential pension benefits. But, again, that is not the motivation for, nor the major effect of, this way of assessing social security benefits. The objective is rather to achieve some intragenerational redistribution across earnings brackets.

This kind of income redistribution can also help mothers, but the link with childbearing is countered by a noncontributory benefit ("spouse benefits") paid to the dependent partners of old-age pensioners. An insured individual's pension benefit is increased by 50 percent when his or her partner reaches the retirement age. At the same time the dependent partner's own pension benefits are reduced on a one-for-one basis against this "dependents' allowance." Since the benefit is not conditional on the spouse's labor force participation, many working women effectively face a higher (net) marginal tax[3] than "first-earner" males. As the benefit is not conditional on time spent rearing children, spouses who stay out of the labor force to take care of their children do not have any advantage over childless ones.

4.1.2   United Kingdom

Things are not too different in the United Kingdom. Recall that for individuals with a full lifetime record of work, benefits provided by the UK State Basic Pension scheme are not linked to their earnings. Workers who take leaves of absence to care for their children are not entitled to any extra payment. At the same time Basic Pensions are inspired by some notion of how long a standard work biography should last. In order to qualify for a full Basic Pension, a person must have 44 years of contributions.[4] Pro-rata reductions are made if the number of qualifying years is between 11 and 44. Spouses with no, or just low, pension benefits of their own are entitled to a "category B" retirement pension on top of the breadwinner's "category A" pension. The former are limited to a maximum of 60 percent of a full Basic Pension. As in the United States, these noncontributory benefits are not contingent on having reared children or having taken time out to care for one's children.

There is nevertheless one aspect in which the UK system is much more generous than US Social Security in rewarding parental child-care obligations. The number of years for which contributions have to be made in order to qualify for a full Basic Pension can be reduced to a minimum of 20 years if the other years were devoted to a number of specified "home responsibilities." Taking care of children is prominent among these responsibilities. Since living with at least one child under the age of 16 is presumed to engender home responsibilities (for as long as this situation lasts), mothers—and, alternatively, fathers—who have maintained some degree of labor-force attachment despite an extended parental leave stand a good chance of qualifying for a full Basic Pension. However, no more than 27 percent of women (as against 95 percent of men) of retirement age are currently receiving a full Basic Pension, and another 45 percent have a reduced basic pension linked to their own employment record.[5] This suggests that most currently retired women have worked for less than 20 years.

4.1.3   Germany

Specific elements of child-related pension benefits were introduced in the German *Gesetzliche Rentenversicherung* in 1986 and have been expanded since on a number of occasions.[6] Currently, for each child born in 1992 or later, mothers—and, alternatively, fathers—are granted additional pension entitlements (*Anrechnung von Kindererziehungs-*

zeiten) equal to those that a person with average earnings would gain by paying contributions for three more years. For children born before 1992, the entitlement is the equivalent of only one year of contributions. Until 1996, child-related entitlements were subject to certain limits, stating that the contributions notionally credited to a person should not exceed 75 percent of average contributions per year, and that they were set off by regular contributions on a one-for-one basis.[7] Since 1996, benefits deriving from this rule are simply added to regular earnings-related benefits.[8]

Another link between pension entitlements and childbearing was introduced in 2002. Since that year, earnings-related pension entitlements acquired over the first ten years since the birth of a child are increased by a complicated, highly redistributive, formula that favors working mothers with low wages. The additional entitlement is zero if earnings are either zero or higher than average earnings. The maximum that can be gained under this rule is equal to the additional entitlements that would be gained if one made additional contributions equal to one-third of the average. Starting from that same year, widows' and widowers' benefits have been made contingent on number of children (before 2002, these survivors' benefits depended only on the deceased partners' entitlements).

Yet another link is entailed by the definition of total pension benefits for individuals with fragmented work biographies. Up to ten years per child (*Kinderberücksichtigungszeiten*) can be "disregarded" when assessing the average annual contributions that are imputed to certain types of nonparticipation periods (for training, extended unemployment spells where claims on unemployment benefits have expired, etc.).

In Germany as elsewhere, child-related pension benefits were originally intended to fill gaps in the typical mother's work record. Up to a point the earliest rules were designed to discourage women with very small children from working. The major effect of later reforms has been to increase the public pension entitlements of mothers regardless of their labor force participation. Today women—as well as men[9]— can qualify for a modest pension by just rearing two children.[10]

4.1.4 France

In France there is a long tradition of offering child-related benefits through the tax and public transfer system. This is true also of the old-age pensions provided by the *Régime Général*. Since 1974 the actual number of years of contribution is being artificially augmented by two years per child for mothers who have taken care of their children for at least nine years before the children reached the age of sixteen (*majoration de durée d'assurance pour enfants*).[11] An important effect of this rule is that provided that they have maintained a sufficient degree of labor force participation, mothers can retire up to two years earlier than the statutory limit for each child they have. This is one of the earliest examples of a child-related element in public pension benefits throughout the industrialized world.

For mothers who bring up three or more children, the pension is increased by an additional 10 percent (*majoration de retraite pour enfants*). In principle, both types of benefit are granted regardless of whether or not the mothers worked during the first two or more years following the birth of a child. On the other hand, the amount of extra benefits that a mother can earn under these regulations is dependent on her average wages during periods of actual contributions, and on the number of years for which she actually made contributions. If the mother effectively withdrew from the labor market following the birth of the child, the amount of the benefit will be small.

Since 1983 the augmentation of the number of years of contributions applies also to fathers who take parental leave (*majoration de durée d'assurance pour congé parental*). The maximum leave permitted is three years, and the augmentation is limited to the effective length of the leave. The same applies, as an auxiliary legal entitlement, to mothers who cannot take advantage of the full augmentation mentioned earlier. For mothers earning very low wages, there is a further child-related benefit equal to the current minimum pension benefit or, under certain conditions,[12] to a higher amount (*allocation aux mères de famille*) increasing with the number of children.

Therefore the French public pension scheme goes out of its way to reward parental child-care activities. A distinctive feature of the rules we have sketched is that they clearly go beyond filling potential gaps in the employment records of working mothers. On the other hand, since the French follow the continental social insurance model,[13] spells of nonparticipation following childbirths reduce other (earnings-related) pension entitlements more than they would if the system were of the Anglo-Saxon social security type.

4.1.5   Italy

The 1995 reform of the Italian public pension system strongly increased the potential for large gaps in individual earnings careers to affect pension entitlements. Although female labor force participation in Italy is low by international standards,[14] this would have added to the opportunity cost of rearing children. To compensate for that, the 1995 package introduced, for the first time, child-related elements in the Italian public pension scheme. These benefits, however, are very limited.

According to current legislation, working mothers who give birth to a child are credited with fictitious contributions (*contributi figurativi*, or *accredito figurativo*) for the five months—two before and three after a child is born—that women are required to stay out of employment (*assenza obbligatoria*),[15] and for up to six more months of voluntary parental leave (*assenza facoltativa*). The latter may be taken at any time during the first three years of a child's life. In either case the entitlements arising from these credits are calculated on the basis of earnings actually forgone (as against average earnings as in Germany). If, instead of withdrawing from the labor market altogether, the mother works part-time, the loss of pension entitlements is made up for using a similar procedure. Smaller *contributi figurativi* are credited for voluntary leaves exceeding six months, or taking place between the fourth and the eighth year of the child's life.[16] Since 1994 Italy also has rules designed to make sure that mothers who happened to be outside the labor force when their children were born are credited fictitious contributions for at least the period of *assenza obbligatoria*.[17]

Therefore the Italian pension system tries to compensate parents for at least part of the opportunity cost they actually incur by raising children. In addition to that, parents—mothers or fathers—are allowed to buy extra cover in the public pension scheme for any period of *assenza facoltativa*, and for any period of extended parental leave. Last but not least, the statutory age of retirement for women is reduced by four months per child,[18] up to a maximum of 12 months. Alternatively, mothers can opt for a more favorable conversion coefficient,[19] which will effectively treat them as if they had been working for up to two years longer than they actually have. When compared to the other rules mentioned here, the effects of these last two measures may well turn out to be substantial.

Regarding the introduction of child-related pension benefits, the Italian public pension scheme has thus moved some way in the direction of France and Germany. So far, however, the child-related elements remain limited in scope by continental European standards, and their effects seem likely to be substantial only for mothers who discontinue their labor force participation for a short period.

4.1.6   Sweden

In Sweden too, the new *Inkomstpension* includes a considerable amount of additional fertility-related benefits (*extrapension för barn*). As in Italy, the new scheme envisages "notionally defined contributions," implying that special measures are needed to make up for the effects of parental leaves on individual pension entitlements. In the old system, men or women who had spent at least 15 years in employment did not suffer a pension loss if they withdrew from the labor market to have children unless this affected the amount earned in their "best 15 years."

The new rules contemplate several alternative methods of crediting parents with fictitious contributions during the first four years after a child is born. Depending on the choice made by the parents, the rules can apply indifferently to the father than to the mother. If no choice is made, the benefits accrue to the parent who has acquired lower pension entitlements in the relevant period of time. The different methods yield different results, depending on the amount earned by the beneficiary in the year preceding, and those following, the birth of a child. For each of these years, the method actually applied is the one most favorable for the particular parent.

Typically the wages that a Swedish parent earns are substantial in the year before a child is born, but low or even zero during the (short) period of parental leave that follows. In a majority of cases, the most favorable alternative is thus to fictitiously raise the contributions credited to the parent for these low-wage years to the level of the last year in full employment. If the wages earned in the year preceding the birth are low, however, the most favorable alternative is to fictitiously raise the amount of contributions credited in the years following the birth to at least 75 percent of the average earnings of current contributors. For parents who earn higher-than-average wages when their children are small, the most favorable method involves crediting them with contributions calculated on the basis of a so-called income base amount (*inkomstbasbelopp*, equivalent to about 20 percent of average earnings) on top of contributions actually made.

Against the background of a rate of female labor force participation (*and* a total fertility rate) that is remarkably high by European standards, the new Swedish pension system strikes a compromise between two immediate aims: to fill any lapses in individual earnings careers relevant for the calculation of future pension benefits and to use the pension scheme to reward child rearing as such, regardless of whether or not parents withdraw from work for a certain period of time.

4.1.7 Japan

In the Japanese flat-rate National Pension Scheme the rules relevant for women, with or without children, are similar to those that apply in Anglo-Saxon countries. Regardless of whether or not they have a work record of their own, married women are entitled to receive the universal basic pension as a spouse benefit. Furthermore working-age married women do not have to pay the (lump-sum) contributions required of all other working-age individuals covered by the universal pension scheme when they are out of work. As in all pure social security schemes, there is neither a specific relation between pension entitlements and child rearing nor any gap to be filled in a mother's earnings record.

Specifically child-related benefits are present, by contrast, in the Employees' Pension Scheme. There women or men taking parental leave do not have to pay contributions for the time they are suspended from their (formally continuing) employment relationship.[20] For a maximum of one year of parental leave, the worker accumulates pension entitlements calculated on the basis of earnings forgone. Amendments are being considered, but none has been approved so far.

4.2 A Synopsis of Measures

Having explained how children and child rearing activities affect pension benefits in our sample of industrialized countries, we will now try to say something about the relative weight of child-related pension benefits. To make things comparable across countries, we will again build on simulations generated by the CESifo Pension Model. In chapter 2 we were essentially looking at the (male) breadwinner in a one-earner family, participating in the public pension scheme.[21] Here we extend the analysis to a two-earner family with at least one child. Separately, we will consider also the case of single mothers. Although we allow for limited behavioral responses to policy differences, these simulations are still accounting exercises like those carried out in chapters 2 and 3.

We have seen that, where they exist, child-related pension benefits can take many different forms. Where they do not exist, other features of the pension system (flat-rate benefits, spouse benefits, etc.) substitute for them to some extent. We have also seen that the effects of these different measures vary with the family's earning profile. It is very hard, especially in a comparative perspective, to disentangle the effects of fertility-related pension benefits from those of other kinds of child benefits, including tax breaks, on a family's net lifetime income. We will thus limit ourselves to looking at the way in which net household wealth—defined for present purposes as the present value of lifetime wages net of pension contributions, plus pension benefits of any kinds—is affected by childbearing in existing pension systems. We disregard unearned income, and all kinds of tax other than pension contributions.[22] We also neglect conventional child benefits, already examined in chapter 3.

Taking the gross lifetime earning profile of a typical primary earner (assumed to be in full-time employment throughout his active life) as given, we calculate (1) the household earnings and pension contributions associated with alternative work records and wage rates of a secondary earner, who might spend time looking after children, (2) the changes in pension entitlements that arise from applying a country's standard benefit formula to individuals with fragmented work records, and (3) the impact of special benefit rules applicable only to parents. The question we try to answer is how net household wealth is affected, under different assumptions and institutional arrangements, by a woman's decision to reduce her labor force participation in order to look after a child.

4.2.1   Women's Wage Profiles and Stylized Biographies

As in the similar exercises carried out in earlier chapters, we conveniently assume that working mothers behave the same in all the countries considered. While the rules taken into account when assessing changes in individual pension benefits are country specific, the life-cycle profiles of labor force participation and earnings to which these rules are applied are based on observations taken from Germany, allowing only for limited variation. This procedure can be criticized on a number of grounds but has the merit of permitting comparisons across countries.

An important ingredient of the exercise are the wage equations for men and married women estimated by Fenge et al. (2006) using German micro-data.[23] The results indicate that wage rates depend on individual qualifications and job experience. Another important ingredient is a set of stylized biographies for married women covering, among other things, aspects such as the timing of births, and the pattern of employment following the birth of a child. The list of stylized biographies of wives include a benchmark profile, a baseline profile, and a number of variations on the latter. For married men, we invariably assume that they work full-time from the age of 20 until they reach the statutory retirement age (or, in the US case, the age threshold for claiming full benefits). We will first use our wage equation to impute wage rates to each of these biographies, and then apply the existing rules to calculate pension contributions and benefits at a household level. This will yield estimates for the present value of net earnings and actualized pension benefits for each set of biographies. Most of the results are expressed as deviations from the benchmark.

The benchmark is a married woman who, like her husband, is in continuous full-time work between the age of 20 and the statutory age of retirement.[24] Taking into account the current rules and the changes scheduled for the near future, the statutory retirement age for women and men now aged around 30 is taken to be 65 in the United Kingdom, Germany, Sweden, and Japan. In France, retirement is possible from 60 upward for both men and women, but women with a fragmented work record may have to work longer in order to qualify for full benefits. In Italy, the female (male) retirement age will *rise* to 60 (65) when the latest reform package is fully implemented.[25] In the United States, the age for claiming full benefits is 67.

The baseline profile has a woman giving birth to a child at age 25, taking leave of absence for three years, working 50 percent of a full-time job for the following three years, and 75 percent for another five. At the end of this eleven year hiatus, when the child is in secondary school, baseline-type mothers are assumed to return to full-time work.[26] The assumptions regarding labor force participation of, and wage rates earned by, husbands are the same used in the benchmark. Departures from the baseline profile take the form of (1) alternative work records, (2) alternative wage rate profiles of women, and (3) different numbers of children. Table 4.1 summarizes the assumptions made for each of our stylized biographies. Figure 4.1 shows the earnings profiles associated with the different work records of women (to facilitate cross-country comparisons, results are expressed as percentages of current national averages).

4.2.2 Baseline Case

To make things comparable, we consistently assume that men and women are born around 1975, and have their first baby in the year

Table 4.1
Stylized biographies of women used in the simulations

Scenario	Number of children	Age at birth(s)	Parental leave	Part-time work (50%)	Part-time work (75%)
Benchmark	—	—	—	—	—
Baseline	1	25	3 years	3 years	5 years
Withdrawal	1	25	(total withdrawal until retirement age)		
Extended leave	1	25	6 years	5 years	—
Short leave	1	25	1 year	2 years	3 years
No leave	1	25	—	—	—
2 children	2	25, 28	6 years	3 years	5 years
3 children	3	25, 28, 31	9 years	3 years	5 years
Low earnings[a]	1	25	3 years	3 years	5 years
High earnings[b]	1	25	3 years	3 years	5 years

Note: All women are assumed to take up full-time work at age 20. Apart from the case of "withdrawal," women return to full-time work after their period of absence or reduced labor force participation.
a. 75 percent of lifetime earnings in the baseline scenario.
b. 175 percent of lifetime earnings in the baseline scenario.

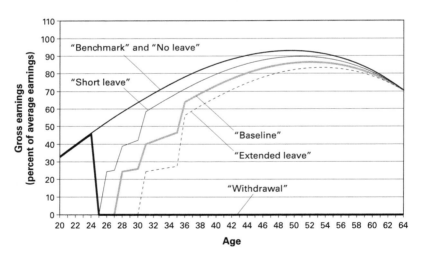

Figure 4.1
Stylized earnings profiles of typical mothers.

Table 4.2
Net household wealth in the baseline scenario

	Husbands		Benchmark women		Baseline case mothers		
	Net earnings	Pension benefits	Net earnings	Pension benefits	Net earnings	Pension benefits related to	
						Work record	Child-rearing
United States	756,094	89,478	486,583	15,083	376,642	12,236	—
United Kingdom	733,640	45,775	481,314	9,614	376,310	9,614	—
Germany	676,877	65,846	434,134	48,047	333,899	40,506	7,406
France	424,221	63,028	272,407	44,916	210,573	34,910	5,306
Italy	319,663	69,993	191,725	51,280	145,654	40,977	1,636
Sweden	631,322	48,276	407,986	42,149	318,520	34,743	3,263
Japan	899,532	91,670	576,441	26,918	443,670	21,452	405

Source: CESifo Pension Model.
Note: All numbers indicated in the table are year 2000 present values measured in euros (using OECD purchasing power parities for non–eurozone countries).

2000. Results are condensed in the form of present values in the year 2000 of the net wage and pension benefit streams.[27] All figures are expressed in euros, using OECD PPPs to account for cross-country differences in the cost of living. While male net earnings, and pension benefits, do not change as we move from the benchmark to the baseline case,[28] female net earnings and pension benefits generally decrease. For females, we distinguish between "standard" pension benefits (related to the woman's own work record) and extra benefits related to child rearing. The former tend to be reduced when women work less than in the benchmark scenario. The latter tend to make up for (part of) this difference. In principle, these child-related benefits can even give a mother *more* than she loses by spending time with her children. Due to the opportunity cost of taking care of children, however, net household wealth is unambiguously lower in all the baseline cases considered than in the benchmark.

Table 4.2 summarizes the results for the case of a couple where the husband works full-time throughout his active life, and the wife's biography conforms to our baseline assumptions (benchmark results are reported for comparison). In making cross-country comparisons, it should be kept in mind that nominal earnings and pension benefits

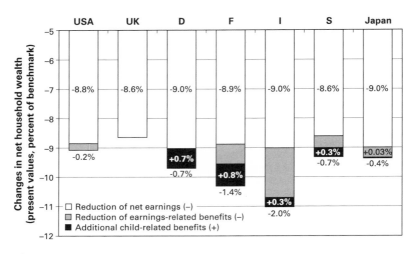

Figure 4.2
Changes in net household wealth—Baseline scenario.

may vary as a result of a variety of factors, including differences in wage rates, in the generosity of the public pension scheme and, last but not least, in the accuracy of PPP equivalencies. The allocation of the pension benefits between the marriage partners is influenced by the existence and generosity of "derived" benefits such as spouse and survivor pensions.[29] Age of retirement, and the length of the retirement period, are another important source of cross-country variation. Other things being equal, pension benefits are obviously higher in countries where people retire earlier,[30] or live longer.[31]

Figure 4.2 shows the same results in terms of percentage changes in net household wealth between the baseline and the benchmark. These changes are the end result of (1) reductions in net earnings due to discontinuities in the wife's work record, (2) consequential reductions in earnings-related benefits, and (3) compensations in the form of child-related benefits (where they exist). In the United States, for example, net earnings are 8.8 percent lower in the baseline scenario than in the benchmark, and earnings-related benefits add a loss of 0.2 percent. As there are no child-related pension benefits, net household wealth is 9 percent lower in the baseline case than in the benchmark. In the United Kingdom, net earnings are 8.6 percent lower. As baseline mothers are entitled to receive the full amount of the flat-rate Basic Pension, there is no loss of regular pension benefits.[32] Therefore net household wealth is 8.6 percent lower in the baseline case than in the benchmark. In France, the reduction in net earnings is 8.9 percent. Earnings-related benefits fall 1.4 percentage points, but there are child-related benefits (worth 0.8 percentage points of total net lifetime earnings in the benchmark case). The final result is a reduction in total benefits of approximately 0.6 percentage points, and a reduction in net household wealth of approximately 9.5 percent.

The downside of the social security type of schemes adopted by Japan, United Kingdom, and United States is that paying pension contributions is not really profitable for mothers, and for married women in general. As is true also of social insurance schemes, any change in a married woman's labor force participation has an impact on household net earnings regardless of whether she has children or not. In a social security scheme, however, most of what a woman pays in contributions when she does work is effectively lost (this is due to the redistributive nature of these schemes).

The loss of total pension entitlements is unconditionally zero only in the United Kingdom. It is fully made up for through child-related pension entitlements only in Germany.[33] There is a loss of pension entitlements in the United States (worth −0.2 percent of benchmark net lifetime earnings) and Japan (−0.4 percent), where child-related entitlements are inexistent or negligible. There is a loss of benefits also in Sweden (−0.4 percent) and France (−0.6 percent), where child-related benefits compensate for about half of the reduction in earnings-related benefits. The loss is highest in Italy (−1.7 percent), where public pension benefits are now very strongly conditioned by individual earnings and contributions, and child-related components are still very small.

Taken in isolation, child-related pension benefits are most important in France, where they amount to 0.8 percent of the net lifetime earnings of a benchmark two-earner couple. They are substantial (0.7 percent in Germany, 0.3 percent in Sweden and Italy) also in the other countries where the standard benefit formula establishes a strong link between earnings and benefit entitlements. By contrast, they have very little effect in Japan (0.03 percent), and are totally absent in the United States and the United Kingdom. Where they are present, child-related pension benefits make up entirely for the loss of regular benefits only in Germany.[34] In Germany and Sweden they limit the total loss to the level observed in the United States, or to within the range of those observed in the United Kingdom and Japan.

As an aside, we now look at the consequences of parental leaves and child-related pension entitlements on the net earnings and pension

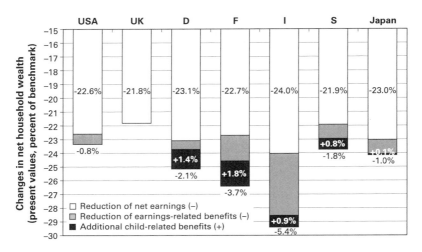

Figure 4.3
Changes in net household wealth for single mothers—Baseline scenario.

benefits accruing to single mothers under our baseline assumptions. In this case we disregard any (former) husband's earnings and benefits (implying that we do not include alimony in our calculations, and ignoring the possibility that the woman is widowed). Figure 4.3 shows the results for a single mother with one child, under baseline assumptions about her labor force participation and earnings profile.[35]

The impact of reduced labor force participation on net earnings and earnings-related pension entitlements is of course stronger in the case of a single benchmark woman than in that of a couple. That apart, the results for single mothers are qualitatively the same as those shown in figure 4.2. The only difference worth mentioning is that child-related pension benefits do no make up for the loss of earnings-related benefits—not even in Germany, where they do in the case of a one-earner couple. A reason is that as single women do not qualify for survivor benefits, any loss of entitlements associated with their own work record is potentially more important for these women than for a couple. This is particularly true of Germany where survivor pensions include a child-related element.

4.2.3 Alternative Patterns of Labor Force Participation

Table 4.3 refers to the case of a married couple where the woman stays out of the labor force a shorter or longer time than assumed in the

Table 4.3
Changes in net household wealth—Alternative work records

Country	United States	United Kingdom	Ger-many	France	Italy	Sweden	Japan
Withdrawal							
Net earnings	−35.5%	−35.8%	−35.3%	−35.3%	−33.7%	−35.7%	−35.2%
Pension benefits related to . . .							
Work record	−1.2%	−0.8%	−4.1%	−6.2%	−9.4%	−3.8%	−1.7%
Child-rearing	0.0%	+0.4%	+0.5%	+0.3%	+0.1%	+0.3%	+0.03%
Extended leave							
Net earnings	−12.6%	−12.4%	−12.8%	−12.6%	−12.8%	−12.3%	−12.8%
Pension benefits related to . . .							
Work record	−0.4%	−0.1%	−1.0%	−2.3%	−2.9%	−1.0%	−0.5%
Child-rearing	0.0%	+0.1%	+0.5%	+0.6%	+0.3%	+0.3%	+0.03%
Baseline							
Net earnings	−8.8%	−8.6%	−9.0%	−8.9%	−9.0%	−8.6%	−9.0%
Pension benefits related to . . .							
Work record	−0.2%	0.0%	−0.7%	−1.4%	−2.0%	−0.7%	−0.4%
Child-rearing	0.0%	0.0%	+0.7%	+0.8%	+0.3%	+0.3%	+0.03%
Short leave							
Net earnings	−4.5%	−4.4%	−4.6%	−4.6%	−4.6%	−4.4%	−4.6%
Pension benefits related to . . .							
Work record	−0.1%	0.0%	−0.3%	−0.6%	−1.0%	−0.4%	−0.2%
Child-rearing	0.0%	0.0%	+0.7%	+0.4%	+0.4%	+0.2%	+0.03%
No leave							
Net earnings	0.0%	0.0%	0.0%	0.0%	0.0%	0.0%	0.0%
Pension benefits related to . . .							
Work record	0.0%	0.0%	0.0%	0.0%	0.0%	0.0%	0.0%
Child-rearing	0.0%	0.0%	+0.7%	+0.3%	+0.3%	+0.1%	0.0%

Source: CESifo Pension Model.
Note: All numbers indicated in the table are percentage changes of present values of expected net household wealth (i.e., earnings net of pension contributions plus pension benefits) against the benchmark scenario of a couple without children where both partners are working full-time from age 20 until retirement age.

baseline case. The results are again expressed as percentage deviations from benchmark household net lifetime wealth. We continue to distinguish changes in benefit entitlements due to a variation in the woman's work record from changes due to the operation of special rules applicable only to mothers who take care of children. It is clear from this table that most of the change in net household wealth is due to the reduction in net household earnings associated with a spell of nonparticipation by the mother. This reduction is about the same in all the countries considered.

Where changes of benefit entitlements are concerned, UK National Insurance easily retains its top position (smallest loss in the highest number of cases). Indeed the case of definitive withdrawal from the labour market is the only one where a British mother suffers any loss of lifetime pension benefits.[36] In all other cases mothers in the United Kingdom end up qualifying for a full State Basic Pension.[37]

In the United States and in Japan, public pension benefits are earnings-related, though not as strongly as in continental Europe. Child-related benefit rules are nonexistent, or not very prominent. As a consequence relative losses in benefit entitlements get smaller as the mother's participation in the labor market gets longer. The maximum loss, associated with the case of definitive withdrawal from the labor market, is smaller than in all other countries except the United Kingdom. At the same time expected pension benefits of a mother with no leave do not exceed those of a woman without children.

By contrast, in countries where public pensions are strongly conditioned by earnings (or contributions levied on earnings), definitive withdrawal leads to very heavy loss of entitlements. If the woman was employed for only five years before the withdrawal, the reduction in earnings-related benefits is about 4 percent of net lifetime earnings in Germany and Sweden, more than 6 percent in France, and 9 percent in Italy. Child-related benefits, ranging between 0.1 and 0.5 percent of lifetime earnings, are not even remotely sufficient to compensate for these losses. At the other extreme, however, in all these countries women who take no maternity leave at all are entitled to receive child-related benefits on top of their earnings-related benefits. Therefore these women end up with higher pension benefits, and higher net household wealth, than childless benchmark women. The premium for rearing one child amounts, in their case, to between 0.1 and 0.7 percent of the net lifetime earnings of a benchmark couple (between 2.5 and 15 percent of a benchmark woman's pension). This suggests that compensating mothers for potential losses of earnings-related benefits was not the only goal pursued by the legislator in introducing child-related components in public pensions. Redistribution, or providing an incentive to have children, could have been among the motivations.

Looking more closely at the pattern of child-related pension benefits in the countries that provide such benefits, we detect another type of cross-country heterogeneity, not fully revealed by the calculations reported in table 4.3. In Sweden, the amount of child-related benefits tends to decrease as we move from the "withdrawal" to the "no-leave" case. In France, by contrast, child-related benefits are highest in the (intermediate) baseline case. In Germany, child-related benefits vary inversely with the length of time for which mothers stay out of the labor force. In Italy and Japan, child-related benefits do not appear to be much affected by the mother's work pattern.

4.2.4   Mothers with Different Earning Abilities

We now look at earnings profiles that differ from the baseline for the assumptions made about the woman's wage rate. We retain the baseline assumptions regarding fertility (only one child) and employment pattern. (Husbands are again assumed to be identical in all the scenarios considered.) Table 4.4 shows the results. Here "low earnings" means that the woman earns around 75 percent, and "high earnings" that she gets around 175 percent, of average female earnings over her entire life cycle. The two earnings profiles are obtained by adjusting the relevant dummy variables in the Fenge et al. (2006) wage equation so as to obtain the wage rates of, respectively, women who completed only secondary schooling, and women with completed university education.[38] Changes in net earnings again account for most of what happens to net household wealth, but cross-country differences are now greater than when we were looking at the effects of female participation.

Our definition of high earners implies that the wage profile of a mother falling in this category reaches its highest point (at about 140 percent of economywide average wages) when she is in her 50s. As a consequence, in Sweden and Japan, high-earnings women hit the ceiling on earnings covered by the national public pension scheme. This limits the level of earnings-related benefits accruing to this category of women in those countries. Conversely, our definition of low earners

Table 4.4
Changes in net household wealth—Level of earnings

Country	United States	United Kingdom	Ger-many	France	Italy	Sweden	Japan
Low earnings							
Net earnings	−16.6%	−16.2%	−16.8%	−16.7%	−16.4%	−16.5%	−16.8%
Pension benefits related to . . .							
Work record	−0.6%	−0.1%	−1.6%	−2.6%	−4.0%	−1.5%	−0.7%
Child-rearing	0.0%	+0.1%	+0.6%	+0.6%	+0.2%	+0.3%	+0.02%
Baseline							
Net earnings	−8.8%	−8.6%	−9.0%	−8.9%	−9.0%	−8.6%	−9.0%
Pension benefits related to . . .							
Work record	−0.2%	0.0%	−0.7%	−1.4%	−2.0%	−0.7%	−0.4%
Child-rearing	0.0%	0.0%	+0.7%	+0.8%	+0.3%	+0.3%	+0.03%
High earnings							
Net earnings	+14.3%	+13.6%	+14.1%	+14.4%	+12.7%	+14.7%	+14.2%
Pension benefits related to . . .							
Work record	+0.8%	0.0%	+1.7%	+1.9%	+3.7%	+1.0%	+0.6%
Child-rearing	0.0%	0.0%	+1.0%	+1.2%	+0.6%	+0.4%	+0.06%

Source: CESifo Pension Model.
Note: All numbers indicated in the table are percentage changes of present values of expected net household wealth (i.e., earnings net of pension contributions plus pension benefits) against the benchmark scenario of a couple without children where both partners are working full-time from age 20 until retirement age.

implies that young British women falling in that category do not meet the lower earnings limit required to qualify for a full State Basic Pension. However, the "home responsibilities" rule restores their pension benefits to the full level.

Wage rate differences apart, all the women considered in table 4.4 are assumed to have the same career pattern. The term of comparison is again the benchmark household (couple with no children, both partners in full-time employment at average wages throughout their active lifetime). Therefore any difference in benefits relating to the woman's work record reflects a difference in the rules applied by the different countries, particularly in the strength of the contribution-benefit link implicit in the benefit formula. For mothers with a limited period of parental leave, changes in earnings-related benefits are consequently absent in the United Kingdom, limited in the United States and Japan, but substantial in France, Germany, Italy, and Sweden. Where they exist, child-related benefits reduce the net loss of pension entitlements for women in the low-earnings group, and increase the advantage over an average earner for those in the high earnings one. The same is true with regard to changes in net lifetime earnings.[39]

Note that the amount of child-related pension benefits to which a woman is entitled increases with the level of earnings in France, Germany, and Italy. By contrast, it appears to vary little in Japan and Sweden. That is because, in the first three countries, child-related pension benefits tend to reflect the actual opportunity cost of time spent with children. In the other two, by contrast, these benefits seem to be based on some notion of what an extra birth is worth for society, independently of what it costs the parents.

4.2.5   Mothers with Different Numbers of Children

Finally, we turn to another source of variation from the baseline biography, the number of children. Table 4.5 shows what happens to married couples where a mother of average earning capacity gradually returns to work after taking parental leave, in the case where she has two and in the case where she has three children (instead of just one as in the baseline biography). In each case we adjust the length of the period of reduced participation to take account of increased domestic responsibilities (see table 4.1). Once again, longer periods of parental leave associated with higher numbers of children clearly affect the parents' net earnings pretty much the same in every country. By contrast, changes in pension entitlements are negligible or absent in some countries, considerable in others, depending on the nature of the public pension scheme.

In the United Kingdom, increasing the number of children does not make a difference to expected pension benefits because the longer absences from the labor market (another three years in the case of mothers of two children, six in that of mothers of three) are invariably excused under the "home responsibilities" rule. In Japan and the United States, earnings-related pension benefits are subject to small reductions as the periods of absence and part-time work increase with the number of children. This confirms our earlier remark that in these countries the second earner's work does not really pay in terms of pension benefits. Since there are no, or next to no, compensating measures[40] the loss of benefits increases with the number of children.

Table 4.5
Changes in net household wealth—Number of children

Country	United States	United Kingdom	Ger-many	France	Italy	Sweden	Japan
Baseline (one child)							
Net earnings	−8.8%	−8.6%	−9.0%	−8.9%	−9.0%	−8.6%	−9.0%
Pension benefits related to . . .							
Work record	−0.2%	0.0%	−0.7%	−1.4%	−2.0%	−0.7%	−0.4%
Child-rearing	0.0%	0.0%	+0.7%	+0.8%	+0.3%	+0.3%	+0.03%
Two children							
Net earnings	−11.9%	−11.8%	−12.2%	−11.9%	−12.1%	−11.6%	−12.1%
Pension benefits related to . . .							
Work record	−0.3%	−0.1%	−0.9%	−2.2%	−2.8%	−1.0%	−0.5%
Child-rearing	0.0%	+0.1%	+1.1%	+1.2%	+0.3%	+0.6%	+0.03%
Three children							
Net earnings	−15.7%	−15.5%	−16.0%	−15.6%	−15.9%	−15.3%	−15.8%
Pension benefits related to . . .							
Work record	−0.5%	−0.1%	−1.3%	−2.8%	−3.7%	−1.3%	−0.5%
Child-rearing	0.0%	+0.1%	+1.5%	+1.7%	+0.5%	+0.8%	+0.03%

Source: CESifo Pension Model.
Note: All numbers indicated in the table are percentage changes of present values of expected net household wealth (i.e., earnings net of pension contributions plus pension benefits) against the benchmark scenario of a couple without children where both partners are working full-time from age 20 until retirement age.

The loss of earnings-related benefits is stronger in France, Germany, Italy, and Sweden. With the exception of Italy,[41] however, the level of child-related benefits increases considerably with the number of children. As a consequence the loss of benefits is lower in these countries than in Japan or the United States. The loss increases with the number of children in France and Italy, is roughly invariant in Sweden, and tends to fall in Germany. In the latter the amount of child-related pension benefits accruing to a mother of two or three again more than fully compensates for the loss of earnings-related benefits. In all four continental European countries child-related pension benefits could more than compensate for the loss of earnings-related benefits if the mother chose to work more than we have assumed in our calculations.[42]

In terms of changes in net household wealth, making up for reductions in earnings-related pension entitlements is clearly of limited significance. The United Kingdom, where child-related pension benefits are negligible, is consequently the country with the smallest loss of net household wealth, closely followed by Germany and Sweden (where fertility-related pension benefits matter), the United States and Japan. France comes next. Italy is a long way behind with the largest loss of net household wealth.

Summing Up

The number of children is now an important determinant of total pension entitlements in a number of industrialized countries. Child-related elements are much more prominent in social insurance schemes, where they serve to compensate for the negative effects of a strong contribution-benefit link, than in social security schemes, where the link is weak. It is thus not entirely clear which type of scheme is more generous toward women with children. What is clear is that the social security schemes considered are at best neutral toward (involve no loss of earnings-related benefits as a result of) childbearing activities, while the social insurance ones tend to subsidize mothers with a strong labor force attachment.

The way child-related pension benefits were introduced in the different countries is extremely interesting. In Germany and France, they were an addition to existing earnings-related benefits. In Italy and Sweden, by contrast, the introduction of the new benefits was paralleled by substantial cuts in existing entitlements. In the last two countries child-related benefits therefore substitute in some measure for earnings-related ones. Since any benefit increase unaccompanied by an increase in contributions adds to the implicit debt associated with any pay-as-you-go public pension scheme, it might be argued that the maneuver will reduce the public debt, or at worst leave it constant, in Italy and Sweden, but will increase it in France and Germany. Is that right?

By definition, child-related pension benefits are conditional on the birth of a child. In due course the child will pay taxes and pension contributions. So long as the benefits accruing to the parents do not exceed the contributions made by the child, child-related pension benefits will then reduce the total (explicit plus implicit) public debt if they replace earnings-related pension benefits. If they are introduced in addition to earnings-related pension benefits, they will raise or lower the total public debt depending on whether the taxes and contributions collectively paid by the children born in response to the policy is smaller or larger than the child-related pension benefits collectively received by the parents. Therefore it all depends on the elasticity of the fertility rate. It would thus be wrong to argue that the new pension benefits will necessarily add to the total public debt if they are in addition to existing ones. Depending on how strongly potential parents respond to the introduction of these specific benefit entitlements, it is rather true that the policy is likely to reduce the debt more in Italy and Sweden, than in France and Germany. We will come back to this issue in chapter 8, when we can count on a model of fertility behavior.

5   Life-cycle Adjustments and Intergenerational Transfers: Theory

Having examined the policies adopted in a number of countries, we now want to make sense of them. Before we can do that, however, we must understand how people respond to them. In the present chapter we outline a number of different explanations of how individuals behave, with the focus on life-cycle adjustments and intergenerational transfers. Paul Samuelson was among the first to see the connection between the two:

Let us assume that men enter the labor market at about the age of twenty. They work for forty-five years or so and then live for fifteen years in retirement. Naturally, . . . men will want to consume less than they produce in their working years so that they can consume something in the years when they produce nothing . . . .

If there were only Robinson Crusoe, he would hope to put by some durable goods which could be drawn on in his old age. He would, so to speak, want to trade with Mother Nature current consumption goods in return for future consumption goods . . . .

For the present purpose, I shall make the extreme assumption that nothing will keep at all. Thus no intertemporal trade with Nature is possible. If Crusoe were alone, he would obviously die at the beginning of his retirement years.

But we live in a world where new generations are always coming along. . . [C]annot men during their productive years give up some of their product to bribe other men to support them in their retirement years? (Samuelson 1958)

The answer to this rhetorical question is clearly yes, if there is a way of making sure that the bribed person will deliver his side of the deal 20, 30, or 40 years later. Samuelson's own solution is in what he calls "social contrivances": contract law and its associated enforcement apparatus, money that ". . . gives workers of one epoch a claim on workers of a later epoch . . ." (Samuelson 1958). Legal-tender money and contracts enforceable through the courts are different expressions of a more fundamental kind of contrivance, the state. Without the state, there can be no assurance that a contract, or a means of payment with no intrinsic value, will not be repudiated by the next generation.

Another contrivance, independent of the state, is the family. Everywhere in the world, in developed as well as in developing countries, young children receive material and personal support from their parents, and elderly parents from their children. Could these intergenerational flows of goods and personal services be taken as evidence of, in Samuelson's terminology, intrafamily "consumption loan arrangements"? Many would argue, we among them, that some of these transfers are genuine gifts, that the giver derives altruistic pleasure from giving. However, as Robertson (1956) put it, altruism is a scarce good that economists should economize. Indeed, as we will see in the next chapter, the hypothesis that intrafamily transfers are *systematically* generated by altruistic motivations appears to be rejected by the data. Therefore, to be on the safe side, we will mostly assume that intrafamily transfers spring from mutually beneficial arrangements.

But, if intrafamily transfers are intergenerational exchanges rather than gifts, the enforcement problem comes back to the fore. What difference does it make if a deal is transacted between members of the same family, rather than perfect strangers? A difference, as Ben-Porath (1980) noted, is that members of the same family have an informational advantage. They know more about each other's personal characteristics, and have lower costs of monitoring each other's moves, than those of perfect strangers. This mitigates the adverse selection and moral hazard problems but does not take care of contract enforcement. We thus find it more productive to think of the family not as a market but as an organization with its own system of governance, and to talk of rule rather than contract enforcement.

A useful way of characterizing an organization is to describe its fundamental rules, its *constitution*. Economic theory tells us that it may be in everyone's interest to agree first on a constitution allowing agents to safely renounce the dominant strategy in a prisoner's dilemma type of situation, and then to optimize individually subject to the constitution (Buchanan 1987). Although originally conceived with reference to city or nation states, the constitution concept can be applied also to smaller groupings, such as clubs, professional associations, and, indeed, families. We will see in the next chapter that the hypothesis of a family constitution is not rejected by the data.

5.1   A Constitutional Theory of the Family

Standard life-cycle theory assumes that each person makes provision for his own old age by saving (Modigliani 1986). Individual decisions are assumed to be coordinated only by the market. Another body of literature interprets the desire to have children as a demand for old-age support (Leibenstein 1957; Neher 1971). Both these approaches assume that individuals are ultimately selfish. The constitutional approach to the economic theory of the family encompasses both these modeling traditions by treating saving and child rearing as alternative ways of providing for old age (Cigno 1993, 2006). In this extended framework, individual decisions may be coordinated not only by the market but also by self-enforcing family constitutions. In the present section we outline the constitutional model under the simplifying assumptions that the state of the world is certain and constant over time, that individuals are selfish, and that only market goods give utility. In the closing section we will argue that relaxing these assumptions increases the descriptive power of the model without changing its predictions in any fundamental way.

Let the life cycle consist of three periods, labeled $i = 0, 1, 2$. A person is said to be young in period 0, adult in period 1, and old in period 2. Adults are able to produce income and to reproduce. The young and the old can do neither. At any given date a family consists of individuals at three different points of the life cycle. That is important because it provides an opportunity for mutually advantageous intergenerational arrangements. Differences of sex and other personal characteristics also provide scope for cooperation, this time among members of the same generation, but we abstract from them at the present stage to concentrate on the intergenerational dimension.

Given a wage rate w, an adult can earn

$$y = wl \tag{5.1}$$

by supplying l units of labor. By bearing a fixed cost p for each child, she can also have up to a maximum of m children.[1] To avoid carrying too many constants around, we will include the child's period-0 subsistence consumption in p. In addition to the child's subsistence consumption, p will include also all the actual expenses other than the child's above-subsistence consumption and opportunity costs associated with the birth of a child.

The lifetime utility of an individual is assumed to be given by

$$U = u_0(c_0) + u_1(c_1 - v(l)) + u_2(c_2),$$ (5.2)

where c_i denotes above-subsistence consumption in the ith period of this person's life, and $v(l)$ the money equivalent of the disutility of labor. The functions $u_i(.)$ are assumed increasing and concave, with $u_i'(0) = \infty$. The function $v(.)$ is assumed increasing and convex.

Given these premises, a family constitution can be described as a set of (unwritten, typically unspoken) rules prescribing that each adult family member must pay (1) at least z to each of her children, if she has any, and (2) at least x to her parent, conditionally on the parent having complied with the constitution. The clause attached to rule 2 makes it in every adult's interest to punish transgressors. That is important because only an adult can punish another adult. Neither children nor old people have the means to do so. It stands to reason that x will be at least sufficient to keep the old alive. Since an old person can have more than one adult child, the amount x that she is entitled to receive from each child will take account of the number of children. In general, x will therefore be conditional on the fertility level of the last generation. Having assumed that the state of nature is certain and the same for every generation, however, every generation will choose to have the same number of children. So x will be the same for every generation. How will an adult respond to such a constitution?

5.1.1 No Assets or Credit Markets

We will start by assuming, like Samuelson, that there are no capital markets, and that "nothing will keep at all." The young and the old must then be supported by the adults of the day in order to survive. Since people are self-interested, it has to be shown that it may be in the interest of the latter to support the former. A direct exchange is not conceivable, however, because an elderly parent has no way of forcing her children to honor an informal arrangement supposedly made when the latter were still young. Let us see if a family constitution can do the trick.

If everyone complies with the constitution, a person consumes $c_0 = z$ when she is young,

$$c_1 = wl - x - (p + z)n$$ (5.3)

when she is an adult, and

$$c_2 = xn \tag{5.4}$$

when she is old. Having already lived her youth, an adult will then choose (l, n) so as to maximize utility over what is left of her life cycle,

$$u_1(wl - x - (p + z)n - v(l)) + u_2(xn).$$

The solution will satisfy

$$v'(l) = w \tag{5.5}$$

and

$$\frac{u_1'(wl - x - (p + z)n - v(l))}{u_2'(xn)} = \frac{x}{p + z}. \tag{5.6}$$

Since an adult spends $(p + z)$ on each of her children in the current period, and receives x from each of them in the next, the right-hand side of (5.6) is the marginal return to money spent on children. According to (5.5), a person will work until the marginal disutility of labor equals the wage rate. According to (5.6), she will have children to the point where her marginal rate of substitution of present for future consumption equals the marginal return to money spent on children.[2]

Let $n(z, x, w)$ be a complier's demand for n. The constitution is feasible if

$$x + n(z, x, w)(p + z) \leq lw. \tag{5.7}$$

If it is feasible, the constitution is also self-enforcing in the limited sense that the best individual response to everyone else complying with it is to do the same. The allocation of resources that results from every family member complying with the constitution is thus a Nash equilibrium. Since complying implies threatening one's own parent of punishment if she does not also comply, and the threat is credible because carrying it out is in the complier's own interest, the equilibrium is subgame perfect. In equilibrium the threat is never carried out because everybody complies.

5.1.2 Assets and Credit Markets

Now suppose that there are durable goods and capital markets. Define r as the interest factor. As it is now possible to provide for old age by accumulating durables, an adult can contemplate flouting the family constitution. If she decides not to pay her parent x, however, she cannot expect to get anything from her children when she becomes old. She will then set n equal to zero and save the amount of income s that maximizes $u_1(wl - v(l) - s) + u_2(rs)$. Since an extra unit of future consumption costs $(1/r)$ units of current consumption, her choice of s satisfies

$$\frac{u_1'(wl - v(l) - s)}{u_2'(rs)} = r. \tag{5.8}$$

That is indeed the story told by standard life-cycle theory. People save to the point where their marginal rate of substitution of current for future consumption equals the current interest factor. A family constitution offers current adults the possibility of providing for old age by having children instead of, or as well as, saving. In a sense the constitutional model therefore incorporates and extends the life-cycle theory of saving. At any date the adults of the day have two strategies, *comply* with the constitution or *go it alone* in the market. It is clear that go-it-aloners have no interest in having children. We will show in a moment that under conditions of certainty, compliers have no interest in saving either.

The payoff of the go-it-alone strategy is the maximum utility that the agent can achieve by an appropriate choice of (l, s),

$$v(r, w) = \max_{l,s}\ u_1(wl - v(l) - s) + u_2(rs). \tag{5.9}$$

This choice of (l, s) satisfies (5.5) and (5.8). The effects of changes in r or w on $v(r, w)$ are

$$v_w = lu_1'(wl - v(l) - s), \quad v_r = su_2'(rs). \tag{5.10}$$

The payoff of complying, provided that the agent's children also comply, is the maximum utility that an adult can achieve by an appropriate choice of n, subject to the constitution,

$$v^*(w, x, z) = \max_{n}\ u_1(wl - v(l) - x - (p + z)n) + u_2(xn). \tag{5.11}$$

The choice of n associated with this strategy satisfies (5.5) and (5.6). The effects of changes in x, w, or z on $v^*(w, x, z)$ are

$$v_x^* = -u_1'(wl - v(l) - x - (p + z)n) + nu_2'(xn), \tag{5.12}$$

$$v_w^* = [l - p'(w)n]u_1'(wl - v(l) - x - (p + z)n), \qquad (5.13)$$

$$v_z^* = -nu_1'(wl - v - x - (p + z)n). \qquad (5.14)$$

The allocation brought about by everyone complying with the constitution is a subgame perfect Nash equilibrium if and only if

$$v^*(w, x, z) \geq v(r, w). \qquad (5.15)$$

In what follows we will refer to the right-hand side of (5.6) as the *domestic interest factor*, and denote it by r_d. Since a complier pays her parent a fixed amount x, regardless of how many children she chooses to have, it is clear that if r_d were lower than, or even just equal to r, there would be no way that an adult could recover the fixed cost of complying. A necessary condition for (5.15) to be true is thus that

$$r_d \equiv \frac{x}{p + z} > r. \qquad (5.16)$$

We can then view the constitutional prescriptions as a kind of two-part tariff. By paying a fixed membership fee x, an adult acquires the right to receive a marginal return r_d, greater than the market interest factor r, on any money she chooses to spend on children. In view of (5.16), a complier will not save.[3]

The point is illustrated by figure 5.1. The convex-to-the-origin curve is an indifference curve. The straight line with horizontal intercept y and slope r represents the budget constraint facing a go-it-aloner. The straight line with horizontal intercept $y - x$ and slope equal r_d represents the budget constraint facing a complier. For (5.15) to be satisfied, r_d must be at least equal to the slope, at point g, of the indifference curve through e.

Notice that plan g contains less current and more future consumption than plan e. That is because the opportunity cost of current consumption is higher for a complier than for a go-it-aloner. Recall that income not consumed is lent to the market in plan e, transferred to the agent's parent and children in plan g. If the agent chose e, she would then save $s^e = y - c_1^e$. If she chose g, she would spend $y - c_1^g$ for her elderly parent and young children. Since c_2 is equal to nx, she would have $n^g = c_2^g/x$ children. In the picture, r_d is such that the agent is indifferent between e and g. In view of (5.15), she will then comply. But, even a small increase in r would induce her to switch to the go-it-alone strategy. We will thus call this kind of agent a *marginal player*.

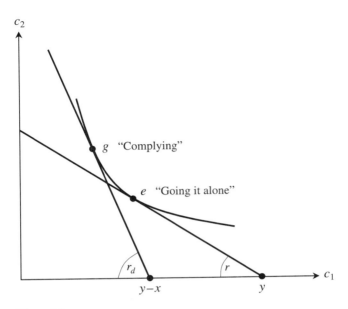

Figure 5.1
The marginal player.

While making it disadvantageous for compliers to lend to the market, (5.16) makes it advantageous for them to borrow from the market in order to finance additional births. But there are obvious limits to this arbitrage operation. First, fertility cannot increase without bound because it will eventually hit the physiological ceiling. Second, there is no legal mechanism through which an entitlement arising from an informal family arrangement can be transferred to another person. Such an entitlement cannot thus be offered as collateral to obtain credit from the market. We will then assume that compliers cannot borrow from the market at all (but nothing of substance changes if we allow borrowing up to some positive amount).

Figure 5.2 shows the set of constitutions that can be supported by a subgame perfect Nash equilibrium. The set consists of all the (x, z) pairs that satisfy (5.15). The boundary of the set is the locus of the (x, z) pairs that make (5.15) into an equation. This boundary does not cut the horizontal axis because z cannot be negative. It cuts the vertical axis, however, because adults would be happy to subscribe to a constitution that did not oblige them to make transfers to their children (above the subsistence level, included in p). The slope of the boundary is given by

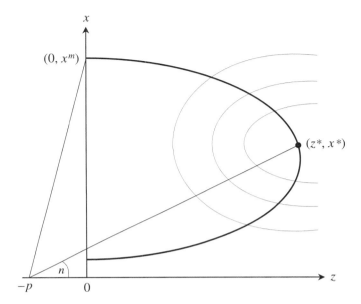

Figure 5.2
Nash-frontier and the renegotiation-proof family constitution.

$$\frac{dz}{dx} = \frac{(p+z)n - x}{nx}. \tag{5.17}$$

Since

$$\frac{d^2z}{d(x)^2} = -\frac{p+z}{(x)^2} \tag{5.18}$$

is negative, z is maximized at the point, shown in figure 5.2 as (z^*, x^*), where

$$r_d = n. \tag{5.19}$$

Therefore the amount transferred to each young child is largest in the constitution that induces parents to have a number of children equal to the domestic interest factor.

Since v_r is positive in view of (5.10), a rise in r would shift the boundary inward. Intuitively that is because the lowest rate of return to children that makes complying with the constitution at least as attractive as going it alone in the market will increase too. This can be seen also from figure 5.1. If r increased, the constitution associated with r_d would no longer satisfy (5.15). By contrast, a rise in w would shift the boundary outward. In view of (5.10) and (5.13) both v_w and v_w^* are in fact positive, but v_w^* is larger than v_w because, in view of (5.16), the opportunity cost and thus the marginal utility of current consumption is higher if the agent complies than if she goes it alone. While an exogenous rise in the interest rate would make the set of potentially enforceable constitutions smaller, an exogenous rise in the wage rate would thus make it larger. For w sufficiently low, or r sufficiently high, the set may be empty (no constitution may be sustainable as a Nash equilibrium).

5.1.3   Self-enforcing Family Constitutions

If the set defined by (5.15) is not empty, an infinite number of constitutions may be sustainable as subgame perfect Nash equilibria. Some of them will entail a high payment (as high as z^*) to the young and a low one to the old; others will entail a high payment to the old and a low one (as low as zero) to the young. Which will prevail?[4] As decisions are taken by adults, who will not be young again but some day become old, one might think that the constitution that gives as much as possible to the old, and nothing above the subsistence level to the young, will prevail. In figure 5.2 this constitution is represented by point $(0, x^m)$. But we will see that this is not right. For a set of rules to persist, it must be self-enforcing not only in the sense that the best response to everyone else complying with it is to do the same but also in the stronger sense that the constitution is not amendable.

At any date t, any member of generation t is at liberty to propose a new constitution. Will subsequent generations take any notice? Not if (1) the old constitution satisfies (5.15), and (2) no other constitution satisfying (5.15) makes generations t, $t + 1$, $t + 2$, etc., better off. If condition 2 is satisfied, the only way a person can offer her children a better deal than the existing constitution, and not loose in the bargain, is to pay her own parent *less* than the existing constitution requires. That, however, means defaulting on the existing constitution. Her children would then be better off upholding the existing constitution, which entitles them to pay nothing to their parent, than acquiescing to the proposed new one. A sustainable constitution is then renegotiation-proof if it is not Pareto-dominated by any other sustainable one. If such a constitution exists, it will prevail.[5]

Let us now look at the properties of renegotiation-proof family constitutions. At any given date the adults of the day are interested only in their own adult and old-age consumption, but their children are interested also in their own youthful consumption. A family constitution is then renegotiation-proof if it maximizes the lifetime utility of the representative family member,

$$U(l, n, w, x, z) = u_0(z) + u_1(wl - v(l) - x - (p + z)n) + u_2(xn), \qquad (5.20)$$

subject to (5.15). The first-order conditions for a maximum are (5.5), (5.19), and

$$\frac{u_0'(z)}{u_1'(wl - v(l) - x - (p + z)n)} = (1 + \lambda)n$$

$$= (1 + \lambda)\frac{u_1'(wl - v(l) - x - (p + z)n)}{u_2'(xn)}, \qquad (5.21)$$

where λ is the Lagrange multiplier of (5.15).

If (5.15) is not binding $(\lambda = 0)$, (5.21) tells us that the agent will equate her children's marginal rate of substitution of youthful for adult consumption to her own marginal rate of substitution of adult for old-age consumption, and have a number of children equal to the common value of these two marginal valuations of current consumption. Taken together with (5.19), it also tells us that the number of children will be set equal to the domestic interest factor. If (5.15) is binding $(\lambda > 0)$, (5.21) tells us that the agent will set her own marginal rate of substitution equal to the number of children and thus, in view of (5.19), to the domestic interest factor, but *lower* than her children's marginal rate of substitution.

We are used to thinking of equality of marginal rates of substitution as a necessary condition for efficiency. That is true here too, but not in the ordinary Pareto sense because the Pareto criterion applies only to situations where the number of individuals is given. In a situation like the present one, where the existence of certain individuals (the children) depends on a decision taken by another individual (an adult), we can apply the *quasi*-Pareto criterion proposed by Baland and Robinson (2002), according to which an allocation A is deemed preferable to an allocation B if the utility of the parent *and* the average utility of the children are higher in A than in B. The reference to an average utility allows for the possibility that the number of children differs between A and B.

Cigno (2006) argues that the number of children, and the allocation of consumption between, and over the life cycle of, parent and children will be efficient in the Baland-Robinson sense if (5.15) is not binding. Otherwise, the agent will have an inefficiently high number of children and allocate an inefficiently low level of consumption to each of them while they are young. The argument is that if (5.15) is not binding, and the children consequently value a marginal increase in their current consumption more than the parent values a marginal increase in hers, the utility of the parent and the average utility of the children would be higher if (1) n is chosen lower than r_d and (2) the parent gives each of these children more than z while they are young, in exchange for a transfer higher than x when she is old. As there is no way of enforcing such a deal because the constitution does not require a child to pay her parent anything more than x, the number of children will be too high, and their current consumption too low.

If (5.15) is not binding, the renegotiation-proof constitution can lie anywhere inside the frontier. If (5.15) is binding, by contrast, the renegotiation-proof constitution is represented by point (z^*, x^*), where the amount transferred to each child is the largest compatible with a Nash equilibrium because that is the only point of the frontier where r_d is equal to n. This proposition can be illustrated with the help of figure 5.2.

Substituting from (5.5) and (5.19), we can express U as a function of (w, x, z) only. The contours of this function in the (z, x) plane have slope

$$\frac{dx}{dz} = -\frac{(p+z)u_0'(z) - xu_1'(wl - v(l) - x - (p+z)n)}{-(p+z)u_1'(wl - v(l) - x - (p+z)n) + xu_2'(xn)}.$$

Therefore they circle around the point that satisfies (5.21). In figure 5.2 this point happens to lie just inside the frontier, close to (z^*, x^*). There is no special reason why that should be true in general. Recalling that the frontier shifts inward as the market interest rate rises relative to the wage rate, however, the probability that the renegotiation-proof constitution will be (z^*, x^*), or a point just to the left of it, is an increasing function of (r/w). Conversely, the probability that the renegotiation-proof constitution will be efficient is a decreasing function of (r/w). If we interpret z as private educational expenditure as in Anderberg and Balestrino (2003), the model tells us that if the parent's wage rate is sufficiently low, or the interest rate sufficiently high, the parent will spend too little on her children's education.[6]

5.2 Public Intervention

We now use the analytical framework we have just developed to predict the effects of public intervention on individual behavior and aggregate outcomes. We will focus on the two policy instruments described in chapters 2, 3, and 4, namely pensions and child benefits. The supporting evidence will be presented in chapter 6. The choice of policy package will be discussed in chapters 7 and 8.

5.2.1 Pension Policy

The effects of pension policy are usually analyzed under the assumption that (1) individuals can re-arrange consumption over their life course only by saving or dissaving, (2) the pension scheme is of the social security ("Beveridgean") type, and (3) the pension scheme breaks even.[7] The behavioral effects taken into account are usually those concerning household savings and the supply of labor. In this subsection we extend the analysis in four important directions. We allow for the possibility that a person might use the family network as an alternative to the market in making provision for old age. We also allow for the possibility that the pension scheme is of the social insurance ("Bismarckian") type, and we pay due notice to the fact that pension schemes often have deficits, and occasionally generate a surplus. Finally, we look at the way pension policy affects not only the incentive to work and save but also the decision to have children. The way this policy affects the decision to invest in a child's human capital, though logically belonging here, will be dealt with later, in the normative context of chapter 7.

Let us briefly recall some of the concepts introduced in chapter 2. A pension scheme reduces i's disposable income by the contribution θ^i in adulthood and increases it by the benefit η^i in old age. The scheme is said to be *actuarially fair* if, at the time of retirement, the expected value of future benefits is equal to the capitalized value of the contributions made. In the absence of uncertainty, this simply means that

$$\eta^i = \theta^i r. \tag{5.22}$$

If a person's treatment is *more* than actuarially fair,

$$\eta^i > \theta^i r, \tag{5.23}$$

that person is getting a present from someone. If a whole generation of contributors receives more than actuarially fair treatment, the present is coming from other generations, typically from future ones. If a person's treatment is *less* than actuarially fair,

$$\eta^i < \theta^i r, \tag{5.24}$$

either that person is being obliged to make a present to someone or the scheme is badly run. If a whole generation of contributors receives a less than actuarially fair treatment, and the scheme is well run, that generation is paying for the presents made to other generations, typically to earlier ones.

If a public scheme is of the Beveridgean type, individual benefits may be the same for everyone or vary with certain personal characteristics, but the benefits are in any case unrelated to individual contributions (there is thus no need to keep track of the latter). If the scheme is designed to break even, it will be more than fair to those a the bottom of the income distribution (and maybe also to other deserving categories; see chapter 2), fair to those in the middle, unfair to those at the top. The scheme can afford to be fair to more people only if it runs a deficit. If it makes a surplus, it will find it difficult to be fair even to those in the middle.

If the scheme is of the Bismarckian type, individual benefits increase with individual contributions (it is thus necessary to keep track of the latter). Each participant has his own balance sheet, so overall financial balance is less of a constraint on a government that wants to treat one category of citizens differently from another. All the same, if the scheme is allowed to run a deficit, the government can afford to be more than fair to a larger number of categories. If it makes a surplus, the government cannot be generous to too many. Here too there is a connection between actuarial fairness and overall financial balance.

Go-It-Aloners

Let us see how individual behavior is modified by the introduction or expansion of a public pension scheme, under the standard assumption that the only way a person can otherwise smooth consumption over his life cycle is by saving or dissaving (i.e., on the assumption that all agents go it alone in the market). The analysis is based on Cigno (2007). As we saw in chapters 2 and 4, the pension contribution required of individual i typically increases with his income,

$$\theta^i = \theta(y^i) < y^i, \quad \theta'(y^i) > 0. \tag{5.25}$$

If the scheme is Beveridgean, η^i is effectively a lump-sum transfer, and $\theta(.)$ an earmarked income tax (the *social security tax*). Given such a scheme, the agent will supply labor to the point where the money equivalent of the marginal disutility of labor equals the marginal increase in take-home pay,

$$v'(l^i) = [1 - \theta'(y^i)]w^i. \tag{5.26}$$

If (5.26) is compared with (5.5), it is clear that the scheme distorts labor decisions by the wedge introduced between the wage rate and the marginal take-home pay. Having assumed increasing marginal disutility of labor ($v'' > 0$), and further assuming that the marginal pension contribution does not decrease as income increases ($\theta'' \geq 0$), adults will work less than they would have done without the pension scheme.

Let us see what happens to life-cycle decisions. If θ^i is no greater than the amount s^i that i would have saved without the scheme, or i is able to borrow the excess back from the capital market, the marginal rate of substitution of present for future consumption will be equated to the interest factor, as in (5.8). Otherwise, the scheme will cause i to be credit-rationed. The marginal rate of substitution will in that case be larger than the interest factor, and the life-cycle allocation of consumption will consequently be distorted. The life-cycle distortion can be avoided by ensuring that no one is forced to contribute more than he would have saved without the scheme (in practice, requiring the very poor to contribute nothing or very little), but there is no way of avoiding the labor distortion. Therefore a Beveridgean scheme can increase a person's utility only if the benefits paid to that person are sufficiently greater than the capitalized contributions made by that same person to more than compensate him of the utility loss caused by the labor distortion. If the scheme has to break even, it *may* raise utility for the very poor but will reduce it for everyone else.

If the pension scheme is Bismarckian, individual benefits are an increasing function of individual contributions,

$$\eta^i = \eta(\theta^i), \quad \eta'(\theta^i) > 0. \tag{5.27}$$

As a consequence the marginal benefit of supplying labor is now the sum of an increase in current take-home pay, and an increase in the current-consumption equivalent of future pension benefits.

Consider first the case where the benefit formula, $\eta(.)$, is actuarially fair. In this case, i will supply labor to the point where

$$v'(l^i) = \left[1 + \left(\frac{u_2'((s^i + \theta^i)r)}{u_1'(y^i - v(l^i) - s^i - \theta^i)}r - 1\right)\theta'(y^i)\right]w^i. \tag{5.28}$$

If i is not credit-rationed, (5.28) simplifies to (5.5). There is then no labor distortion. Intuitively, that is because an actuarially fair pension contribution is *not* a tax on labor but a postponed wage payment. If the agent is not credit-rationed,[8] she is then indifferent between receiving a euro while she is still working or r euros when she retires. If the agent is credit-rationed, however, the expression in round brackets on the right-hand side of (5.28) is negative but greater than -1. The whole right-hand side of the equation is then smaller than w^i, but larger than $(1 - \theta'(y^i))w^i$. Therefore an actuarially fair Bismarckian scheme does not distort labor decisions directly. It does so indirectly if saving decisions are distorted by credit-rationing. Even if credit is rationed, a Bismarckian scheme will nevertheless discourage labor less than a Beveridgean scheme would.

Consider next the case where the benefit formula is not actuarially fair. The difference between the capitalized value of the contributions and the present value of the benefits,

$$\vartheta^i = \theta^i - \frac{\eta^i}{r}, \tag{5.29}$$

constitutes an *implicit tax*[9] if it is positive, and an *implicit subsidy* if it is negetive.

The agent will now supply labor to the point where

$$v'(l^i) = \left[1 - \theta'(y^i)\left(1 - \frac{u_2'(s^i r + \eta(\theta^i))}{u_1'(y^i - v(l^i) - s^i - \theta^i)}\eta'(\theta^i)\right)\right]w^i. \tag{5.30}$$

If the agent is not credit-rationed, (u_1'/u_2') will be chosen equal to r, and (5.30) will then simplify to

$$v'(l^i) = \left[1 - \theta'(y^i)\left(1 - \frac{\eta'(\theta^i)}{r}\right)\right]w^i. \tag{5.31}$$

It should be clear from (5.31) that the scheme distorts labor decisions even when the agent is not credit-rationed. The agent will supply too little labor if the benefit formula is less than actuarially fair ($\eta' < r$), too much labor if it is more than actuarially fair ($\eta' > r$). If the agent is credit-rationed, the life-cycle allocation of consumption will be distorted too. Since (u_1'/u_2') is now larger than r, credit-rationing reinforces the labor distortion caused by an implicit pension tax, reduces that caused by an implicit pension subsidy.

Compliers and Go-It-Aloners

If people have the option of either complying with a family constitution or going it alone in the market, the policy analysis becomes more complicated. This is because different agents may adopt different strategies, and a number of them may switch from one to the other in response to policy. We will start by assuming that the scheme is Bismarckian, and that both η^i and θ^i are lump sums. This way we do not need to worry about labor distortion (we do that toward the end of the subsection). We also suppose that θ^i is no greater than the amount that i would have saved in the absence of a pension scheme if she decides to go it alone. Saving decisions will then be distorted only if the scheme is not actuarially fair.

If the scheme is actuarially fair to everyone, the effect of θ^i on the payoff of going it alone for agent i,

$$\frac{dv(r, w^i)}{d\theta^i} = -u_1'(y^i - \theta^i - v(l^i) - s^i) + ru_2'((\theta^i + s^i)r), \qquad (5.32)$$

is equal to zero in view of (5.8). The effect on the payoff of complying can be written as

$$\frac{dv^*(w^i, x^i, z^i)}{d\theta^i} = -u_1'(y^i - \theta^i - v(l^i) - x^i - (p + z^i)n^i)$$

$$+ \frac{x^i}{p + z^i} u_2'(\theta^i r + x^i n^i)$$

$$+ \left(r - \frac{x^i}{p + z^i}\right) u_2'(\theta^i r + x^i n^i). \qquad (5.33)$$

Since the sum of the first two right-hand-side terms of (5.34) is zero in view of (5.6), and the third is negative in view of (5.16), the whole expression is negative. Therefore the introduction of a pension scheme per se makes complying less attractive. The policy forces compliers to accept a lower marginal return on some of their money. As a result the

proportion of the adult population who comply with some family constitution will decrease. Those who switch from the comply strategy to
the go-it-alone strategy will stop having children and start saving.

Let us now look at the effects of the policy on the behavior of infra-
marginal players. If j is an infra-marginal complier, the fertility effect
of θ^j,

$$\frac{dn^j}{d\theta^j}$$

$$= -\frac{(p+z^j)u_1''(y^i - \theta^i - v(l^i) - x^i - (p+z^i)n^i) + x^j r u_2''(\theta^i r + x^i n^i)}{(p+z^j)^2 u_1''(y^i - \theta^i - v(l^i) - x^i - (p+z^i)n^i) + (x^j)^2 u_2''(\theta^i r + x^i n^i)},$$
(5.34)

is clearly negative. Because the effect on the share of compliers in the
adult population is negative too, aggregate fertility will fall. If j is an
infra-marginal go-it-aloner, by contrast, what is negative is the saving
effect of θ^j:

$$\frac{ds^j}{d\theta^j} = -\frac{u_1''(y^i - \theta^i - v(l^i) - s^i) + r u_2''((\theta^i + s^i)r)}{u_1''(y^i - \theta^i - v(l^i) - s^i) + r^2 u_2''((\theta^i + s^i)r)} = -1.$$
(5.35)

Aggregate saving can thus rise or fall.

Let us now see what happens if the scheme is not actuarially fair. The
effect of the implicit tax on the payoff of going it alone for agent i,

$$\frac{dv(r, w^i)}{d\vartheta^i} = -r u_2'((\theta^i - \vartheta^i + s^i)r),$$
(5.36)

is clearly negative. The effect on the payoff of complying,

$$\frac{dv^*(w^i, x^i, z^i)}{d\vartheta^i} = -r u_2'((\theta^i - \vartheta^i)r + x^i n^i),$$
(5.37)

is negative too, but smaller than (5.37) in view of (5.16), (5.6), and (5.8).
An implicit tax has thus the effect of reinforcing the negative effect of
the pension scheme on the share of compliers in the adult population.
By contrast, an implicit subsidy tends to offset it.

If j is an infra-marginal complier, the fertility effect of ϑ^j,

$$\frac{dn^j}{d\vartheta^j} = -\frac{(p+z^j)u_1''(y^i - \theta^i - v(l^i) - x^i - (p+z^i)n^i)}{(p+z^j)^2 u_1''(y^i - \theta^i - v(l^i) - x^i - (p+z^i)n^i) + x^2 u_2''(\theta^i r + x^i n^i)},$$
(5.38)

is negative. An implicit tax (subsidy) will reinforce (tend to offset) the negative effect of the scheme on aggregate fertility. If j is an infra-marginal go-it-aloner, by contrast, what is negative is the saving effect of ϑ^j,

$$\frac{ds^j}{d\vartheta^j} = -\frac{u_1''(y^i - \theta^i - v(l^i) - s^i)}{u_1''(y^i - \theta^i - v(l^i) - s^i) + r^2 u_2''((\theta^i - \vartheta^i + s^i)r)}. \tag{5.39}$$

An implicit tax (subsidy) thus makes it more likely that the scheme will reduce (increase) aggregate saving.

We can illustrate these predictions diagrammatically by looking at how a marginal player would respond to the policy. In figure 5.3 the budget line has horizontal intercept y and slope r if the agent goes it alone, and horizontal intercept $y - x$ and slope r_d if she complies. Without the policy, the endowment point is d in the first case, f in the second. The utility-maximizing consumption plan is e if the agent goes it alone, g if she complies. Since e lies on the same indifference curve as g, the agent will comply, have c_2^g / x children, and save nothing.

Let us now introduce an actuarially fair pension scheme. If the agent goes it alone, the relevant budget line will remain the same, but the

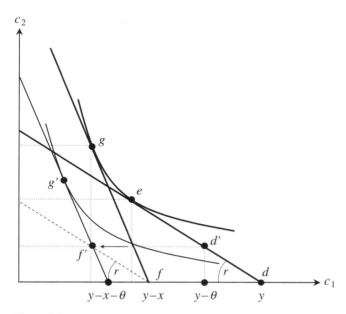

Figure 5.3
Effects of an actuarially fair pension scheme.

endowment point will move to d'. If we assume that d' lies to the right of e as pictured, the utility-maximizing consumption plan will remain e.[11] By contrast, if the agent complies, the budget line will shift inward, parallel to itself, until it goes through the new endowment point, f'. The utility-maximizing consumption plan will then be g'. Since g' lies on a lower indifference curve than e, the marginal player will respond to the policy by switching to the go-it-alone strategy, saving $(y - \theta - c_1^e)$ and having no children.

The behavior of infra-marginal compliers can be deduced from the same diagram by asking what the marginal player would have done if the go-it-alone strategy were not available. The answer is that she would have reduced her fertility to $c_2^{g'}/x$, and continued to save nothing. The behavior of infra-marginal go-it-aloners can be similarly deduced by asking what the marginal player would have done if the comply strategy had not been available in the first place. Without the policy, she would have gone it alone, had no children, and saved $(y - c_1^e)$. From this we deduce that the policy induces infra-marginal go-it-aloners to save less, and inframarginal compliers to have fewer children. Since it also induces marginal players to have fewer children, and to save more, the effect on aggregate fertility is clearly negative, but the effect on aggregate saving is ambiguous.

Figure 5.4 shows what happens if the scheme is *less* than actuarially fair $(\vartheta > 0)$. The implicit tax shifts the budget lines associated with the two strategies further inward. The endowment point moves from d' to d° if the agent goes it alone, and from f' to f° if she complies. The marginal player's resolve to switch to the go-it-alone strategy is clearly strengthened. To see the effect of the implicit tax on an infra-marginal complier, let us again assume that a go-it-alone strategy is not available. This agent will then respond to the implicit tax by having fewer children, c^{g°/x. To see the effect on infra-marginal go-it-aloners, we will assume instead that a comply strategy was not available in the first instance. Without the implicit tax, the agent would have saved $c_1^{d'} - c_1^e$. With the implicit tax, she will save a larger amount, $c_1^{d^\circ} - c_1^{e^\circ}$. Therefore the implicit pension tax induces infra-marginal compliers to have fewer children, and infra-marginal go-it-aloners to save more. The effect on aggregate fertility is negative. The effect on aggregate saving is positive.

Figure 5.5 shows what happens if the scheme is *more* than actuarially fair $(\vartheta < 0)$. The implicit subsidy shifts both budget lines outward. The endowment point is now d'' if the agent goes it alone, and f'' if she

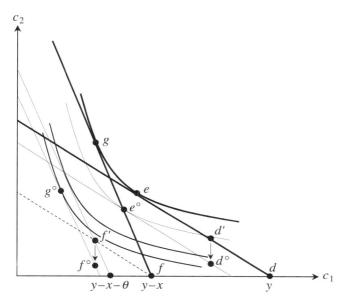

Figure 5.4
Effects of a less than actuarially fair pension scheme ($\vartheta > 0$).

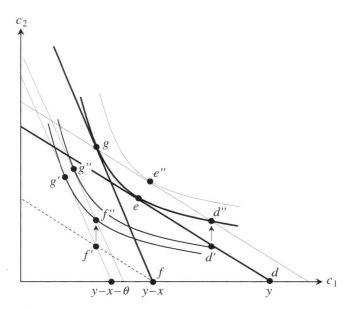

Figure 5.5
Effects of a more than actuarially fair pension scheme ($\vartheta < 0$).

complies. It is plausible that the budget line associated with the comply strategy will not lie any farther out than if there were no pension scheme[12] and so, as pictured, the marginal player's resolve to switch to the go-it-alone strategy will not be affected. To see the effect on infra-marginal compliers, let us again assume that a go-it-alone strategy is not available. The agent will then have $c_2^{g''}/x$ children, which is more children than without the implicit subsidy. To see the effect on infra-marginal go-it-aloners, assume instead that a comply strategy is not available. Without the implicit subsidy, the agent would have saved $c_1^{d'} - c_1^e$. With the implicit subsidy, she will save the smaller amount $c_1^{d''} - c_1^{e''}$. The implicit subsidy will thus raise aggregate fertility and have an ambiguous effect on aggregate saving. There is thus a slight asymmetry between the effect of an implicit pension subsidy, and that of an implicit pension tax.

Our preceding discussion was based on the assumption that y is not affected by the policy. But we know that if the pension scheme is Beveridgean, it reduces the incentive to work and hence income. The budget lines of compliers and go-it-aloners alike will then lie further inward than they would if their labor decisions were not affected. Correspondingly current and future consumption will be lower for everyone concerned. As this implies, go-it-aloners will save less and compliers will have fewer children. This way the policy reduces the aggregate saving more and raises aggregate fertility less than it would in the absence of a labor distortion. If the scheme is Bismarckian, the effect on a person's income will depend on whether or not this particular person is fairly treated by the scheme, and on whether or not she is credit-rationed. How that modifies our predictions regarding aggregate saving and fertility depends on who is getting an implicit subsidy and who is paying an implicit tax, and also on who is credit-rationed and who is not. Because, however, a Bismarckian scheme distorts labor decisions less than a Beveridgean one, and any distortion will be in one direction for some and in the opposite direction for others, we will be content with the aggregate predictions obtained under the assumption that labor decisions are not distorted at all.

These predictions differ sharply from those of standard life-cycle theory, according to which an actuarially fair pension scheme will definitely reduce aggregate saving, and any implicit subsidy (tax) will make this reduction larger (smaller). The reason is of course that life-cycle theory assumes everybody to be a go-it-aloner, while the present model offers agents the alternative of complying. They differ also from those of the dynastic model, according to which an actuarially fair pension scheme would definitely reduce saving as in life-cycle theory, since it reduces the demand for old-age consumption. The fertility effect will be zero even if the number of children is a choice variable, since the relative wealth position of the parent and child generations is not affected. An implicit pension subsidy (tax), by contrast, will make the parent generation relatively richer (poorer). If fertility is exogenous as in Barro (1974), the subsidy (tax) will induce parents to make larger (smaller) bequests, and thus to increase (decrease) the amount saved. If fertility is endogenous as in Becker and Barro (1988), the subsidy (tax) will induce parents to make larger (smaller) bequests to each child. As the marginal cost of children will consequently rise (fall), parents will choose to have fewer (more) children. The fertility effect of a pension scheme will thus be negative or positive depending on whether the scheme is more or less than actuarially fair. The saving effect will be ambiguous in either case.

As was already pointed out, while a Bismarckian scheme can be fair to everyone, a Beveridgean scheme cannot. But either kind of scheme can be more or less than actuarially fair to everyone. In the first case, it will generate a deficit. In the second case, it will make a surplus. In general, the probability that a person will receive an implicit pension subsidy (pay an implicit pension tax) increases with the size of the deficit (surplus) generated by the scheme. Since implicit taxes and subsidies affect behavior, this establishes an important link between aggregate saving and fertility, on the one hand, and the current account balance of the pension scheme, on the other. That link is exploited in some of the econometric analyses reviewed in chapter 6.

5.2.2 Child Benefits

Child benefits are subsidies paid to parents, not to children. Unlike the pension benefits examined in the last subsection, they are paid when the beneficiary is in the active period of life and not retired. Paying parents φ for each child that is born is equivalent to reducing p. The effects on the payoff of complying,

$$\frac{dv^*(w^i, z^i, x^i)}{d\varphi} = n^i u_1'(y^i - x^i - (p - \varphi + z^i)n^i), \tag{5.40}$$

and on the fertility of an infra-marginal complier,

$$\frac{dn^i}{d\varphi} = \frac{-u_1'(y^i - v(l^i) - x^i - (p - \varphi + z^i)n^i)}{(p + z^i)^2 u_1''(y^i - v(l^i) - x^i - (p - \varphi + z^i)n^i) + (x^i)^2 u_2''(x^i n^i)}$$

$$+ \frac{n^i(p + z^i)u_1''(y^i - v(l^i) - x^i - (p - \varphi + z^i)n^i)}{(p + z^i)^2 u_1''(y^i - v(l^i) - x^i - (p - \varphi + z^i)n^i) + (x^i)^2 u_2''(x^i n^i)},$$

(5.41)

are thus positive. Since the payoff of going-it-alone is not affected, the share of compliers in the adult population, and the fertility of each infra-marginal complier, will then increase.

Child benefits have thus the effect of raising aggregate fertility and reducing aggregate saving. Their effects on saving and fertility are best understood by looking at figure 5.6. Without the policy, the agent's best plan would be e if she went it alone, g if she complied. Since e and g lie on the same indifference curve, the agent will comply. With the policy, the budget lines associated with the two strategies shift to the left. The one associated with complying becomes steeper. The best consumption plan is now e' if the agent goes it alone, g' if she

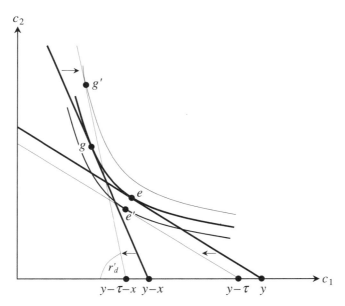

Figure 5.6
Effects of child benefits on the marginal player.

complies. Since g' is on a higher indifference curve than e', the marginal player will continue to comply but will have more children ($c_2^{g'}/x$ rather than c_2^g/x) than she would without the policy. Some inframarginal go-it-aloners, those close enough to the margin, will switch to the comply strategy, have more (than zero) children, and save less (zero) than they would without the policy. Those further from the margin will save more or less depending on income elasticity. Aggregate fertility will thus rise, and aggregate saving may go either way.

These predictions are the same as those of the endogenous-fertility version of the dynastic model, but different from those of life-cycle theory, and of the exogenous-fertility version of the dynamic model. In the last two models, child benefits are treated as a lump-sum subsidy. If all agents happen to have the same number of children, paying each agent φ times her number of children, and taking the same amount of money away from her by a lump-sum tax, will have no effect whatsoever (and be utterly pointless). If different agents have different numbers of children, however, the policy will redistribute in favor of households with more children. Agents with many children will then be induced to save more, and agents with few to save less. The aggregate saving effect of the policy is thus ambiguous (the effect on aggregate fertility is zero by assumption). In a dynastic model with endogenous fertility, by contrast, the policy induces parents to have more children and to make lower bequests to each child. The aggregate fertility effect is thus positive, and the aggregate saving effect ambiguous, as in the family constitution model.

5.2.3   Male and Female Wage Rates

If we replace the assumption that all households include only one adult of the female sex, with the assumption that go-it-alone households include only one adult of either sex but complier households include a man and a woman, we find that male and female wage rates have differential effects on behavior. To simplify, suppose that all childless adults, women and men, divide their time between leisure and income raising activities, while women with children spend all their time caring for their children.[13]

By these assumptions we can leave the budget constraint of a go-it-alone household as it is and rewrite the budget constraint of a complier household as

$$c_1 + (p(w_f) + z)n = w_f + l(w_m)w_m - x,$$

where w_m denotes the man's wage rate, w_f the woman's wage rate, and $l(w_m)$ the man's labor supply. Since $l(.)$ satisfies (5.5), $l'(w_m) = 1/v'(w_m)$. The cost of a birth, now denoted by $p(w_f)$, is defined to include also the opportunity cost of maternal time. The function $p(.)$ is assumed increasing and convex. The payoff of the comply strategy is then

$$v^*(w_f, w_m, z, x)$$
$$\equiv \max_n [u_1(w_f + lw_m - v(l(w_m)) - x - (p(w_f) + z)n) + u_2(xn)].$$

Before introducing sex differentiation, we had established that the marginal effect of the wage rate on the payoff of complying is positive, and larger than the marginal effect on the payoff of going it alone. That remains true of the man's wage rate but not of the woman's. The marginal effect of w_f on the payoff of the go-it-alone strategy is clearly positive. Since p increases with w_f, if we allow n or w_f to become large enough to make $np'(w_f)$ at least equal to unity, the marginal effect on the payoff of the comply strategy will be negative:

$$v^*_{w_f}(w_f, w_m, z, x)$$
$$= (1 - np'(w_f))u_1'(w_f + lw_m - v(l(w_m)) - x - (p(w_f) + z)n), \quad (5.42)$$

While an increase in the male wage rate will raise the share of compliers in the adult population, an increase in the female wage rate will lower it. Since the domestic interest factor r_d, defined in (5.16), and consequently a complier's demand for children are decreasing in w_f, a rise in the female wage rate will reduce aggregate fertility. The aggregate saving effect is ambiguous for both wage rates.

These predictions differ from those of both life-cycle theory and the dynastic model, where both wage rates affect saving positively. The endogenous fertility version of the dynastic model predicts, the same as the present model, that the male wage rate has a positive, and the female wage rate a negative, effect on fertility (or rather, it would if we introduced differential wage rates the way we have done here). Figures 5.7 and 5.8 illustrate the predictions of the constitutional model, again by reference to the behavior of a marginal household. Because this household will split into two if its adult members switch from the comply to the go-it-alone strategy, the decision variables must be inter-

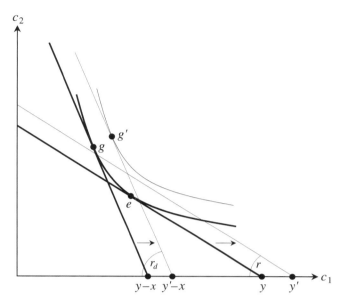

Figure 5.7
Effects of the male wage rate.

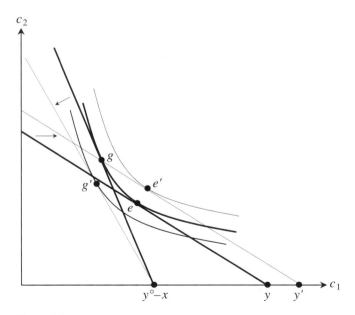

Figure 5.8
Effects of the female wage rate.

preted as referring to a single (two-adult) household before the switch, to the sum of two (one-adult) households after it.

Figure 5.7 shows the effects of the male wage rate. A rise in w_m shifts both budget lines outward. Since the one associated with the comply strategy is steeper than the one associated with the go-it-alone strategy, the payoff of the former increases more than the payoff of the latter. Some infra-marginal go-it-aloners (close to the margin) will thus switch to the comply strategy. These new compliers will reduce their saving (to nothing) and increase their fertility (from nothing to some positive level). Assuming a marginal propensity to consume lower than one, those who still go it alone will save more. The marginal player will still comply but will now have more children ($c_2^{g'}/x$ rather than c_2^g/x). The same is true of infra-marginal compliers. The aggregate fertility effect of the wage change is thus positive, but the aggregate saving effect is ambiguous.

Figure 5.8 shows the effects of the female wage rate. A rise in w_f shifts the budget line associated with the go-it-alone strategy outward. The one associated with the comply strategy becomes less steep. Assuming that w_f or n is "large," however, the horizontal intercept remains the same. The couple will go it alone (their separate ways), their fertility will fall to zero, and their saving will become positive. Infra-marginal compliers also will have fewer children. Infra-marginal go-it-aloners will save less. The aggregate fertility effect of the wage change is negative, but the aggregate saving effect is still ambiguous.

5.3   Uncertainty, Personal Services, and Altruism

We have reasoned so far as if there were no uncertainty, all goods were provided by the market, and individuals were selfish. Relaxing these assumptions increases the descriptive power of the model but does not change its positive implications in any fundamental way. The normative implications will be discussed in the next chapter.

If the state of the world is uncertain, there may be scope for mutual insurance arrangements among members of the same family, either of the same generation as in Kotlikoff and Spivak (1981), or of adjoining generations as in Di Tella and MacCullogh (2002). That, however, raises once again the problem that an informal agreement cannot be enforced through the courts (neither of the papers mentioned deals with the issue). Can a family constitution help? Were it possible to make constitutional prescriptions fully conditional on the state of the world, the family constitution story would go through essentially unchanged. If that is prohibitively costly, however, the constitution will have to rely on simple rules of the kind that an adult is excused from supporting her parent if, through no fault of her own, her own income falls below a certain level. That will make it risky to invest in children. But investing in conventional assets is risky too. If the two kinds of risk are not positively correlated, it may then be worthwhile for a risk-averse complier to do some precautionary saving, in addition to having children.[14] Uncertainty gets rid of an unrealistic feature of the basic constitutional mode, namely that people who have children do not save.[15] That makes no qualitative difference to the aggregate saving and fertility effects of pension policy, and to the aggregate fertility effects of child benefits. But it makes the aggregate saving effect of child benefits ambiguous, since go-it-aloners will still save collectively less while compliers save collectively more.

Now suppose that the market does not supply perfect substitutes for the personal services a young person receives from a parent, or an elderly person from a grown-up child. A flow of personal services from parents to young children can be easily incorporated in a dynastic model by making the utility of the beneficiaries a function of these services. The same cannot be said about the flow of services from grown-up children to elderly parents. A different route is followed by Cox (1987) who hypothesizes intrafamily exchanges of money for personal services. To the extent that these exchanges take place between persons at different points of the life cycle (but sex differences matter too), we may regard this as an extension of the basic life-cycle model. Assuming, however, that the agent is indifferent between selling her time to the labor market or to an elderly relative, while the elderly relative is not indifferent between buying the service from the labor market or from the agent (e.g., a daughter), because the two kinds of service substitute for each other at a diminishing rate, either the agent will extract all the consumer surplus from the elderly person, or the allocation will be inefficient. The elderly person will be exploited in either case.

Could a family constitution take care of that? Cigno and Rosati (2000) allow for the possibility that the family constitution requires adult family members to deliver either a specified sum of money or a variable combination of goods and personal services yielding the same utility as that sum of money. By permitting agents to supply the cost-minimizing mix of money and own time,[16] this extension makes (5.16) easier to satisfy, and thus raises the probability that an enforceable family constitution exists. The model's predictions regarding saving and fertility behavior remain essentially the same, but the extended model makes predictions also about the flow of personal services. In particular, it predicts that credit-rationing raises the probability that an agent will make monetary transfers, because it induces her to switch from a go-it-alone to a comply strategy. This is in sharp contrast to the prediction of both the dynastic and the exchange model, that credit rationing can only reduce the probability of giving money.

Cigno (2006) examines the implications of introducing parental altruism into the constitutional model. There are two possibilities. If all parents are so rich and altruistic that they not only make transfers to their young children in excess of the amount prescribed by the constitution but also take less than the constitution entitles them to receive from their grown-up children,[17] the constitution is obviously irrelevant. If either of the constitutional prescriptions is binding, however, the existence of self-enforcing family constitutions will affect behavior in very much the same way as in the basic model. The only difference of substance altruism makes is that the domestic interest rate does not need to be higher than the market interest rate. If the two rates are equal, the allocation is efficient not only in the Baland-Robison sense but also in the dynamic one.

6 Life-cycle Adjustments and Intergenerational Transfers: Evidence

We have seen that different views about the mechanism that generates voluntary transfers to the young and the old have different implications for the way in which saving and fertility respond to the introduction of a compulsory pension scheme, and to social transfers in general. In the present chapter we will try to discriminate empirically between these different views. That is important from a broad welfare perspective. But there is also a narrow interest in finding out which is the right model because saving and fertility, hence growth, have direct implications for the financial viability of public pension systems.

6.1 Micro-data Evidence

In developing countries, but also in some highly developed ones such as the United States, different categories of workers (e.g., private and public employees) face different pension rules; some categories have no public pension cover. The resulting disparities in individual benefit entitlements, or "pension wealth," may be exploited to estimate the behavioral response to pension policy. An official memorandum of the US Congressional Budget Office, CBO (1998), surveys the findings of fourteen empirical studies based on US individual or household data.[1] Ten of these studies arrive at (median) estimates implying negative elasticities, ranging between -1 and -0.2,[2] of private saving with respect to pension wealth. However, the 2-standard errors band does not include a range of positive pension effects in only three of these ten studies.[3] At least five of the remaining studies find a negative effect of pensions on saving that is not significant at the 5 percent level.[4] It would thus seem that US data do not lend clear support to the standard life-cycle theory proposition that public pensions crowd out household saving. More important, as none of these studies takes fertility to be endogenous and none of them controls for any implicit pension tax or subsidy, we cannot take these findings as either a validation or a confutation of the competing theories outlined in the last chapter, which attribute an important role to intergenerational transfers.

In many other developed countries, pension rules are the same for everyone. The effects of pension policy can then be estimated only if there is a change in these rules, and provided that the researcher disposes of panel data. Using the Dutch Socio-Economic Panel, Alessie, Kapteyn, and Klijn (1997) find that participation in a mandatory occupational pension scheme encourages, rather than substitutes for, voluntary saving. However, since occupational pensions present fiscal advantages, this cannot be taken as a confutation of life-cycle theory. It may simply mean that the income effect of the new scheme dominates the substitution-effect.

A number of micro-level studies examine the effect of child benefits on fertility,[5] and these studies generally find this effect to be positive in the case of monetary transfers and insignificant in cases of in-kind transfers and price subsidies (particularly for child care services).[6] Studies estimating the fertility effect of the man's and the woman's wage rate generally find that the former is positive, and the latter negative.[7] Taken together, these findings amount to a rejection of the hypothesis that fertility is exogenous, and of the standard textbook account of saving decisions, but do not allow us to discriminate among alternative models of joint saving and fertility determination. In what follows we look at a number of studies focused on transfer behavior. Some of these studies appear well suited for testing alternative theories, and thus for indirectly establishing, if not the size of saving and fertility effects of public intervention, at least the sign.

6.1.1   Intrafamily Transfers

Individuals expend time and money on their children when these are very young, and make them mostly monetary transfers at later stages. These downward monetary transfers are substantial. For the United States, Greenwood and Wolff (1992) calculate that private money transfers account for nearly two-thirds of the growth in total household wealth between 1962 and 1983. Over the same period, more than half of the wealth of persons aged 40 to 49, and as much as 85 percent of the wealth of persons aged less than 40, came from *inter-vivos* transfers. People make transfers also to their parents. In countries where the old are on the whole comparatively well provided with cash through public pensions or personal saving, however, these upward transfers appear to consist primarily of time.

The 1968 to 1988 waves of the Panel Study of Income Dynamics conducted in the United States by the Institute for Social Research of the University of Michigan reveal that 24 percent of American children receive money from, but less than 3 percent give money to, their parents. By contrast, more than 30 percent of children receive personal services from, and more than 27 percent give personal services to, their parents.[8] The 2001 wave of the British Household Panel Survey similarly reveals that less than 2 percent of adults never visit their non-coresident mother (and that a little over 2 percent of mothers is never visited by their non-coresident children). Nearly 47 percent of adults visit their non-coresident mother at least once a week (nearly 41 percent of mothers is visited by non-coresident children at least once a week).[9] A similar picture emerges from the 1992 *Enquête Trois Générations* conducted in France by Caisse Nationale d'Assurance Vieillesse,[10] and from the 1987 to 1991 wave of the *Indagine Multiscopo* conducted in Italy by Istituto Nazionale di Statistica.[11] It would be interesting to have a money value for the time and personal services given or received to compare with the amount of money given or received at different points of the life cycle, but this cannot be done by evaluating time transfers at market values.[12]

The timing of the different types of transfer is revealing. By way of illustration, we show, in figure 6.1,[13] the age distribution that emerges from the Italian *Multiscopo*, but a similar pattern occurs also in the other surveys mentioned. It transpires that a household is most likely to give help to other households if its head is in middle life, most likely to receive help if its head is either young or old (we will see that the same age pattern applies to transfers between members of the same household). Figure 6.2 shows the age distribution of giving and receiving separately for money-intensive and time-intensive forms of help.[14] While confirming the life-cycle pattern of figure 6.1, the two panels of figure 6.2 add the important detail that the young get mostly money and the old mostly time. The percentages reported in these diagrams may seem small, but that is only because they include neither transfers between members of the same household (which, in Italy is likely to include children up to the age of 30, and their grandparents) nor mere visiting or calling over the telephone. The percentages would get much

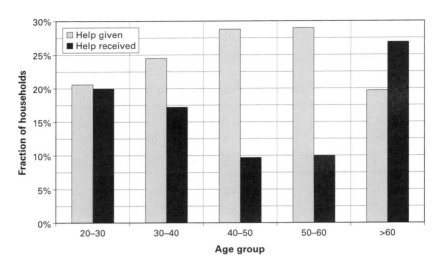

Figure 6.1
Transfers made/received by age group.

larger if we added transfers to or from coresidents, and counted visits and telephone conversations as transfers of time.

This kind of information is interesting in its own right. Being intimately connected with the motivations for having children, and accumulating assets, it also helps to discriminate among alternative theories of household behavior. We now look briefly at the way transfer behavior is affected by earnings and assets, and then at a test based on the effect of credit-rationing.

6.1.2 *Effect of Income on Transfer Behavior*

Both the dynastic model, and the life-cycle model with money-for-services exchanges (the "exchange" model), outlined in the final section of the last chapter predict that the higher a person's own earnings or assets, the higher is the probability that she will make a monetary transfer, and the lower is the probability that she will receive one. Dynastic models say something more specific, which may be exploited to construct a test of the hypothesis that money transfers are genuine gifts. In these models the agent regards the consumption of her loved ones as a good. If this person is rich enough for it to be in the interest of every other member of the family to go along with what she

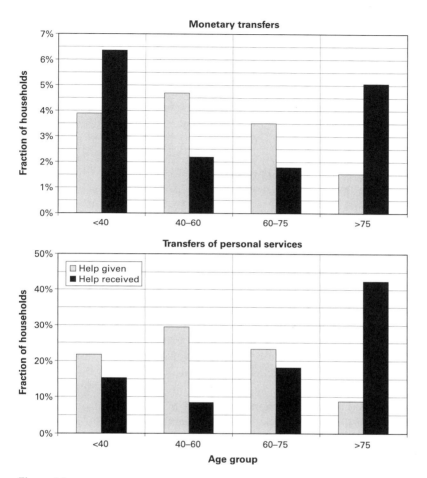

Figure 6.2
Transfers made/received by type of transfer.

decides,[15] the consumption levels of those making or receiving transfers will depend not on their own income and assets but on the income and assets of the entire family network. Adding a money unit to the income of the person or household that makes the transfers, and subtracting it from the income of the person or household that receives them, would then leave the consumption plans of benefactor and beneficiary unchanged. If that were true, we should observe that the amount of money voluntarily transferred is reduced by exactly one unit. Another way of putting this is to say that the derivatives of the amount of money voluntarily transferred with respect to the benefactor's and beneficiary's incomes should add up to unity.

Altonji, Hayashi, and Kotlikoff (1992) test the first of these propositions ("income pooling") for the United States by comparing consumption and income patterns in networks of related households. If these households were linked by altruistic transfers, we should not observe a correlation between household consumption and household income, but we do. The data indeed show that own income is a strong predictor of own consumption. Also for the United States, Altonji, Hayashi, and Kotlikoff (1997) test the second proposition (the "derivative property"), and find that the sum of the derivatives is way below unity. Both propositions are thus rejected, but this does not necessarily imply that altruism as such (i.e., altruism without the subsidiary assumption of a benign family dictator) is rejected too. Altruism as such appears to be rejected by evidence reported in Cox (1987), and Cox and Jakubson (1995), that private transfers do not behave in the way one would expect if they really were gifts.

The constitutional model predicts that, if the private benefactor is an infra-marginal complier or an infra-marginal go-it-aloner, taking money away from her and giving it to her beneficiaries would have no effect on her transfer behavior. Only a marginal player would respond to the policy by switching to the go-it-alone strategy, and thus making no transfers. Evidence that own consumption is positively correlated with own income, or that money received from the government does not substitute one for one for money received from relatives, is thus more damaging to the hypothesis that the data are generated by either the dynastic or the exchange model, than to the hypothesis that they are generated by the constitution model but not enough to discriminate between the two hypotheses. If we want to do that, we need to find an instance where observed transfer behavior is consistent with optimization in the domain restricted by the presence of a family constitution, and not with optimization in the domain restricted by its absence. Credit-rationing is such an instance.

6.1.3 *Effect of Credit-Rationing on Transfer Behavior*

All the theories we have examined predict that households or individuals are more likely to receive money transfers if they are credit-rationed than if they are not. In the dynastic model, altruistic adults will intervene to relax the credit rationing faced by their children. In

the exchange model, a person is more willing to supply personal services in exchange for cash if she is credit-rationed than if she is not. In
the family constitution model, the only persons receiving transfers are
the young and the old, neither of which is allowed to borrow. The effect of being rationed in the credit market on the probability of *receiving* money transfers cannot thus be used to discriminate empirically
among competing theories.

By contrast, the effect of being rationed on the probability of *making*
money transfers allows one to distinguish between the family constitution model, on the one hand, and the dynastic and exchange models,
on the other, because credit-rationing reduces the rationed person's
lifetime wealth. The dynastic model predicts that if a person becomes
poorer, she will buy less utility for (transfer less money to) her loved
ones. The exchange model predicts that this person will spend less for
personal services. The constitution model, by contrast, predicts that
credit rationing may induce a person to switch from the go-it-alone to
the comply strategy, and thus to start make more transfers. The last
proposition is illustrated in figure 6.3 for the basic case where transfers
are exclusively monetary, but the argument goes through also in the

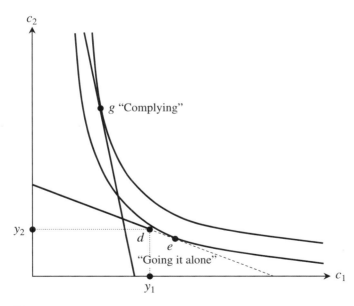

Figure 6.3
Effects of credit-rationing.

more general case where the constitution can be complied with by giving personal services instead of money.

Consider an individual with current income y_1, and future income y_2.[16] In the absence of a binding credit ration, this person will go it alone. She will then choose the consumption plan e, which implies borrowing the amount $c_1^e - y_1$ from the market. If she is not allowed to borrow at all, the go-it-alone strategy will restrict this person to the endowment point d. She will then be better off by complying with the family constitution and choosing the consumption plan g, which yields a higher level of utility than d. The effect of a zero ration is thus to raise the amount of money transferred to others from zero to $y_1 - c_1^g$. So long as borrowing the permitted maximum puts the borrower on a lower indifference curve than the consumption plan g, that is true also if the ration is greater than zero.

The diagram assumes that children are as safe as houses. In reality, however, domestic investments are risky because grown-up children might not want, or be able to, pay parents their dues. As we saw in the last chapter, risk-averse compliers may thus find it optimal to borrow less than their full ration. It still remains true, however, that some agents will make transfers (comply) if they are effectively rationed, and not make transfers (go it alone) if they are not. The finding of a *positive* effect of rationing on the probability of giving money, or on the amount given, would thus be consistent with the hypothesis that individual behavior is conditioned by a family constitution, and reject the hypothesis that individuals are driven by either altruistic or exchange motivations.[17] We now look in some detail at a paper that tests the constitution hypothesis against the other two using Italian data on credit-rationing and monetary transfers.

The Bank of Italy Biannual Household Survey provides household-level information on expenditure and asset holdings, and individual information concerning the age, sex, education, labor market status, earnings, and relationship with one another of all household members. These surveys also give us the number and ages of any non-cohabiting parents or children of the household head or head's partner, and include questions on whether any household member was denied credit by a financial institution, or refrained from applying in the belief that it would be denied, in the course of the interview year. Normally they also provide information on monetary help *received* by any member of the household from non-coresident "friends or relatives" in the course of the interview year. Exceptionally, however, the 1991 edition asked about the amount of monetary help that any member of the household might have *given* to non-coresident "friends or relatives." Cigno et al. (2006) use this unique data set to test the hypothesis that transfer behavior in Italy is conditioned by the existence of family constitutions, against the hypothesis that money transfers are either gifts, or payment for services rendered. Since the constitution model predicts that transfers are made by persons in middle life with children, the authors consider only households where the head or the head's partner has children (living in or out of the parental home). This selected sample is then divided into two subsamples, one with head still working and the other with head retired.

For each subsample, and for the whole sample of households with children, the authors estimate first a probit model of the probability of making a money transfer taking credit-rationing as exogenous. The controls include all the remaining individual and household characteristics, including earnings, assets, and the share of liquid assets in the total portfolio. They find that being rationed increases the probability of making money transfers by 7.9 percent (with a t-statistic of 3.83) in the full sample, by 8.1 ($t = 3.6$) in the subsample with the household head working, and by 7.6 ($t = 1.36$) in the one with the head retired. These results are consistent with the family constitution hypothesis in that they show that households with the head still working are significantly more likely to make monetary transfers if they are credit-rationed, while households with the head retired are not significantly affected by credit conditions.

However, since a binding credit ration is partly the result of choice (if one does not wish to borrow, one cannot be rationed), there could be an endogeneity problem, and the estimates may be biased. The authors then use dummies for homeownership and area of residence to identify the auxiliary equation of the probability of being rationed.[18] To check for possible weakness of these instruments, the authors regress the rationing variable on the full set of explanatory and instrumental variables, and test whether the latter could be rejected by an F-test. As the F statistics are well above the threshold value of 10, the authors conclude that the instruments are not weak in a statistical sense. The two equations (for the probability of making a money transfer, and for the probability of being rationed) are estimated simultaneously by the maximum likelihood method. In the two subsamples as in the full sample, the probability of being credit rationed is lower for homeowners and decreases as the place of residence moves from south (the reference area) to north.

In the full sample credit-rationing has a significantly positive effect on the probability of giving money.[19] Other things being equal, a 1 percent increase in the probability of being rationed raises the probability of making a transfer by 0.17 percent. Credit-rationing has a significantly positive and slightly larger effect (0.18 percent) also in the subsample of households with head not retired. By contrast, the probability of being rationed has no significant effect in the subsample of households with the head retired. These findings appear to reject the null hypothesis that self-enforcing family constitutions do not exist. This is the paper's main result. In the full sample, and in both subsamples, income and assets have a significantly positive, but extremely small, effect on the probability of giving money. While not rejecting alternative explanations, this finding is better explained by the family constitution model, where income or asset changes affect transfer behavior only if they induce the agent to change strategy, than by models that do not contemplate strategy switches.

In the full sample, and in the subsample with the head working, the probability that someone in the household will give money to a noncoresident "friend or relative" is significantly and positively affected by the number of children aged up to the age of 30 living out of the parental home. By contrast, this probability is negatively affected by the number of children living in. The parents of the household head, and of the head's partner, living either in or out of the household, have no significant effect on the probability of giving money. From this it may be inferred that money transfers go essentially to the children of the household's head, or of the head's partner, and that this is true not only of transfers between households but also of transfers within households (unrecorded in the survey). This does not necessarily mean that elderly parents get nothing. It may mean that transfers to the old are essentially in the form of personal services. Figures 6.1 and 6.2, constructed with data from ISTAT's almost contemporaneous *Multiscopo* survey, confirm that this is indeed the case.

6.2 Macro-data Evidence

Direct evidence of the effects of pensions and child benefits on saving and fertility behavior can be found in aggregate national data. The pitfalls of aggregation are well known. On the other hand, macroeconometric studies based on long time series (as distinct from cross-country data) have some advantage over microeconometric analyses of cross-sectional, or even panel, data when it comes to assess the effects of policy on the joint determination of lifetime saving and fertility. Because of the irreversibility of fertility outcomes the effects of policy do not lend themselves to be analyzed on the basis of observations "before and after" a single policy change, or even through short panel data. An individual or a couple will think again about how many children to have, when to have them, and how much to save for old-age and bequest purposes only if the change appears to be permanent. Furthermore the adjustment may take place through imitation. It may thus take some time for people to change their expectations, and even longer for most of them to change their lifetime plans, in response to a policy change. During that time the government may change its collective mind, and adjust or overturn the original policy in the light of how people are responding to it.

For ready comparison we summarize in table 6.1 the predictions of the different theories examined in the last chapter, regarding the sign of the effects of various policies and exogenous variables on the aggregate fertility rate, n, and the aggregate household saving–income ratio, s. The "pension coverage" row indicates the predicted effects of an increase in either the proportion of the population covered by compulsory pension arrangements, or in the average level of cover, under the assumption that the pension formula is actuarially fair. The "pension subsidy" row shows the effects of an increase in the implicit pension subsidy (reduction in the implicit pension tax). The "child benefits"

Table 6.1
Policy effects predicted by different models

	Exogenous fertility		Endogenous fertility	
	Life cycle s	Dynastic s	Constitution (n, s)	Dynastic (n, s)
Pension coverage	$-$	$-$	$(-, \pm)$	$(0, -)$
Pension subsidy	$-$	$\pm$	$(+, \pm)$	$(-, \pm)$
Child benefit	$\pm$	$\pm$	$(+, \pm)$	$(+, \pm)$
Female wage rate	$+$	$+$	$(-, \pm)$	$(-, \pm)$
Male wage rate	$+$	$+$	$(+, \pm)$	$(+, \pm)$

Note: n = fertility rate, s = saving–income ratio.

row shows those of an increase in the child benefit rate fully financed by an earmarked lump-sum tax on all agents. The last two rows show the effects of after-tax male and female wage rates. The signs indicated in the "exogenous fertility" columns assume that the number of children varies randomly across agents. Subject to all kinds of *caveat*, comparing the predicted with the estimated signs may permit to discriminate among the theories considered.

6.2.1 Aggregate Effects of Pensions and Child Benefits Policies

Using cross-country data, Feldstein (1980) finds a negative correlation between public pension coverage and voluntary household saving, but Graham (1987) throws doubt on this result. Feldstein (1982) finds the same negative correlation in aggregate time series. Commenting on existing time-series analyses of saving and pensions, CBO (1998) remarks that the results are highly sensitive to the way in which expected pension benefits are included in the estimation. Indeed Leimer and Lesnoy (1982, 1985) show that the negative correlation found by Feldstein (1980, 1982) is due to, among other things, arbitrary assumptions about future replacement rates. With alternative, more consistent assumptions, the correlation is positive in most cases. A further problem with all these macroeconometric studies of saving behavior is that like their microeconometric counterpart examined in the last section, they take fertility as exogenous and do not control for the possible presence of an implicit pension subsidy or tax. If fertility is actually endogenous, the estimates may be biased. If there is an implicit pension subsidy or tax, and this is correlated with the size of the pension program, it is not clear whether the effect estimated is that of the forced saving, of the intragenerational redistribution, or of the intergenerational redistribution aspect of the policy.

Using international cross sections, Hohm (1975), Entwisle and Winegarden (1984), and several others find a negative correlation between public pension coverage and fertility. None of theses studies control for the possible presence of child benefits. More recent cross-country studies treat saving and fertility as jointly determined. Ehrlich and Zhong (1998) find that pension coverage has a negative effect on saving, fertility, and growth. By contrast, Zhang and Zhang (2004) find that pension coverage has a negative effect on fertility, positive effects on educational investment and per-capita income growth, and no significant effect on saving.[20] Because they treat saving and fertility as jointly determined, the last two studies are an improvement on earlier studies of saving or fertility behavior. Like their predecessors, however, they do not control for child benefits, nor for any implicit pension subsidy or tax.

A number of single country time-series studies attempts to disentangle the effects of pension coverage from those of any implicit pension subsidy or tax, and in one case also from that of child benefits. Cigno and Rosati (1992) use a co-integration model to estimate the long-term effects of pension policy on saving and fertility in Italy. The paper shows that pension coverage has a positive long-term effect on voluntary household saving, and a powerfully negative one on fertility. Controlling for the expansion of financial markets, which offer people an alternative to the family and the state in making provision for old age, the paper finds that as much as three-quarters of the total fertility reduction that occurred in Italy between 1930 and 1984 can be attributed to the increase in the proportion of the population covered by mandatory pension arrangements. The pension deficit is found to have a negative effect on saving but no significant effect on fertility. Again using co-integration models, Cigno and Rosati (1996, 1997) find the same sign pattern in post–Second World War time series for Italy, Japan, the United Kingdom, United States, and West Germany. The child benefit rate is used as an explanatory variable only for the United Kingdom, where it has a positive effect on fertility and an insignificant one on saving.

6.2.2 A VAR Model for Germany

In all the macroeconometric models cited the direction of causation is *assumed* to run from policy to household saving and fertility. In what follows, we report in somewhat greater detail on a recent study where the direction of causation is left to be determined by the data. Cigno, Casolaro, and Rosati (2003) re-do the Cigno and Rosati (1996) analysis for West Germany using the vector autoregressive (VAR) approach, which allows for all possible interactions and directions of causation between the variables. The data are better than in the earlier study, not only because they are the longest time series (1960–1995) that will ever be available for West Germany[21] but also because they are based on a more stringent definition of pension benefits.

In this study fertility is represented by the total fertility rate and saving by the household saving rate. Male and female wage rates are measured net of marginal income tax and are thus partly a reflection of policy. The interest rate is represented by the yield on long-term government bonds. Pension coverage is measured as the ratio of the number of persons receiving pension payments to the number of persons over the age of 65. The implicit pension subsidy is proxied by the pension fund deficit, the yearly difference between pension benefits and pension contributions. Over a sufficiently long run of years, it may be expected that the deficit (surplus) in the annual account of the pension administration will tend to behave like the surplus (deficit) in the lifetime account of the representative agent. In steady state the two concepts coincide. The child benefit rate is defined as the sum total of public cash payments and tax allowances accruing to parents of young children, divided by the number of children.[22]

To estimate a VAR model, all the regressors must be stationary. Preliminary testing showed that the series are stationary in first differences and that the variables are thus $I(1)$. Given co-integration, it is always possible to apply the Granger representation theorem (Granger 1987) to the autoregressive structure, and thus to formulate a VAR model in ECM (error correction model) form. This allows the short-term dynamics of the system to be influenced by deviations from long-term equilibrium, and makes it possible to estimate the long-term elasticities together with the coefficients that describe the adjustment to displacements from the long-term path. The matrix of the coefficients that characterize the stationary long-run equilibrium, and the one that characterizes the short-run adjustment process, can be separately estimated by maximum-likelihood techniques.

The authors start by estimating an unrestricted ECM with eight variables (fertility rate, household saving rate, social security coverage, social security deficit, child benefits rate, male and female wage rates,[23] interest rate) and a constant term. Plotting the residuals, and examining the results of the recursive estimation, reveals a structural break in the child benefits series in 1986, the year in which federal policy changed drastically with the introduction of fertility-related pension benefits (*Anrechnung von Erziehungszeiten*) and a substantial expansion of conventional child benefits (*Kindergeld, Erziehungsgeld*, and *Kinderfreibetrag*). This break is taken care of by the introduction of a dummy for that year. The plot of the fertility variable reveals a sharp fall between the end of the 1960s and the first half of the 1970s. This coincides with the diffusion of the contraceptive pill. The actual adoption of this technical innovation reflects shifts in both the demand for, and supply of, contraception. The factors determining the demand for contraception are the same that determine the demand for children and may thus be thought to be adequately represented by the variables already in the model. The factors determining the supply of contraception are not represented however. The authors deal with that by including a step-dummy in the co-integration vector for the 1968 to 1975 period.

The rank of the co-integration matrix is determined by examining the eigenvalues of the companion matrix. This reveals the presence of six unit roots in the eight-variable model, with two co-integration vectors, one for the saving rate and the other for the fertility rate. The authors then go on to estimate a vector ECM, with a constant term (not restricted in the co-integration space), two lags for each of the eight variables, an unrestricted dummy to account for the break in the child benefits series, and a step dummy in the co-integration space to account for the shift in the supply schedule of contraception. The two co-integration vectors are identified by setting the long-term effects of fertility on saving, and of saving on fertility, equal to zero. The null hypothesis of a wrong overidentifying restriction is rejected at a high significance level.[24] Confirming the hypothesis of a policy discontinuity in 1986, the dummy for that year is significant in the fertility equation. Confirming the hypothesis of a shift in the supply schedule of contraception between the end of the 1960s and the first half of the 1970s, the step-dummy is significant in both equations. The estimated long-term elasticities are reported in table 6.2 (the standard errors are shown in brackets).

Fertility is affected negatively by social security coverage, and positively by the social security deficit, the child benefits rate, and the

Table 6.2
Estimated social policy effects in Germany

	Fertility	Saving
Pension coverage	−0.22 (0.08)	0.46 (0.15)
Pension deficit	0.07 (0.01)	
Child benefit	0.23 (0.02)	0.05 (0.03)
Female wage rate	−4.78 (0.59)	−7.45 (0.93)
Male wage rate	4.78 (0.59)	8.67 (0.93)
Interest rate	0.04 (0.01)	0.06 (0.01)

Source: Cigno, Casolaro, and Rosati (2003).
Note: Long-term effects; all variables other than the interest rate are in logs (standard errors in brackets).

interest rate. The fertility effects of male and female wage rates are, respectively, positive and negative. The finding that the effect of the child benefit rate is very small by comparison with those of the wage rates should not come as a surprise. Given the very high cost of having a child,[25] the child benefits rate would have to be very large indeed to cover a significant fraction of the cost of parenthood. Saving is positively affected by social security coverage, but not by the social security deficit, which is insignificant. The saving effects of the male and female wage rates are, respectively, positive and negative. That of the real interest rate is significantly positive but very small. The finding of a negative effect of the female wage rate on aggregate household saving is empirically novel (aggregate studies use income or earnings as the explanatory variable), and this implies that the woman's wage rate raises household expenditure more than household earnings.

The finding that in the long run the exogenous variables have non-zero effects on the fertility rate rejects the hypothesis that fertility is exogenous. The finding that, again in the long run, pension coverage has a negative effect on the fertility rate and a positive one on the saving rate, and that the implicit pension subsidy (proxied by the pension fund deficit) has a positive effect on the fertility rate, rejects the dynastic model. By contrast, the family constitution hypothesis is not rejected. These empirical results are consistent with those of the cross-country study by Zhang and Zhang, and of the earlier time-series studies by Cigno and Rosati on France, Germany, Italy, Japan, the United Kingdom, and the United States.

Let us now look at the short run. The matrix of the estimated coefficients representing the short-term behavior of the economy shows that apart from fertility itself only the two wage rates react to a divergence of the fertility rate from its long-term path. By contrast, not only saving but also fertility, the two wage rates, and the social security deficit respond to deviations of the household saving rate from its long-term course. While, in the long term, causation runs from policy to saving and fertility behavior, it is clear that, in the short term, there is also some reverse causation. In this respect it is interesting to discover that, in Germany, a temporary slackening of household saving induces the policy maker to either increase the social security deficit or reduce the surplus, rather than to curtail pension coverage. The finding that wage rates responded to variations in the fertility rate, but the interest rate did not respond to variations in the saving rate, seems to indicate that over the observation period, labor was less mobile than capital.

7   Policy: What Ought to Be Done?

Given that many public pension systems are in financial difficulty, should they be closed down, downsized, reformed, or bolstered with additional measures? Questions such as these cannot be addressed from the limited perspective of the system's own financial viability. They need to be looked at from the viewpoint of society at large. Given that the variables affected by public pensions (saving, fertility, etc.) are also influenced by child-related benefits, the two cannot be dealt with in isolation. In the present chapter we will reason as if we were starting to design a system of public transfers from scratch. The issue whether it is sensible to change what is already there will be faced in the next chapter.

Let us start by asking ourselves what is the logic of obliging people to participate in a pension scheme. A commonly used argument is that the young do not see far enough into the future to make adequate provision for old age (Diamond 1977; Aaron 1982). Another is that, in a compassionate society, the less able would otherwise be tempted to free-ride on the rest of the population (Hayek 1960, ch. 19; Hammond 1975). The first argument does not require much explanation, and the second is based on the following reasoning: if the characteristics of a certain person are such that try as she may, she is unlikely to earn much more than the subsistence minimum, she will rationally refrain from saving in the expectation that public compassion will not allow her to starve when she is old. The former is an argument for obliging everyone to make provision for old age in *their own* interest, and the latter is an argument for obliging everyone to contribute to a pension fund in *everyone else's* interest.

We do not find the first argument very satisfactory, since it implies time inconsistency, and it is thus difficult to reconcile with the standard economic assumption of rational behavior. If people are myopic, it does in any case offer a rationale for some degree of compulsion, not necessarily for public provision. The second argument is not really convincing either, since it does not seem very sensible to interfere with the life-cycle decisions of millions of people, with all the administrative costs and deadweight losses this is likely to cause, for the sake of bringing relief to a relatively small number of persons. Redistribution of lifetime wealth can be carried out by a variety of means other than old-age pensions. If a small number of people are still very poor when they reach old age, they can be helped by measures targeted specifically at them.

Now let us look at the arguments in favor of child benefits. The usual one is either that children should be subsidized because society values their well-being more than their parents do (an externality argument), or that households with children are poorer than childless households with the same level of income (an equity argument). The first argument is based on a linguistic misunderstanding, namely that child benefits are paid to children. Child-related cash benefits are paid to parents, who then must decide whether to spend the money on their children or on themselves. Even earmarked cash benefits, such as scholarships, and transfers in kind, such as free education or school meals, may end up replacing expenditures that parents would have otherwise undertaken out of their own resources. The second argument holds water if fertility is exogenous, and children bring no utility. If children bring utility, some couples may have to be compensated for having too many children, but others may have to be compensated for having too few. If fertility is endogenous, fertility-related transfers are an inducement to have more children. The final result could then be a larger rather than smaller number of poor children (Cigno 1986).

A less widely appreciated argument is that—since children are not transferable, but money is—income redistribution in favor of households with children may help bring about an efficient allocation of parental time. Suppose that some people are comparatively better at raising children and others at making money. There is then a clear efficiency argument for relaxing the budget constraint of women (or couples) with a comparative advantage in raising children, since that will allow them to specialize further in the activity at which they are comparatively more proficient. But there could also be an equity argument for redistributing in the opposite direction. Suppose that some of those who have a comparative advantage in raising children have also an absolute advantage. These persons may be so good at raising children, or like children so much, that their utility in the absence of policy would be higher than that of persons with a comparative advantage in raising money. If that is the case, the policy maker faces another trade-off between equity and efficiency considerations (Cigno 2002).[1]

These introductory remarks should make it clear that there are no simple answers to the questions raised at the start of this chapter. In what follows, we will try to answer them with a minimum of formality, first in a full information framework with capital as the only asset and then in an asymmetric information framework with production of human capital.

7.1 Optimal Policy in a Simple Framework

We will assume that utility is given by equation (5.2) of chapter 5, implying that people derive utility only from their own consumption and disutility only from their own labor. Suppose that all individuals are the same, that there is no uncertainty, and that labor and physical capital are the only factors of production. Further assuming that production is characterized by constant returns to scale, income per adult at date t is given by

$$y^t = f(k^t), \tag{7.1}$$

where k^t is capital per adult at date t, and $f(.)$ is a concave production function. Further assuming that international capital movements are unrestricted, and that the economy is "small," the interest rate may be taken as exogenous.

Let us call generation t the one that reaches adulthood at date t so that the date of the action coincides with the generation of the actor. Under this convention, y^t and k^t can be described also as the capital and income per adult of generation t. Abstracting from changes in life expectancy, the aggregate population growth factor between date t and date $t+1$ is equal to the fertility rate of generation t, n^t. The resource constraint is then

$$k^t - r^t d^t + f(k^t) = \frac{c_2^{t-1}}{n^{t-1}} + c_1^t + (p + c_0^{t+1} + k^{t+1} - d^{t+1})n^t, \tag{7.2}$$

where d^{t+1} is the per-capita foreign debt of generation $t+1$.[2]

7.1.1 Social Optima

For a social optimum the marginal rate of substitution of present for future consumption must be the same for all generations alive at any given t, and equal to one plus the marginal product of capital at that same date,

$$\frac{u_0'(c_0^t)}{u_1'(c_1^t - v(l^t))} = 1 + f'(k^t) = \frac{u_1'(c_1^{t-1}v(l^{t-1}))}{u_2'(c_2^{t-1})}. \tag{7.3}$$

Additionally the marginal product of capital must equal the interest rate,

$$f'(k^t) = r^t - 1, \tag{7.4}$$

and the marginal disutility of labor must equal its marginal product,

$$v'(l^t) = f(k^t) - (r^t - 1)k^t. \tag{7.5}$$

That is all that would be needed if the population profile were given. Since the size of future generations is itself an object of choice, we need a criterion for picking a population profile out all possible ones. As a preliminary to that, we must decide whether we are concerned only with the well-being of existing individuals, or also with that of individuals yet to be born. Aristotelian ethics, classical theories of the social contract (from Hobbes to Kant), and more recent contributions such as Harsanyi (1955) or Binmore (1994, 1998), refer to the "common good" of a given set of individuals. If our concern extends to the unborn, we must look elsewhere for normative advice.

The only philosophical approach with direct implications for population issues is utilitarianism. This comes in two main variants.[3] John Stuart Mill identifies the common good with the utility of the average individual. The objective of society should thus be to maximize

$$W^0 = \sum_{t=0}^{\infty} (\delta)^t U^t, \qquad 0 < \delta \le 1, \tag{7.6}$$

where δ is a generational weighing factor. By contrast, Jeremy Bentham argues that the common good is measured by aggregate utility. Society should then maximize

$$W^0 = \sum_{t=0}^{\infty} (\delta)^t N^t U^t, \qquad 0 < \delta \le 1, \tag{7.7}$$

where

$$N^t \equiv \prod_{j=0}^{t} n^{j-1} \tag{7.8}$$

is the number of persons in generation t. These two visions of the common good come to the same thing if the population profile (the size of each generation) is given, but not otherwise.

If social preferences are represented by the Millian welfare function (7.6), the choice of n^t must satisfy

$$\frac{u_2'(c_2^t)}{u_1'(c_1^t - v(l^t))} \frac{c_2^t}{n^t} = p + c_0^{t+1} + k^{t+1} - d^{t+1} \tag{7.9}$$

for each t. The left-hand side of this equation represents the social benefit of an extra birth at date t. Since the new person would produce goods at date $t + 1$, the benefit is given by generation t's marginal valuation, expressed in terms of its current consumption, of the future adult's contribution to the old-age consumption of generation t, (c_2^t/n^t). The right-hand side represents the social cost of an extra birth at date t. This is a sum of two elements. The first is the cost of bringing a new person into the world, and providing for that person's consumption through childhood $(p + c_0^{t+1})$. The second is the difference between the cost of equipping the future adult with k^{t+1} units of capital, and the foreign debt, d^{t+1}, that this person will inherit from generation t. In steady state (7.2), (7.3), and (7.9) imply

$$n = \delta r. \tag{7.10}$$

In view of (7.4) this is nothing other than the discrete-time version of the *modified golden rule* of capital accumulation.

If social preferences are represented by the Benthamite welfare function (7.7), the criterion for putting another person into the world at date t is

$$\frac{\delta W^{t+1}}{u_1'(c_1^t - v(l^t))} + \frac{u_2'(c_2^t)}{u_1'(c_1^t - v(l^t))} \frac{c_2^t}{n^t} = p + c_0^{t+1} + k^{t+1} - d^{t+1}. \tag{7.11}$$

Compared with (7.9), the marginal benefit of an extra birth now includes an extra term $[\delta W^{t+1}/(u_1'c_1^t - v(l^t))]$. Since W^{t+1} is the socially weighted average of the utility of a person born a date t, and of the utilities of all her descendants, this term represents society's marginal valuation of the utility of generation $t + 1$ in terms of adult consumption at date t. The benefit of an extra birth at t is thus larger for Bentham than for Mill. In steady state the conditions for a Benthamite optimum imply

$$1 = \delta r. \tag{7.12}$$

This is very restrictive because it implies that the rate at which society discounts the utility of future generations must be equal to the internationally determined interest rate. Since the latter is exogenous, this can happen only by chance. If present and future persons are given equal dignity ($\delta = 1$), (7.12) can be satisfied only if the interest rate happens to be zero.[4] We will thus stick by Mill.

7.1.2   Laissez-faire Equilibria

Suppose that no self-enforcing family constitution exists. Can individual decisions coordinated only by the market lead to a social optimum, or at least to an efficient allocation of resources given the population profile? Notice that since r^t is exogenous, (7.4) implicitly determines the domestic stock of capital per adult at date t. Therefore domestic saving has no effect on the domestic stock of capital per adult.[5] Income per adult is then effectively exogenous. If the internationally determined rate of interest is constant over time, per-capita income is constant too.

We know from chapter 5 that at any date t, consumers borrow or lend until

$$\frac{u_1'(c_1^{t-1}v(l^{t-1}))}{u_2'(c_2^{t-1})} = r^t, \tag{7.13}$$

and supply labor until its marginal disutility is equal to the current wage rate,

$$v'(l^t) = w^t. \tag{7.14}$$

On the other hand, producers equate the marginal product of capital to the interest rate as in (7.4), and the marginal product of labor to the wage rate,

$$f(k^t) - (r^t - 1)k^t = w^t. \tag{7.15}$$

Therefore (7.4) and (7.5) as well as the second equation in (7.3) are satisfied. Since young children cannot borrow, there is nothing to ensure that the first equation in (7.3) is satisfied too. Therefore there is no reason to believe that the allocation of consumption will be efficient given the population profile. Even if that were true by chance, the population profile would still be wrong. There is in fact nothing to ensure that the population criterion (7.9) is satisfied. Since a child costs at least p, and yields no return, selfish people have no incentive to raise children. If fertility is endogenous, the economy will then end with generation 0.

The incentive to raise children is provided by a self-enforcing family constitution. However, we know from chapter 5 that if such a constitution exists,

$$\frac{u_1'(c_1^i v(l^i))}{u_2'(c_2^i)} = \frac{x^i}{p + z^i} > r. \tag{7.16}$$

Under the present assumption that all individuals are the same, there is either a self-enforcing constitution common to all families or none at all. In the second case, no one has children, and the economy disappears with generation 0. In the first, everyone has children, but (7.13), and therefore the second equation in (7.3), is not satisfied. Either way, there is scope for public intervention.

In reality individuals are heterogeneous. Some may thus comply with some family constitution and have children, but others may go it alone and have no children. Since the share of compliers in the adult population is a decreasing function of the interest rate (see chapter 5), the lower the interest rate, the further the allocation of consumption from a Pareto optimum given the population profile. Conversely, the higher the interest rate, the further is the population profile from the one that satisfies the modified golden rule. Therefore it is not true that either no one has children or everyone has too many. The same can be said, even without heterogeneity, if the return to complying is uncertain, and risk-averse compliers thus provide for old age partly by having children, and partly by saving (see chapter 5). Even so, there is still scope for policy.

7.1.3 First-best Pensions and Child Benefits

Imagine to have maximized the Millian social welfare function subject to the resource constraint and found that the socially optimal consumption, labor and fertility plan is $(c_0^{t*}, c_1^{t*}, c_2^{t*}, l^{t*}, n^{t*})_{t=0,1,2,\dots}$, where c_j^{t*} is the period-j consumption of each member of generation t. Since young children cannot provide for themselves, and assuming that parental actions are observable, the government can implement this plan by using a combination of two schemes. The first is a stylized *pension scheme* that charges each member of generation t a lump-sum contribution θ^t in period 1 and pays her a lump-sum benefit η^{t+1} in period 2. The second is a stylized *child benefit scheme* that charges every member of generation t a lump-sum tax τ^t and pays her a per-child benefit φ^t, in period 1. Introducing the former without the latter would give rise to a *positive externality*.[6] When deciding whether to have another child, atomistic agents have in fact no way and no reason to take into account the fact that one more future worker will increase social welfare by relaxing the government budget constraint. In order to achieve a social optimum, the government must thus use pensions and child benefits together (we may regard φ as a *Pigovian subsidy*).

Since the government can observe how may children are born, and how much their parents feed them, all it has to do is set

$$r\theta^t = c_2^{t*}, \quad \varphi^t = p + c_0^{(t+1)*}, \quad \tau^t = (p + c_0^{(t+1)*})n^{t*} \tag{7.17}$$

and offer the adult members of each generation t the following "forcing contract":[7]

$$\eta^{t+1} = \alpha^{t+1} \quad \text{if } n^t = n^{t*} \quad \text{and} \quad c_0^{t+1} = c_0^{(t+1)*},$$

$$\eta^{t+1} = \beta^{t+1} \quad \text{otherwise,} \tag{7.18}$$

where

$$\alpha^{t+1} = c_2^{t*} \quad \text{and} \quad \alpha^{t+1} > \beta^{t+1}. \tag{7.19}$$

An agent will thus get a higher pension if she has the right number of children, *and* spends the right amount for each child, than if she does not.[8]

The adult members of generation t can then either (1) beget n^{t*} children, spend $(p + c_0^{t*})$ for them, and save nothing, or (2) have no children and save. For β^{t+1} sufficiently lower than α^{t+1}, the payoff of the first course of action will be higher than the payoff of the second, and higher also than the payoff of complying with any family constitution. The government can thus induce the agent to implement the socially optimal plan.[9] By so doing, however, the government would destroy the possibility that a self-enforcing family constitution might exist. Put another way, the government would replace any voluntary intrafamily arrangement with its own mandatory transfer system.

Notice that if society gave each generation the same weight ($\delta = 1$), the optimal rate of population growth would equal the interest rate. It would then make no difference whether pensions are fully funded or pay-as-you-go. By contrast, if later generations were given less weight than earlier ones ($\delta < 1$), the socially optimal rate of population growth would be lower than the interest rate. In that case the pension scheme could still be pay-as-you-go, but it would then have to make a deficit.[10]

The public transfer system we have just described looks remarkably like a family constitution, with η in place of x, and φ in place of z.[11] But there is an important difference. Since the government, unlike the family, has the power to coerce, the former does not need to pay over the odds to persuade agents to comply with its rules. In a full information setting, the public transfer system is thus superior to any spontaneous arrangement. In the presence of asymmetric information, however, this superiority may well be undermined by the family's informational advantage. The asymmetry may concern either the agent's personal characteristics or her actions. We will briefly deal with the former here, and come back to the latter later in this chapter.

Suppose that p or w vary across agents. If these personal characteristics are known to other members of the same family, but not to the government, we have an adverse selection problem. The government could then resort to policies that do not require a knowledge of the personal characteristics of every agent or induce agents to reveal them.[12] Since these policies are distortionary, a first best is out of reach. It is an open question whether the government can do better or worse, with its power of coercion, than families with their informational advantage. An additional argument for not trying to displace intrafamily arrangements altogether is that the personal services offered by the agent's own parents or children are not perfectly substitutable with those offered by the market (i.e., by complete strangers).[13] The family constitution's ability to secure those services for the young and the old is one of the possible explanations for the resilience of such informal arrangements in the face of expanding public transfer systems (see chapters 5 and 6). By both arguments it seems unlikely that the second-best policy will wipe out all spontaneous intrafamily arrangements.

7.2   Human Capital, Uncertainty, and Moral Hazard

In section 7.1 we assumed that income is produced with capital and labor only. We now introduce human capital as an additional factor of production. Since human capital is an indicator of personal capabilities—in particular, of ability to produce income—it cannot be separated from the person who has them. If a person dies, her human capital disappears with her. If a person emigrates, her human capital goes abroad with her. Assuming, however, that people do not move across national frontiers as freely, or as quickly, as capital in the usual sense, domestic investment in human capital will affect the domestic stock of this factor, hence the domestic level of income per adult resident. This complicates the analysis but does not change the conclusions reached in a simpler framework. With or without self-enforcing family constitutions, the laissez-faire solution cannot be depended on to deliver a socially optimal solution.[14]

In addition to introducing human capital, we now allow for the fact that some individual actions are either unobservable by the government or observable only at high cost. Among these actions is the amount of time or money that parents invest in their children's broadly defined education.[15] We also recognize that a person's earning ability (or, more generally, success in life) is not entirely determined by how much her parents spent for her education. To some extent, it will depend also on luck (DNA, state of the economy, being in the right place at the right time, etc.). So earning ability is to be regarded as a random variable. In such circumstances parental investments in children will determine not their children's earning ability but the probability distribution of that ability. Of course, a person's earning ability will eventually become known, but that will not be enough for the government to infer how much education the person received as a child.

We also replace the unrealistic assumption that people can choose how many children to have, with the more realistic one that parents can only choose their reproductive behavior (frequency of intercourse, contraceptive practice) and that this will condition the probability distribution of ending up with $0, 1, 2, \ldots$, children. Like the assumption that the government cannot observe how parents allocate their money and their time between themselves and their children, this gives rise to a moral hazard problem. It also changes the means and ends of population policy. Since the government observes how many children are actually born, but can neither observe nor infer the reproductive behavior that contributed to that outcome, an agent cannot be made to have any specified number of children by simply threatening her with a monetary penalty (the "forcing contract" idea). Let us now look at the ends.

Maximizing an intergenerational social welfare function such as (7.6) makes sense if the number and characteristics of the persons alive tomorrow can be determined with certainty by those alive today. It does not make much sense, however, if the number and characteristics of the persons alive tomorrow are random variables. In that case we should be talking of *potential*, rather than future, persons.[16] The most fundamental objection to the application of utilitarian criteria to potential persons is that it runs counter to the methodological individualism principle on which Western-style economic thinking is built. According to that intellectual tradition, welfare assessments must be based on judgments made by individuals. From this it follows that (1) only actual persons can formulate such judgments and (2) welfare assessments relating to *alternative* sets of individuals cannot be compared. Thus, if two states of the world contain different populations, the mean (or the sum) of the utilities of the individuals that exist in one state cannot be compared with the mean (or the sum) of the utilities of the individuals that exist in the other.

Given that the size and composition of the next generation are uncertain, policy can be judged only by its effects on the well-being of existing individuals. This does not mean that future generations will be exploited, but instead that the well-being of potential persons will come into the picture only insofar and inasmuch as the well-being of an actual person is affected. This is anathema to decent people who regard it as their moral duty to do what they think is good for future generations. But that is precisely the point. They can only do what *they* think is good for people yet to come. There is thus no contradiction between saying that actual people, or some of them, are concerned for the well-being of potential people, and saying that welfare judgments can only be based on the preferences of actual people.

7.3 Policy Optimization as a Principal-Agent Problem

When it comes to justifying public intervention, economists tend to look first for efficiency arguments. We saw, for example, that a pension scheme on its own is a source of inefficiency because it generates a population externality. In a full-information environment this externality can be cured by introducing child benefits or educational subsidies alongside pensions. Does the prescription change if the actions of current adults can only condition the probability distributions of the number, and earning ability of their children? Having assumed that these actions are not observable by the government, the policy optimization takes the form of an *agency problem*, with the government in the role of principal and parents in that of agents.

In earlier sections we characterized a social optimum first, and then compared it with a laissez-faire equilibrium where individual actions are coordinated only by the market, or by the market and a self-enforcing family constitution. In the present asymmetric information context we will find it convenient to first characterize individal behavior given the policy, and then to inquire what the policy should optimally be. The analysis draws on Cigno, Luporini, and Pettini (2003) and Cigno and Luporini (2003).

7.3.1   Parents as Government Agents

Let the human capital of this adult be represented by her wage rate, w_0, and that of each of her children by their future wage rate, w. Whereas w_0 is known, w is a random variable with given density conditional on the amount of education invested in each child, e. Similarly the number of children, n, is a random variable with given density conditional on the reproductive action b. The utility of a current adult is given, once again, by (5.2) of chapter 5.[17]

To simplify, we assume that current adults are identical, each adult supplies one unit of labor, and any money spent on a child on top of p is educational expenditure. Depending on whether p is just monetary expenditure, or a full cost including also the opportunity cost of the minimum amount of time that a parent must spend with a child, w_0 will then represent the actual or the full income of a current adult. With the generational label omitted, the residual lifetime utility of a current adult is determined ex post (i.e., when the actual values of n and w are revealed) by

$$U = u_1(c_1) + u_2(c_2). \tag{7.20}$$

In the uncertain environment the assumed concavity of $u_i(.)$ signifies risk aversion.

Suppose that agents are promised by the government a per-child subsidy φ, payable in period 1 as soon as a child is born, and a further per-child subsidy, possibly contingent on w, $\psi(w)$, payable in period 2 as soon as the child's earning ability is revealed.[18] Let $\tau(w_0)$ be the taxes paid by a current adult with earning capacity w_0, where $\tau(.)$ is an increasing function. Being too numerous to collude, agents take φ, $\psi(.)$, and $\tau(.)$ as given.

Consumption in periods 1 and 2 are given by

$$c_1 = w_0 - \tau(w_0) - [p + e - \varphi]n - s \tag{7.21}$$

and

$$c_2 = sr + \psi(w)n. \tag{7.22}$$

In view of (7.20), it is clear from (7.21) and (7.22) that an adult will have children only if $(\psi + \varphi)$ is at least as large as p, and will invest in a child's education only if ψ increases with w. Since the number of children that will be born is uncertain at the stage when the agent chooses her reproductive behavior, but will be known with certainty at the stage when the agent chooses her labor supply, educational expenditure, and saving, the agent's decision problem is solved by backward induction.

The agent's first step is to choose (e, s), taking n as given. The maximand is the agent's expected utility over all possible realizations of w, $E_w(U)$, where U is determined by (7.20), c_1 is determined by (7.21), and c_2 by (7.22). The agent will then invest in each child's education to the point where the marginal expected utility (arising from the government subsidy contingent on w) of e equals the marginal cost,

$$E_w\left(\frac{dU}{de}\right) = 1. \tag{7.23}$$

If she can, the agent will also borrow or lend until the ex ante marginal rate of substitution of current for future consumption equals the interest factor,

$$E_w\left(\frac{u_1'(w_0 - s - [p + e - \varphi]n)}{u_2'(sr + \psi(w)n)}\right) = r. \tag{7.24}$$

These two conditions associate a level of educational expenditure, e^n, and a saving level, s^n, with each possible realization of n.

The next step is to choose reproductive behavior, b. The maximand is the expectation of $E_w(U)$ over all possible realizations of n, $E_n(E_w(U))$. The value of U is still determined by (7.20). Equations

(7.21)–(7.22) must still hold, but (e, s) is now replaced by (e^n, s^n). Assuming that reproductive behavior carries no immediate costs,[19] the agent will raise b to the point where its expected marginal utility is zero,

$$E_n\left(E_w\left(\frac{dU}{db}\right)\right) = 0. \tag{7.25}$$

7.3.2 Government as Principal

If the tax schedule $\tau(.)$ is taken as given,[20] the policy problem is to choose the value of the per-child subsidy φ and the transfer schedule $\psi(.)$ (i.e., a value of ψ for each possible w). From our earlier considerations the government's maximand is identical to that of each agent, but the choice of policy is subject to the government budget constraint and to the incentive-compatibility constraints that arise from the agent's behavioral response to the policy. The problem is solved by backward induction, the same as that of the agent.

As a first step, the government chooses (e, s) and a ψ for each possible w, taking n and φ as given. The maximand is $E_w(U)$, where U is still determined by (7.20), with c_1 and c_2 given by (7.21)–(7.22). Where revenue is concerned, what matters to the government is not the future w of any particular child but its average value. Assuming that the number of agents is large enough for the expected value of w to coincide with the actual average, the government does not face any financial risk (it does face uncertainty over the realization of each agent's utility, since this is affected by the w of the agent's own children). The government budget constraint can then be written in per-adult terms as

$$\left[\varphi + \frac{E_w(\psi(w))}{r}\right] n \le \tau(w_0) + \frac{n}{r} E_w(\tau(w)). \tag{7.26}$$

The incentive-compatibility constraints are the conditions on the agent's choice of educational expenditure and saving, respectively (7.23) and (7.24). The solution associates a particular value of e and s, respectively denoted by $e^{n,\varphi}$ and $s^{n,\varphi}$, and a particular schedule $\psi(.)$, denoted by $\psi^{n,\varphi}(.)$, with each possible realization of n and choice of φ.

The second step is to choose (b, φ), taking into account the fact that n is a random variable with probability distribution conditional on b. The maximand is now $E_n(E_w(U))$, where U is still determined by (7.20), with c_1 and c_2 given by (7.21)–(7.22), but $(e, s, \psi(.))$ is now replaced by

$(e^{n,\varphi}, s^{n,\varphi}, \psi^{n,\varphi}(.))$. Again, if we assume that the number of agents is large enough for the expected value of the average n (as well as of the average w) to be realized with certainty, the government does not face any financial risk. The government's budget constraint is now

$$\varphi E_n(n) + \frac{E_n(E_w(\psi^{n,\varphi}(w))n)}{r} \leq \tau(w_0) + \frac{E_n(E_w(\tau(w))n)}{r}, \tag{7.27}$$

and the incentive-compatibility constraint is the condition on the agent's choice of fertility behavior (7.25).

Before looking into the properties of the optimal φ and $\psi(.)$, notice that the justification for using these policy instruments rests on an externality argument. Agents are too small to take into account the effects of their choice of b and e on future government revenue. Notice also that if the agent can borrow any amount at the interest rate $(r-1)$, it is a matter of indifference whether the government pays φ in period 1, as we have assumed, or φr in period 2.[21] It does make a difference, however, if the agent cannot borrow against the future government subsidy (the problem is not so much that the subsidy is uncertain as that it cannot be mortgaged). In any case, the government's choice of φ and $\psi(.)$ must be communicated to the agent *before* the latter chooses b, hence e. Let us now look at the properties of the optimal policy.

If the agent's reproductive and educational behavior were observable, the incentive-compatibility constraints on the government's choice of policy would not be binding, and the plan (b^{**}, e^{**}, s^{**}) chosen by the policy maker would be a first best. Since the realizations of the individual n and w are uncertain, but their averages are certain, the government can raise social welfare by ensuring the agent. The first-best plan could then be implemented by promising to pay the agent

$$\varphi^{**} = p + e^{**} \tag{7.28}$$

in period 1, and

$$\psi^{**} = E_w(\tau(w)) \tag{7.29}$$

in period 2, conditionally on the agent choosing (b^{**}, e^{**}). Notice that as ψ^{**} does not depend on the actual w of an agent's children, the principal is offering each agent full insurance against the risk that her children will turn out to have low ability despite the agent's educational investments.[22] Since the government can observe neither b nor e, however, there is a moral hazard problem[23] that makes the first best unattainable.

Let us now place ourselves at the stage of the policy optimization problem where the number of children is already known, but the future earning capacity is still uncertain. The agent cannot be guaranteed a given ψ, regardless of w, because the agent would in that case invest nothing in her children's human capital. She will have an incentive to do so only if ψ increases with w. But that conflicts with the insurance principle. Tension between incentive and insurance considerations is then likely to result in a U-shaped ψ schedule (decreasing in the child's earning and tax-paying capacity at low realizations of w, where insurance considerations are paramount, increasing at high realizations, where incentive considerations tend to predominate),

$$\psi^* = \psi(w), \tag{7.30}$$

as in figure 7.1. The U-shape of the schedule provides a rationale for subsidizing parents of handicapped or educationally subnormal children, besides parents of highly talented children.

A similar argument can be made at the stage where the number of children is uncertain. Since reproductive activity is not observable, would-be parents must be given the incentive to choose the right level of b. That is done by promising

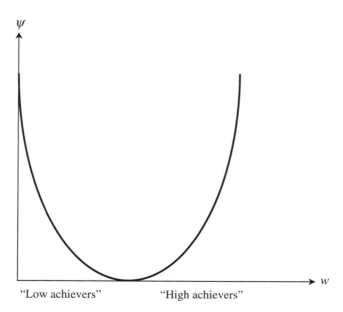

"Low achievers"   "High achievers"

Figure 7.1
Second-best transfer to parents, conditional on a child's earning capacity.

$$\varphi^* = p, \tag{7.31}$$

where p, it must be remembered, covers a child's subsistence consumption but not education. Notice that the threat element (the possibility of a forcing contract) in the population policy is gone, along with the assumption that parents can directly choose how many children to have, and also gone is the command quality of the first-best policy, along with the assumption that reproductive behavior is observable. Since both kinds of subsidy are conditional on results, and results are influenced by parental actions, the policy will obviously distort individual behavior. The outcome is thus a second best.

The second-best policy may be thought of as consisting of two parallel schemes.[24] At any date, one of these schemes pays every current adult a sum φ^* for each child that she has, and charges every current adult

$$\tau(w_0) = \varphi^* n. \tag{7.32}$$

We may interpret this as a conventional *child benefit scheme*. At the same date, the other scheme pays every old person a sum $\psi(w)$ for each child that she has, and charges every adult a sum $\tau(w)$, satisfying

$$E(\psi(w)) = E(\tau(w)). \tag{7.33}$$

We may interpret this as an unconventional *pension scheme* paying benefits conditional on the number and earning ability of the pensioner's own children.[25] How does this compulsory transfer system differ from the voluntary one generated by a self-enforcing family constitution?

It seems reasonable to assume that people cannot observe the reproductive behavior of their relatives any more than the government does. Unlike the government, however, people have a pretty shrewd idea of how other members of their family treat their children. In particular, children know full well how much education they received from their parents. A family constitution can then require every adult to spend a fixed amount z for the education of each child that she happens to have, and to pay her own parent a sum $x(w_0), x'(w_0) > 0$, conditional on her parent having complied with the constitution a period earlier. Conditional on the present adult having complied, the same constitution will in turn require each of her children to pay her $x(w)$ a period hence.

The difference between this constitution and the second-best scheme is that, in the latter, the agent is obliged to pay the government $\tau(w_0)$

anyway. Here, by contrast, the agent will choose to pay her parent $x(w_0)$ only if she intends to have children. Therefore the family constitution must still offer an (expected) return to money spent on children that is higher than the interest factor,

$$\frac{E_w(x(w))}{p+z} > r. \tag{7.34}$$

Everything we said earlier about the chances that self-enforcing family constitutions will bring about an efficient allocation apply here too.

Once again, it is not clear whether the government, with its power of coercion, can do better than families with their informational advantages. All we can say is that the existence of actions observable by members of the same family (in particular, by the directly interested party), but not by the public authority, tilts the balance a little further in favor of families. The second-best policy is thus likely to leave even more space for informal intra-family arrangements than earlier considerations had led us to expect.

7.4   Pensions and Child Benefits in the Presence of Uncertainty and Asymmetric Information

The second-best pension and child benefits system developed in the last section subsidizes parents in proportion to the number of children they have, and pays pension benefits conditional on the number and earning capacity of the pensioner's children,

$$\eta = \psi(w)n. \tag{7.35}$$

In view of (7.33), pension benefits are financed by the taxes paid by current adults, but this is not a conventional pay-as-you-go scheme. In the latter the payments made by current adults go into a common pool, and individual pension entitlements bear no relation to the amount paid by the pensioner's own children. Therefore, in a conventional pay-as-you-go scheme, there is no incentive for adults to produce good tax payers. Indeed, if pension entitlements are earnings-related, the scheme is an incentive to spend more time in the labor market, have fewer children, and spend as little time as possible with them. Here, by contrast, there is a direct link between the pension benefits to which a person is entitled, and the taxes that person's children will pay over their lifetime (the relationship between pension benefits received by the parent and taxes paid by the children is not one for one, how-ever, because there is a certain amount of redistribution in favor of parents of unlucky children). Therefore the system provides parents with the incentive to invest in their children's human capital. Let us see how it works, and whether we need a conventional pension scheme by the side of it.

Suppose that current adults happen to be identical as assumed in the last section. As these individuals enter adulthood, the child benefit scheme induces them to undertake the second-best level of reproduc-tive activity. Partly as a result of that, and partly as a result of chance, some of these people will end up with relatively many children, and some with relatively few or none at all. The pension scheme will in-duce those who have children to undertake the second-best level of educational expenditure. As a result of chance, some of these children will enter adult life with a relatively large earning capacity, others with a relatively small one. Despite the assumption that their parents are identical, the new adults are thus heterogeneous.

The time when children reveal their earning capacity is also the time when their parents retire. The latter will then receive pension benefits increasing with the number and earning capacity of their children. We have already said that the scheme provides some insurance against the risk that a person's own children may turn out to be low earners. What about the risk of having few children, or none at all? That does not matter because agents with few or no children have more money to save. Therefore their old-age consumption need not suffer.

Now suppose that current adults have different w_0.[26] On equity grounds, the general income tax schedule $\tau(.)$ could be designed to re-duce net wage inequality. But that would have an efficiency cost, since it would reduce the incentive for parents to (1) invest in their children's human capital and (2) specialize according to their personal compara-tive advantage. Agents with higher w_0 should thus be allowed to spe-cialize in raising money. Conversely, agents with lower w_0 should be allowed to specialize in raising children.[27] Adults should then be offered the alternative of qualifying for a pension by either raising in-come and paying pension contributions, or raising children (who will in turn be paying taxes or pension contributions). Agents with a com-parative advantage in raising money would then opt for the former, and agents with a comparative advantage in raising children for the latter.

Risk considerations, and real-life complications that are ignored here for the sake of simplicity,[28] would lead some to choose a combination of the two strategies. Simply allowing people to privately buy an annuity (i.e., to choose their own s) would achieve that result if financial markets were perfect. But market imperfections make it desirable for the government to provide also a conventional contributions-related pension scheme. What matters is that the choice of scheme should be left to the individual agent. Any limitation to this freedom, such as "occupational pensions" (see chapter 2) that tie a certain form of pension provision to a certain form of employment, or even to a certain employer, can only be distortionary, and should thus be avoided unless additional considerations come into play.

Pensions, even the newfangled ones we are proposing, should in any case be bolstered with conventional child benefits (cash payments or tax allowances for households with children). Given risk aversion or credit rationing, a parent will prefer a child benefit for certain to an uncertain pension benefit with the same actuarial value. Therefore child benefits are a more cost-effective way of providing agents with the incentive to have children. Since child benefits are not an incentive to invest in a child's human capital (indeed the opposite), however, they are not a substitute for a transfer conditional on the child's future earning capacity. Since that capacity will be revealed only when the child is in middle life, and the parent on the point of retirement, the natural way to provide this further subsidy is, as already indicated, in the form of a pension benefit related to some measure of the child's capabilities.

8   Policy: What Can Be Done?

In the last chapter we reasoned *as if* no public system of pensions and child-related transfers existed, and we were considering creating one (we could have titled it "what ought to *have been* done"). In reality such systems are well established throughout the developed world, and doing away with them is not easy nor even desirable. It is not easy because there are vast bureaucracies with a vested interest in keeping them going, and possibly also a majority of electors with a vested interest in maintaining the status quo. Boldrin and Rustichini (2000) show that a pay-as-you-go pension system, once voted in, would not be voted out by subsequent generations even if it were expected that the return will eventually fall. Not desirable because it would reduce welfare. Since existing public pension schemes are largely unfunded, closing them down would in fact imply replacing a pay-as-you-go mechanism with individual contracts based on the capitalization-and-insurance principle (and it does not matter very much whether these contracts would be issued by the private or the public sector). Breyer (1989), Fenge (1995), and several others have shown that the gains for future generations of moving from pay-as-you-go to full funding can never compensate for the cost to the generations caught in the transition.[1] As for the child-benefit side of the system, this certainly cannot be closed without also abolishing pay-as-you-go pensions, since parents can reasonably object to bearing the full cost of raising future contributors for the benefit of childless pensioners.

Fortunately, however, the public transfer system we ideally want is not altogether different from the one we actually have.[2] As we saw in the last chapter, no matter how the policy problem is formulated, the optimal solution will always include a mix of old-age pensions and child-related transfers, both financed by levies on citizens of working age. There is, however, a fundamental flaw in the design of existing pension schemes, namely that they reduce the incentive to have children and invest in their human capital. Since, in the long run, the internal rate of return of a pay-as-you-go pension scheme cannot exceed the growth rate of total income,[3] this means that the system tends to erode its own profitability. Child benefits improve the situation, on the one hand, because they encourage fertility but make it worse, on the other, because they discourage parental investment in their children's human capital. Although public education takes up the slack to some extent, there are aspects to education that only parents can provide (see chapter 7).

In countries where there is a statutory age of retirement, the problem is exacerbated if the retirement age has not kept pace with the rise in life expectancy. In part, this has to do with organized resistance by workers, and in part, because governments, employers, and trade unions have repeatedly colluded against the interests of future generations and allowed early retirement to be used as a stop-gap solution to adverse economic shocks (as in the 1970s and 1980s). Retirement age is an important issue, and one that is attracting a lot of public attention, but it is essentially a political one. No great amount of economic expertise is needed to recognize that if after retiring at the same age of 63 a man is expected to live 78 years rather than 68 like his father, he will likely have to be supported by the taxpayer for three times as long as his father was. Put another way, longevity is a problem only insofar as people are obliged (or permitted) to retire at a time when they could still produce income. Without that artificial limitation, a rise in life expectancy will only increase social welfare.

The point, in any case, is not whether rising longevity is more or less of a problem than falling fertility. It is rather that public transfers to the aged are not a prominent cause of rising life expectancy (not, at least, in the rich countries we are concerned with). It is rather, as we argued theoretically and empirically in earlier chapters, that pension schemes as presently designed are a major cause of fertility decline and likely also of underinvestment in human capital. For all these reasons we have treated household saving, fertility, and educational investment as endogenous and the retirement age as just another policy instrument (one of the factors determining the level of coverage offered by a public pension scheme). In the present chapter, we draw together the different threads—institutional, theoretical, empirical—of this book and identify a number of possible changes in the structure of existing pension systems. Then we will try to evaluate numerically the likely effects. Most of the changes envisaged constitute a mere strengthening of reforms already under way in a number of countries. The only radical change is that of pensions being matched to the earning capacities of one's children, as suggested by the theoretical analysis of the last chapter.

8.1 An Early Summing-up, and Some Policy Options

Because public pension schemes tend to have a very low level of funding (see chapter 2), their balance sheets are affected more by total income growth than by the interest rate. If pension policy affects the growth rate of total income, this then feeds back to the policy itself. The conventional wisdom is that public pensions are bad for growth because the taxes or contributions needed to pay for them displace voluntary saving, and discourage labor. We have argued theoretically and reviewed empirical evidence that matters are more complicated than this.

We saw in chapter 5 that pension coverage has an ambiguous effect on aggregate household saving, and negative effect on aggregate fertility. By contrast, the pension deficit has a negative effect on saving, and a positive one on fertility. We also saw that a public pension scheme will necessarily discourage labor only if it is of the Beveridgean type. A Bismarckian pension scheme could have the opposite effect, and any distortion it causes is likely to be small. In any case, labor force participation affects the *level* of per-capita income, not the growth rate. For pension policy to have an effect on per-capita income growth via the supply of labor, pension coverage has to be continually increasing, and there are obvious limits to that.

In chapter 6 we produced evidence that pension coverage has a positive effect on household saving and a negative one on fertility, that the pension deficit has a nonpositive effect on saving and a nonnegative one on fertility, and that child benefits have a positive effect on both. We also reported evidence of a positive effect of pension coverage on educational investment. Because the effect was estimated without controlling for child benefits and the pension deficit, the estimate may be biased.

What does all that tell us about the effect of pension policy on the growth rate of total income? The latter is the sum of the population growth rate and the growth rate of per-capita income. The policy affects population growth through the fertility rate. Could it affect per-capita income growth? Probably not (especially if the pension scheme is Bismarckian) through labor participation, as we have just argued, but probably yes through fertility, savings, and education. In the models we used in chapter 7 we assumed that production is governed by constant returns to scale, the interest rate is exogenous (internationally determined), and human capital cannot be passed on from one generation to the next. By these assumptions the growth rate of per-capita income is exogenous. Removing or weakening some of these assumptions, however, may make per-capita income growth endogenous.

Endogenous growth theories rest on one or both of the following combinations of assumptions:

1. Capital and labor are immobile, and there are increasing returns to scale in production.

2. Labor is immobile, and human capital can in some sense be transmitted from one generation to the next.

Hypothesis 1 does not require much explanation. If capital and labor do not move across national frontiers, the more the existing population adds to the domestic stocks of capital and labor by savings and child-bearing, the larger will be the scale of operations of the domestic economy and the productivity of both factors. Hypothesis 2 implies that education raises not only the human capital of the generation being educated but also that of future generations. One way to justify this hypothesis is to assume that the knowledge and skills of today's adults rub off on to today's young (via apprenticeships). Another is to say that at least some knowledge, rather than individual capabilities, of each generation is stored in books and electronic archives to be available for future generations.[4]

The empirical evidence suggests that there may be some truth in the predictions of endogenous growth theory. If there is, pension policy will affect per-capita income growth too. But positively or negatively, and by how much? The estimates of the growth effects of pension coverage mentioned in chapter 6 are contradictory, and may be biased. There are no estimates of the growth effects of the pension deficit. All we can then say is that existing pension policies reduce population growth, and *may* raise per-capita income growth. We do not know what they do to total income growth. Our guess is that they reduce it, but the discussion that follows does not rest on this. We simply look for different ways of making the effects of existing pension systems on population growth less negative, and their effects on per-capita income growth more positive.

One possibility is to reduce the scope of public pension systems to just a (low) safety net for the very unlucky. The argument against this is that public intervention is required because we do not have a complete system of markets. The counterargument is that a reduction in public provision would facilitate the development of financial and insurance markets, and thus make the system less incomplete. Another possibility is to increase the incentive to have children by either raising conventional child benefits or introducing fertility-related pension benefits. The problem with this policy is that, as we saw in chapters 6 and 7, it reduces the incentive for parents to invest in their children's human capital. It thus counters the negative impact of public pension coverage on population growth but may accentuate that on per-capita income growth.[5] Is there any way of increasing the incentive to have children, without reducing the incentive to invest in their education?

In the last section of chapter 7, we argued that the incentive for parents to invest resources (not just money, but also time and effort) in the education of each of their children can come from a pension scheme that makes a couple's pension entitlements an increasing function of their own children's future tax paying capacity. The argument against this is that not everyone wants, or can have, children. There are then two ways one could go. One is to argue that public provision of old-age security is justified only by an externality argument, and that the government should thus give a pension only to those who bear the cost, but do not fully appropriate the benefit, of producing and educating future tax payers. The rest of the adult population should be left to make their own old-age arrangements, or be provided with just a safety net. Another way to go is to argue that market incompleteness makes it desirable to have a public pension scheme for childless people too.

Thus the best alternative to simply running down an existing pension system may be to gradually replace it with two parallel schemes, one providing contributions-related benefits and the other providing benefits related to the earning capacity of the pensioner's children. Both schemes would have to be collectively financed by current taxpayers as in a conventional pay-as-you-go pension system, but with the important difference that the second scheme would offer an incentive to raise children and to invest in their human capital. Since different couples and individuals have different comparative advantages, people should be free to participate in one or both schemes by either specializing fully in raising income or raising children, or by combining the two activities in some proportion over the course of their life. In either scheme the benefits formula would have to take account of the foregoing incentives.[6]

To illustrate the risk considerations, we will now carry out some numerical simulations. As we saw in section 6.1, the existing microeconometric estimates of the effects of pension policy on saving behavior are open to question on a number of scores. Furthermore they capture only the immediate impact of pension policy. We will thus use the macroeconometric estimates of saving and fertility behavior of Cigno, Casolaro, and Rosati (2003) for West Germany. As we saw in section 6.2, these estimates take account of both long- and short-term adjustments, allow for reverse causation, and control for the effects of child benefits and wage rate dynamics. They are also consistent with the available microeconometric evidence regarding the effects of child benefits on fertility choice. Because the direction of causation was found to run from policy to saving and fertility in the long run, while in the short run policy responds to saving behavior, we will limit ourselves to simulating long-term policy effects using the elasticities reported in table 6.2. As we will not take account of any adjustment lags, these simulations will show what *would* happen if saving and fertility behavior adjusted immediately to changes in government policy. For this reason the simulated developments of saving and fertility in the event of a continuation of existing policies are not strictly comparable with the saving and fertility experienced over the sample period, which do reflect adjustments lags.

8.2   Reducing Pension Coverage and Raising Child Benefits

Our first step is to use the estimates reported in table 6.2 to make out-of-sample projections of fertility and household saving to the year 2020, under alternative assumptions regarding the evolution of public policy. Regarding the evolution of the other exogenous variables, we will assume that male wage rates will continue to rise, in real terms, at the average growth rate observed over the sample period (1960–1995), and female wage rates will go on trying to catch up with their male counterparts at the pace observed over the same period.[7] The real interest rate is assumed to remain constant at its 1995 level.

Where pension coverage (measured here as the ratio of total pension expenditure in real terms to number of persons aged 65 or over)[8] and the real child-benefit rate (defined to include child-related income tax allowances, *Kinderfreibeträge*, as well as direct cash transfers, *Kindergeld*)[9] are concerned, we consider six alternative scenarios. In each scenario the pension deficit is assumed to remain constant as a percentage of household disposable income at its 1995 level.

S1 Pension coverage grows, on average, at the 1960 to 1995 average rate (2 percent a year); child benefits remain constant at the 1995 level.

S2 Pension coverage and child benefits grow at the average rate of the sample period (2 percent a year the former, 1.2 percent the latter).

S3 Pension coverage and child benefits remain constant at the 1995 level.

S4 Pension coverage remains constant at the 1995 level; child benefits grow at an average rate of 1.2 percent a year.

S5 Pension coverage decreases at an average rate of 2 percent a year; child benefits remain constant at the 1995 level.

S6 Pension coverage decreases at an average rate of 2 percent a year; child benefits grow at an average rate of 1.2 percent a year.

Typically reforms lose momentum after an initial fervor. To mimic this fact of political life, we have front-loaded changes in pension coverage and child benefits so that the effects of our imagined reforms are felt more strongly in the initial years. Scenario S6 assumes a 40 percent reduction in pension coverage by the year 2020. If that were achieved entirely by cutting annual entitlements, the replacement ratio (pension benefits in the first year after retirement, divided by earnings in the last year of work) guaranteed by the German pension system would go down, in the case of a person with a full working career, from the present 70 percent level to less than 45 percent. But that is not the only way in which pension coverage can be reduced. Keeping in mind that the latter reflects both the average annual pension benefit and the average age of retirement, we have ample scope for achieving at least part of the reduction by curbing retirement ahead of the statutory limit in the first place, and by raising the limit in line with increasing life expectancy in the second.

In addition to these imaginary policy scenarios, we consider four more plausible ones. The first incorporates policy already agreed upon by parliament, and in some measure actually carried out since 1995.[10] The other three assume additional adjustments, not outside the realm of political feasibility, that would considerably strengthen the effects of the reforms already in place. The reform process reflected in these scenarios is messier than those hypothesized in scenarios S1 through S6. For that reason it looks remarkably like the real thing. All these scenarios represent different ways of reducing the level of coverage provided by the existing pension system, without really changing its design. Design changes will be introduced in a further series of scenarios discussed later in the chapter.

APS (actual policy scenario) is a hybrid of things that have already happened, and things that are expected to happen from political decisions that have already been taken. For the years that have lapsed since the end of the sample period, we use actual data. For subsequent years, we assume that the child benefits rate will grow (as in S2) at 1.2 percent a year in real terms, and that pension coverage will evolve, as a result of rules introduced since the end of 1995, in the way predicted by the CESifo pension model.[11] These financial projections reflect the legal framework that has resulted from the amended retirement rules, and stiffer penalties[12] for retiring before the statutory limit, introduced in the late 1990s, and with the 2001 reform.[13]

NEW (no early withdrawal) scenario assumes a more rapid increase in the effective retirement age than is envisaged in APS so that it equals the statutory limit of 65 by the year 2010.[14] Since, under present disability rules, many people retire before the statutory limit, this increase cannot be achieved by merely strengthening the disincentives to early retirement envisaged in APS. Tougher disability rules, incentives for able-bodied persons to stay at work after the statutory age of retirement, or a rise in the statutory age of retirement will clearly be needed.

CPI (consumer price indexation) scenario assumes a US or French style of pension indexation, whereby pension benefits in the first year after retirement are calculated as a given fraction (the replacement rate) of earnings, and subsequently up-rated in line with the cost of living.[15] Pension benefits in Germany are basically indexed to wages *net* of pension contributions. This way, an increase in contributions feeds back to the level of benefits. CPI indexation was applied in Germany as a temporary measure in the year 2000 but was later discontinued (see chapter 2).

NEW + CPI scenario combines the assumptions behind NEW and CPI.

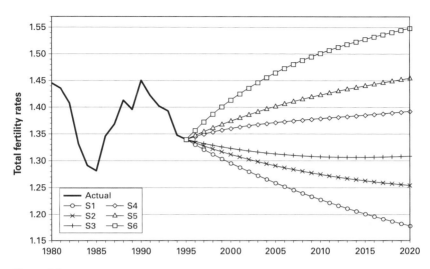

Figure 8.1
Total fertility rates in Germany until 2020—Simulation 1.

Figures 8.1 through 8.4 show the predicted evolution of fertility and household saving from 1995 onward under all these different scenarios.[16] To give the reader a sense of the actual data, the figures include the actual development of these variables over the previous decade and a half.[17]

8.2.1   Fertility Effects

As in chapter 1 the measure of fertility we used was the total fertility rate (the total number of children that a woman would have in a lifetime if, at each point of her life, she experienced the age-specific fertility rate of the women that have that age in the year of observation). Unlike the birth rate (number of births per woman of fertile age), this measure of fertility is independent of age structure and is thus a synthetic (cross-sectional) indicator of the evolution of completed fertility.

Figure 8.1 shows actual fertility rates for the 1980 to 1995 period, and simulated ones (scenarios S1 through S6) for the 25 years that follow. As can be seen immediately, persevering with past policies (scenarios S1 and S2) will accentuate the fertility decline.[18] Even holding pension coverage and the child benefits rate constant in real terms at their 1995 levels, as in S3, will not be sufficient to stabilize fertility. To keep

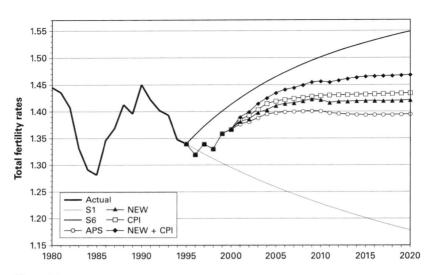

Figure 8.2
Total fertility rates in Germany until 2020—Simulation 2.

fertility from declining further, child benefits (S4) must be increased or pension coverage (S5) reduced. If one did both (S6), the total fertility rate would rise by a fifth of a child per woman over a period of twenty-five years. Completed fertility for women born in 1970 or later would then go up to something between 1.8 and 2 children, that is to say, to the levels currently observed in France and the United Kingdom, way above the levels observed in Italy and Japan. In this scenario German fertility will largely recover the ground it lost between 1960 and 1995, which has strongly contributed to the financial crisis of the German public pension system. It should be kept in mind, however, that if the gap between male and female wage rates closes faster than it has over the sample period, that will partially offset the combined effects of pension retrenchment and child benefits increases.

Note that reducing individual pension entitlements by 2 percent a year, as in S5 and S6, will amount to a cut of about 40 percent over the full twenty-five-year period.[19] Because pension coverage is measured as the ratio between total pension payments and number of persons aged 65 or more, part of the cut can be achieved by curbing early retirement, rather than reducing the average annual pension benefit. That is indeed one of the directions in which policy is beginning to move.

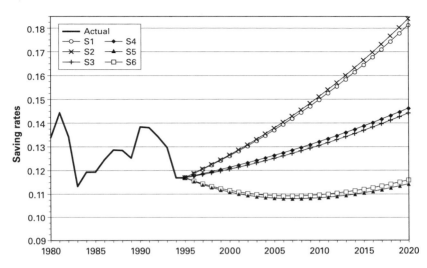

Figure 8.3
Saving rates in Germany until 2020—Simulation 1.

Figure 8.2 shows the fertility implications of APS. The years between 1995 and 1999 have been mostly lost in discussions. A number of piece-meal adjustments carried out since 1999, and finally the 2001 reform, appear to have achieved a reduction in pension coverage sufficient to stabilize fertility by the year 2005 (subject to our early caveats on ad-justment lags and wage rate dynamics). As we said above, this reduc-tion in coverage was obtained by a combination of penalties for early retirement and reductions in annual benefits. The same chart shows also the effects of the other, more realistic scenarios (NEW, CPI, and NEW + CPI). It appears that the gradual implementation of reforms already on the statute book, strengthened by a number of additional rule adjustments, such as the complete eradication of early retirement (NEW) and the uncoupling of pension benefits from current wages (CPI), should be enough to bring us within reach of the S5 scenario.

8.2.2   Saving Effects

We now turn to household saving behavior. The household saving rate declined over the last ten years of the sample period. Figure 8.3 shows that reducing pension coverage in the way envisaged by scenarios S5 or S6 can stabilize the household saving rate at between 11 and 12 percent of household disposable income (since child benefits have only a small effect on saving, and the pension deficit has none, it does not matter what happens to them). Holding pension coverage constant (S3 or S4) will induce a recovery of the saving rate toward the heights of the early 1980s and late 1990s. Allowing pension coverage to rise at the average growth rate of the 1960 to 1995 period (S1 or S2) will drive saving up sharply. Graphically the contrast between this, and what happens to fertility, is striking, and it illustrates the point made in various places of this book that forced saving through a conventional public pension scheme tends to crowd out private investment in children, rather than in conventional assets.

Figure 8.4 shows that APS, NEW, CPI, and NEW + CPI all imply a stable saving rate until such a time as the combined effect of the recent reforms is fully felt. When that time comes (in the simulations, the turning point is around the year of 2005, but remember that these assume instant adjustment), the saving rate will start rising again. The projected saving rate increases are somewhere in between those associated with the two more extreme scenarios, S1 and S6. Despite all the reforms expenditure on pensions does not decrease in APS and does so only slowly in the no-early-withdrawal (NEW), and CPI indexation scenarios.[20]

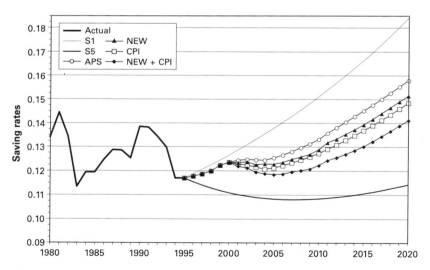

Figure 8.4
Saving rates in Germany until 2020—Simulation 2.

8.3   Reforming the System

We now start to consider the effects of introducing actual design changes along the lines indicated in the first section of this chapter. In the present section, we examine the effects of allowing people to qualify for a pension by rearing children. An element of that, *Kindererziehungszeiten*, was introduced in the German pension system as early as 1986. As we pointed out in chapter 6, however, the econometric estimates on which our policy simulations are based account for this important innovation only through a dummy. The child-benefit elasticities pick up the effects of both *Kindererziehungszeiten* and conventional child-related benefits (*Kindergeld* and *Kinderfreibeträge*) because the two have tended to move together since the former was first introduced in 1986.

Furthermore the new policy instrument has lost some of its more innovative characteristics in the course of the years. When it was first introduced, a parent who withdrew from the labor market to look after a child was credited for one year with a notional pension contribution, set at 75 percent of average earnings. The benefit was thus directly related to a measure, however rough, of the opportunity cost of parental time expended on the child. The condition that the parent should actually withdraw from the labor market in order to qualify for the credit disappeared in 1996. *Kindererziehungszeiten* have thus become just another fertility incentive, not dissimilar in its effects from a conventional child benefit. Since then, the number of years for which the parent qualifies for the credit has been extended from one to three years, and the contributions notionally credited from 75 to 100 percent of average earnings.[21]

8.3.1   *Linking Individual Pension Entitlements to Individual Fertility*

We will now simulate the effects of raising the weight of the fertility-related element of pension benefits at the expense of the earnings-related one. To do so, we convert the former into an equivalent child benefit by discounting it back to the average age of reproduction at the appropriate market rate of interest. At first sight, this might seem to imply that people are indifferent between a sum of money today, and the capitalized value of that same sum of money tomorrow. Were we actually assuming this, we would run into the objection that if it is not possible to borrow, a person will unambiguously prefer the money today. If people responded to the delayed payment in the same way as they respond to the immediate payment, that might lead to an over-estimate of the effects of fertility-related pension benefits. But things are more complicated than that.

Recall that the econometric estimates we are using for these simulations reject simple explanations of household behavior based exclusively on market mechanisms. The numbers are consistent with the predictions of a strategic model of individual behavior according to which adults have a choice of either complying with a set of family norms (a family "constitution") or going it alone in the market (see chapter 5). By this model, if a conventional pension system is introduced or expanded, a number of people who would have otherwise complied will now go it alone. These switchers will save more, and have fewer children, than they would otherwise. The opposite will happen if people can qualify for a public pension not only by working and paying contributions, but also by rearing children. Since the latter is compatible with a "comply" strategy, and compliers get a higher return from investing in children than from lending to the market, a number of persons who would have otherwise gone it alone will now comply. Switchers now have more children, and save less, than they would otherwise.

These considerations do not change the fact that a sum of money to-day is preferable to its capitalized value tomorrow but make it clear that the promise of a pension, combined with the opportunity to implicitly lend to one's own children at more than the market rate of interest, may be more attractive than the immediate payment of a sum of money equal to the discounted value of that pension. We conservatively assume that the two alternatives are equally attractive for the average working-age citizen.

Figure 8.5 shows the fertility implications of a scenario, FRP (fertility-related pensions), that incorporates the NEW + CPI assumptions but allows for an increase in the fertility-related component of pension benefits at the expense of conventional, earnings-related pension benefits. Recall the simulation exercise carried out in section 4.2 that showed the effect on a woman's total pension entitlement of withdrawing from the labor market in order to have a child. We will now set the fertility-related element of pension entitlements so that it neatly fills the gap between the total pension entitlement of a childless woman in the "benchmark" case, and that of a woman with one child in the

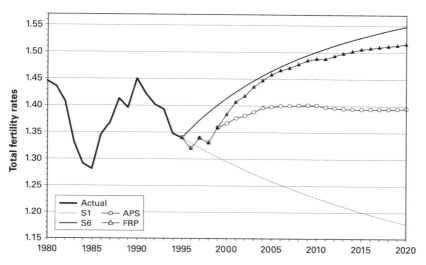

Figure 8.5
Total fertility rates in Germany until 2020—Simulation 3.

baseline case (the latter is taken to represent the typical work pattern of a German mother).[22] In order to make these fertility-related pension entitlements comparable with ordinary child benefits, we convert their present value in an equivalent flow of annual payments over a span of 18 years from the date of birth of the child that motivated the award,[23] and then apply the child-benefit elasticities reported in table 6.2 to these annual payments.

For the sake of comparison, figure 8.5 shows also what happens to fertility in the "actual" policy scenario, APS, and in the two extreme scenarios, S1 and S6 (recall that S1 assumes a continuation of the policies carried out in West Germany over the 1960 to 1995 period, while S6 assumes a gradual increase in the child benefit rate, and a reduction in pension coverage, from the end of that period.) In the FRP scenario, fertility recovers to a level that is comparable with that of the S6 scenario. It would thus seem that similar effects can be obtained by either cutting pension coverage or partially replacing conventional earnings-related pension benefits with fertility-related ones.

Figure 8.6 shows the consequences of FRP for saving behavior. Since child benefits, hence the present value of fertility-related pension benefits, have only a small effect on saving, the saving rate does not recover as strongly as in S6. Since the effect of FRP on fertility is similar to that

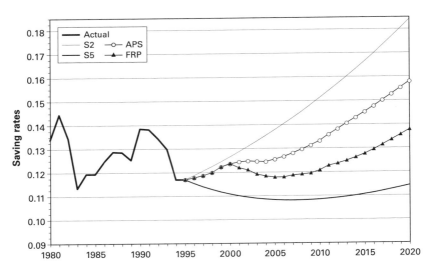

Figure 8.6
Saving rates in Germany until 2020—Simulation 3.

of S6, the total income growth effect of partially replacing earnings-related with fertility-related benefits is thus unlikely to be as large as that of cutting pension coverage.

8.3.2 Linking Individual Pension Entitlements to Own Children's Earning Capabilities

The FRP scenario we have just considered assumes that fertility-related pension benefits are financed, just like regular child benefits, out of general taxation. This implies redistribution from households with few or no children to households with many children. To the extent that several generations pay taxes in the same fiscal year, there is also some intergenerational redistribution. In steady state, however, each generation pays for the child benefits it receives (and that is what is reflected in the long-run estimates of child-benefit elasticities that we are using). The incentive to have children thus arises purely from intragenerational redistribution.

We now try to visualize the effects of the more radical reform outlined toward the end of section 8.1. The reform differs from FRP in that it introduces pension entitlements that increase not with the number but with the collective earning capacity of the pensioner's own children. As already pointed out, that is not what happens in a

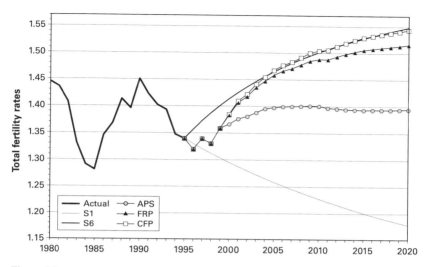

Figure 8.7
Total fertility rates in Germany until 2020—Simulation 4.

conventional pay-as-you-go pension scheme where there is no link between the earning ability of the pensioner's children and the benefits that the pensioner receives. Since no such scheme exists in Germany or anywhere else, there is no way of estimating its effects directly. We will thus have to make imaginative use of the information we have.

Conceptually, the behavioral effect of this policy can be split into two parts. One is the effect of promising every couple a certain amount of money in old age for each child that they have, and financing this expenditure with a poll tax on every member of that same generation. The other is the effect of returning the poll tax to the parent generation, and financing the reimbursement with a poll tax on each of their children. We have already calculated the first of these effects by applying the child-benefit elasticities to the annualized present value of the promised old-age benefits.[24] We now calculate the second effect by applying the estimated pension deficit (implicit pension subsidy) elasticities of saving and fertility to the present value of the new-styled pension benefits.[25]

We thus imagine a CFP (child-financed pensions) scenario, constructed under the assumption that the increase in fertility-related pension benefits envisaged in FRP is financed with the contributions collectively paid by the children of those who receive the benefits, rather than out of general taxation. Figure 8.7 shows that fertility rises more strongly in CFP than in FRP (reported for comparison). Since the pension deficit has no significant effect on household saving,[26] the saving rate (not displayed) behaves as in the FRP scenario.

Subject to every possible caveat, the last simulation seems to show that this more radical reform would stimulate population growth more than fertility-related pension benefits, without any significant effect on saving behavior.[27] The theory thus leads us to expect that CFP would raise also per-capita income growth by inducing parents to invest more in the human capital of each of their children. Although we do not have elements for quantifying this last effect, it seems reasonable to assume that CFP would produce *at least* the same rate of total income growth as any of the alternatives considered so far, without any sacrifice in terms of either higher pension contributions, or lower pension coverage. This confirms the theoretical prediction made in chapter 7, and recalled in section 8.1 of the present chapter, that the reform would obviate an inefficiency of the existing system of public transfers.

Conclusion

We started this book with the observation that public pension systems, some more than others, face a financial crisis. A major cause of this looming crisis is the slowdown in total income growth. Particularly damaging to largely unfunded pension schemes is the fall in the population component of total income growth, and consequently in the number of pension contributors to an ever-increasing number of pension beneficiaries. The question is, Should public pensions be reformed, buttressed with additional measures, such as fertility and education incentives, or cut back? If one is convinced that, in all conceivable circumstances, the cost of government failure is always likely to outweigh the cost of market failure, the answer is obviously that public intervention in all its forms should be kept to the very minimum. In the present context, this means that the government should limit itself to providing a safety net for the old and indigent. If, on the contrary, one is willing to concede that in certain circumstances the cost of market failure could outweigh that of government failure, a more elaborate social transfer scheme might be justified. This is our a stance.

The theory and evidence summarized in this book leads us to conclude that public pension schemes dampen population growth, and possibly also private human capital investment. Since, in the long run, the highest rate of return that a pay-as-you-go pension system can offer to its participants is equal to the rate of total income growth, these systems tend to erode their own profitability. Cutting public pensions back—as most countries have done, some more ferociously than others—might not solve the problem. The econometric evidence indicates that, other things being equal, a cut in the size of the public pension system can help fertility to recover but will reduce aggregate household saving. If saving helps per-capita income growth, cutting pensions back might then not be of help to total income growth.

If cutting down the public pension program means doing away with its contributions-related component, and leaving in place just a flat-rate benefit scheme by way of universal safety net, what is left is pure Beveridge. Because individual benefits will then be largely independent of individual contributions, the latter will be a tax in all but name.[1] If contributions increase with earnings, as is usually the case, this tax will discourage labor and reduce per-capita income. If one takes the road of pension cuts, one must then go the whole way and leave just a very small scheme carefully targeted at those who, through no fault of their own, find themselves in dire poverty when they get old. This will get rid of a big money loser but will not be socially optimal.

The analysis reported in this book suggests that externalities, credit rationing, and insurance considerations justify more substantial public intervention (see chapter 7). The second-best policy includes two essential elements. The first is a child-benefit scheme, not unlike the existing ones (see chapter 3), making transfers to parents from the moment they have children. The second is a two-pronged pension program allowing working-age individuals to qualify for retirement benefits by either, or both, of two methods:

1. Produce income and pay pension contributions.

2. Have children, and invest in their human capital.

Pension benefits earned by method 1 should reflect the lifetime contributions made by the pensioner over his or her own lifetime, with some correction for redistributive and insurance purposes. This method of qualifying for retirement benefits is approximated, in varying degrees, by existing pension systems of the Bismarckian type (see chapter 2). Pension benefits earned by method 2 should reflect the value of the taxes and pension contributions that the pensioner's own children are expected to pay over *their* lifetime—again, with corrections for redistributive and insurance purposes. In some measure, existing pension rules already compensate mothers for contributions not made during periods of absence from the labor market (in the case of Germany, they more than compensate them; see chapter 4). But these compensatory measures are no more than delayed child benefits. By contrast, method 2 relates a person's pension entitlements not only to the number of children but also to these children's earning ability, hence to the amount of taxes and pension contributions that they can be expected to pay over their lifetime.

What we are proposing under method 2, in effect, is that a person's pension be financed, in part or in total, by the pensioner's own children. That is not what happens in conventional pay-as-you-go schemes where the payments made by currently working-age individuals go into a common pool, and serve to pay benefits for *all* currently retired individuals. There is no link between the benefits to which a person is entitled, and the payments made by that person's children. Indeed many of the persons in receipt of a pension today have no children. Under our proposal childless persons could still earn a full pension by method 1, but method 2 would allow parents to earn at least part of their pensions by raising future taxpayers and pension fund contributors. This would give parents an incentive to invest in their children's human capital, and thus encourage those with a comparative advantage in raising children to specialize in that activity more than they would if only method 1 were available. That would favor allocative efficiency.

We mentioned in the Introduction that the public debate on pension reform is focused on the age of retirement and on the disincentive-to-work effect of public pensions, rather than on the disincentive to have children and invest in their human capital. Regarding the disincentive to work, we argued in chapter 5 that this is associated with Beveridgean schemes, where pension contributions are effectively a labor tax, but not necessarily with Bismarckian ones, where pension contributions are a form of forced saving. Regarding the statutory age of retirement (or the minimum age at which a person qualifies for a full pension), our approach has been to treat this as one of the parameters that determine the coverage of a public pension system. Holding it constant in the face of rising life expectancy raises coverage. An actuarially fair pension scheme does not need any such limit. Whichever the age at which a person retires, the expected value of the benefits is equal to the capitalized value of the contributions made up to that point.

In a public pension scheme, however, strict actuarial fairness is generally tempered—as it should be (see chapter 7)—by redistributive and mutual insurance considerations. We think therefore that there should be a "normal" age of retirement, regularly adjusted in line with mortality statistics, and penalties (bonuses) for those who retire earlier (later). The norm should vary not only across cohorts but also across categories of individuals within the same cohort. It should be higher for members of more recent cohorts, who have higher life expectancy, and lower for individuals engaged in physically demanding occupations (mining, heavy metalwork, etc.) or with a personal history of serious illness, who have lower life expectancy. Moves in this direction have already been made, or are under discussion, in most of the countries used as examples in this book.

The public transfer system we are proposing has as its objective the provision of incentives to have children, and to invest in the human capital of each child. We pointed out in chapters 5 and 7 that these objectives can be furthered by the use of indirect taxation to distort prices in favor of goods that constitute an input into the production of human capital, since this lessens the adverse selection and moral hazard problems associated with direct transfer schemes. This avenue is limited, however, by the extent to which it is possible to distinguish child-specific or educational goods from the rest. Another way of correcting for parental under-investment in their children's human capital is through the provision of free or subsidized public education, or through the award of scholarships, but it should be kept in mind that education in a broad sense does not end with school attendance. Much education goes on within the family. A further problem is that educational subsidies substitute for parental expenditure. Some parents would have sent their children to a fee-paying school in the absence of a free one. The same is true of scholarships. The money saved thanks to these subsidies need not be spent entirely on other forms of human capital investment. Therefore public education and price subsidies do not do away entirely with the problem of providing parents with the incentive to invest in their children's human capital at the efficient level.

In chapter 8 we used available estimates of the effects of several kinds of social transfer on household saving and fertility behavior in West Germany to simulate the effects of various policy packages. These simulations show that a reform resembling the one we are proposing could sufficiently restore the incentive to have children and all but eliminate the problems currently facing the German pension administration. Lack of comparable quantitative information prevented us from simulating also the effect of the reform on per-capita income growth (via the household savings rate, and via the rate of parental investment in their children's human capital). Our simulations thus provide only a conservative estimate of the benefits that would ensue from the reform. Pension-based incentives to have children are now present in many of the countries used as examples in this book, but overall, they are very small (see chapter 4), and none provide an incentive to invest in a child's human capital.

Notes

Chapter 1

1. The data used for the figure are taken from the World Bank's (2001) Health, Nutrition, and Population database, and from information provided by the various national statistical offices involved.

2. In Japan, the year 1966 is marked by a singular occurrence. Girls born in that year (the year of the fire-horse according to the Chinese calendar) were expected to make those who would live with them unhappy, even to kill their husbands. This is often said to explain the dip in the number children officially born in 1966. But official statistics may be distorted by a certain amount of misreporting of the date of birth of girls.

3. But not for the same reason. Japan did not experience a baby boom. These are simply generations born in a regime of near absence of birth control.

4. The methodology adopted is mostly that suggested by Edwin Cannan in 1895, and further developed by a number of other authors in the 1940s.

5. In their research, if not in their day-to-day business, demographers nowadays take care to show the probability distribution of outcomes around their baseline scenarios. See, for instance, Alho (1990), Lee and Tuljapurkar (1994).

6. The net migratory flows assumed in these scenarios are based on long-term averages recorded in the past. They are thus high in the United States, at a moderate level in the EU-15, and virtually absent in Japan. In some European countries, especially Germany and Italy, net immigration exceeded these levels during the last decade as large numbers of immigrants arrived from Eastern Europe and, in the Italian case, North Africa. It is assumed that this pattern will not continue. Of course, different assumptions can make a big difference to future population structures. This only strengthens the argument that treating behavior as exogenous is extremely unsafe.

7. Regarding the actual period of labor force participation, a definition based on people aged 60+ per those aged 20 to 59 might appear more appropriate, at least in a European context. However, the alternative definitions mostly affect the *level* of old-age dependency (which are much higher in the alternative case) and the time-path of its (more rapid) increase, while the fundamental pattern of demographic *change* remains the same.

8. Again, the sources are US Bureau of Census (2000), Japanese National Institute of Population and Social Security Research (2002), and Eurostat (2000).

9. For sources, see note 8 above.

10. For a preliminary discussion and some evidence, see, for example, Disney (1996), Hurd and Yashiro (1997), Bosworth and Burtless (1998), Bryant and McKibbin (1998), Miles (1999), Faruqee (2002), or Feyrer (2002).

11. More detailed projections of age-related expenditure, taking precautionary reforms of this kind into account, are given also in OECD (2001a, ch. 4), and EU Economic Policy Committee (2001).

12. The life expectanctcy of those who will be old in 2050 will be different from that of the today's old, not only because of medical advances but also because they have not experienced any widespread war or economic depression during their youth.

13. In terms of total fertility rates, this implies a modest increase over the next two decades. Total fertility tends to fall below completed fertility if younger women have their children later than the older generation. For Italy, Eurostat's baseline scenario actually assumes an increase in completed cohort fertility to a German level.

14. The source is Eurostat (2000).

15. See the striking evidence presented in Oeppen and Vaupel (2002) that maximum life expectancy observed in countries taking the lead in this area at any given point in time exhibits a next to linear increase (by about one year over a period of four years; the adjusted R^2 of this estimate is a striking 98 percent), showing no sign of a slowdown so far for 160 years. As we mentioned earlier, demographers are projecting an increase of less than half this speed for the future.

Chapter 2

1. The only major exception is Australia. But even in Australia there is a minimum income guarantee scheme for the elderly.

2. The interested reader is referred to the specialized literature, for example, Diamond (1977).

3. See Lindbeck and Persson (2003) for an extended discussion.

4. As we will see in section 2.3, even in broadly Beveridgean systems there is usually *some* connection (through the number of years for which contributions are paid, if in no other way) between benefits and contributions.

5. Systems of this kind are hard to come by in practice, certainly in the public sector. If a public pension scheme has any reserves at all, these are usually too small to pay benefits for more than just a few months ahead. In recent years, however, some national pension schemes have started to build up reserves in the expectation of exceptionally large payments, when an exceptionally large generation retires. A few countries have introduced mandatory funded schemes on the boundary between public and private sector.

6. In practice, the switch from DB to DC has often been accompanied by other design changes, aimed at giving individuals more choice over portfolio composition. This additional freedom of choice can raise utility but also administrative costs (on the latter, see Diamond, 2000). Which of the two has risen more is an empirical question.

7. The rate of return used to calculate the capitalized vale of the contributions made should be a risk-free market rate of interest. The risk premium used to calculate the

expected value of the benefits will reflect uncertainty about the insured person's life expectancy at the time of retirement.

8. If insurance companies cannot tailor the individual policies to the true personal characteristics of their clients, there is also an adverse selection problem.

9. That is not true if the scheme is market-based, for example, as in Chile. Even though participation is mandatory, private insurance companies must compete for customers, and thus spend on advertising.

10. In other words, we follow the overlapping generations approach of Samuelson (1958) and Diamond (1965).

11. We are ignoring a number of real-world complications. In particular, we are not deducting a risk premium for insurance against longevity.

12. We will see in chapter 7, this is how it ought to be. It should nevertheless be kept in mind that national income (hence its growth rate) can be calculated in many different ways, and is subject to measurement error. Any statement about the growth rate being higher or lower than any particular number should thus be taken with a modicum of scepticism.

13. Compared to Aaron's original contribution, this should instead be called the *non-Aaron* condition. It actually rules out the case in which Aaron was interested—the social insurance paradox, according to which introducing an unfunded pension scheme makes everyone better off.

14. For example, the most basic link is created if a number of "qualifying years" are required to get a full pension that is otherwise a flat rate (see section 2.1).

15. As some maintain, the life expectancy of the rich is systematically higher than that of the poor. Were this true, it would partly offset the redistributive features built into the benefit formula.

16. Let $(\eta^{t+1}/y^{t+1}) = (\eta^t/y^t) = \alpha$ be the predefined level of benefits. Taking into account the periodic budget constraints for $t+1$ and t implies $\theta'^{t+1} = (\alpha/n^t)$, $\theta'^t = \alpha/n^{t-1}$, and so on. Substituting this into (2.3) yields the result given in the text.

17. See Beveridge (1942) for his draft of the British social security scheme used in the postwar period.

18. A good source of comparative institutional information is the survey of more than 150 "Social Security Programs throughout the World" provided by the US Social Security Administration (2002; accessible via http://www.ssa.gov). In-depth information for a smaller set of countries is given in CESifo's (2006) "Database for Institutional Comparisons in Europe" (DICE, access via http://www.cesifo.de). Here we mainly rely on the recent DICE update in Fenge et al. (2003).

19. Looking at net income is important because different countries apply different rules in taxing wages and pension benefits.

20. More information can be found in the Social Security Administration's Web site, http://www.ssa.gov.

21. The fraction of public-sector employees who are not covered by the Social Security system usually have cover through other, parallel arrangements.

22. For detailed information, see http://www.pensionguide.gov.uk or http://www.dss .gov.uk. Both sources are provided by the Department of Employment and Pensions (formerly: Department of Social Security). As in all other cases, we disregard extra-benefits paid to pensioners with *dependent* children.

23. Other benefits provided by National Insurance are funded with general tax receipts.

24. See the simulations in OECD (2001a).

25. Additionally the state earnings-related pension scheme (SERPS), which still exists for those who did not opt out of it when it ceased to be mandatory, has been given a new lease of life, and now offers a State Second Pension (S2P), calculated according to a benefit formula that is much more redistributive across different earnings levels than the old one.

26. For fuller information regarding current provision, see http://www.vdr.de and http://www.bmas.bund.de, VDR being the German Social Security Administration (*Verband Deutscher Rentenversicherungsträger*) and BMAS being the Federal Department of Labor and Social Protection (*Bundesministerium für Arbeit und Soziale Sicherung*).

27. Adding contributions for health care, long-term care, and unemployment insurance, the total price of social insurance is more than 40 percent of gross wages.

28. Without this cross-subsidy, current contribution rates would be about 2 percentage points higher than they actually are. In a sense, the strategy followed by Germany is the opposite of that adopted by the United States whose Social Security Trust Funds are built up as a "demographic buffer fund."

29. With gross-wage indexation, contribution rates can eventually exceed *any* bound as old-age dependency increases. Net-wage indexation establishes a feedback mechanism between pension benefits and contribution rates, ensuring that the latter are less than 100 percent.

30. The main effect seems to be that private savings, which would have been made anyway, are being re-directed toward the special type of private pension plan that qualifies for the subsidy.

31. Valuable sources of information on institutional details are http://www.retraite .cnav.fr and http://www.legislation.cnav.fr.

32. See information provided at http://www.inps.it.

33. Old-age provision is the only major item of public expenditure in Italy in the area of social protection. This can be inferred from international comparisons of GDP ratios associated of other types of social expenditure, such as unemployment benefits and public health care.

34. For an extended discussion of this new variety, see Disney (1999) or Palmer (2000).

35. The present government is, however, trying to accelerate the transition by pushing through legislation that would require 40 years of contributions, instead of 35 as at present, for retirement before the statutory age (65 for men, 60 for women) from the year 2008.

36. See http://www.fkf.se and http://www.fk.se, the homepages of the Swedish association (*Försäkringskasseförbundet*, FKF) of social insurance administrations (*Försäkringskassan*,

FK). Specific information regarding the new Swedish pension system is also provided via http://www.pension.nu.

37. Actually these "private savings" are collected by the social security administration and then channeled to a semipublic body that acts as a meta-fund manager. This agency carries out aggregate net (re-)investments that arise from the large number of individual transactions, although individuals have full control over their investment strategies. The legal framework for the *Premiepension* scheme is defined to avoid individual noncompliance, and it cuts down overhead and transaction costs to a minimum.

38. Information is provided by the Japanese Ministry of Health, Labor and Welfare via http://www.mhlw.go.jp. An extensive "Annual Report on Health and Welfare", in English, is available at (http://www1.mhlw.go.jp/english/wp_5/).

39. It has taken some time for these ideas to spread. Recently a similar view of unfunded pension schemes was presented in Murphy and Welch (1998), Geanakoplos, Mitchell and Zeldes (1998), and Orszag and Stiglitz (2000).

40. For a fuller discussion, see Sinn (2000) as well as Fenge and Werding (2003).

41. See Sinn (2000) for a formal demonstration.

42. Their work is based on Thum and Weizsäcker (2000), who developed the framework for running calculations for the German statutory pension scheme.

43. The model was originally constructed for the preparation of a report of the Advisory Board of the Federal Ministry of Economics (1998). It portrayed the German statutory pension scheme (*Gesetzliche Rentenversicherung*). Its up-dated version can be adapted, within certain limits, to any similar institution.

44. Calculations for France and Sweden exclude disability pensions (on the contribution as well as on the benefit side), since disability is covered by separate schemes.

45. These assumptions imply that the difference between ng and r increases as n gets smaller. If the difference were assumed to be constant, the qualitative results will remain unchanged, but any increases in ϑ' will obviously be smaller.

46. As we pointed out earlier, in being fully funded or close to it, the second and the third pillar of a pension system tend not to give rise to an implicit tax.

47. As we already noted, the UK and US schemes also redistribute the most between rich and poor members of the same generation.

48. See Fenge and Werding (2004).

Chapter 3

1. For example, European Observatory on National Family Policies (1996, 1998).

2. For example, *Bundesministerium für Familie, Senioren, Frauen und Jugend* (1998), OECD (2002b).

3. See, for example, Mendelson (2003); the volume edited by Bradshaw (2003) contains material on a larger number of countries, but the individual contributions are not integrated to allow for cross-country comparisons.

4. On a smaller scale, similar allowances exist in Italy and Japan.

5. The theory of public finance does not provide unambiguous rules as to how to tax individuals living together. This may be one of the reasons why there are almost as many approaches to taxing families and married couples as there are national revenue codes.

6. In 2001, the participation rates of married or cohabiting (single) mothers with children under 19 years were 68 (68) percent in the United States, 68 (50) percent in the United Kingdom, 67 (66) percent in France, 63 (67) percent in Germany, and 45 (83) percent in Japan (Bradshaw and Finch 2002, tab. 2.5). Numbers for Italy are not available. Variations are much larger, however, if we take into account the number of hours worked on a regular basis.

7. The source for the numbers used in the figure is Bradshaw and Finch (2002, ch. 3) and the materials for their "matrix analysis" of a large set of model families provided at http://www.york.ac.uk/inst/spru/research/summs/childben22.htm.

8. Obviously some of the variation may be due to inaccurate measurement of PPPs or to differences in income across countries. The first source of error should not be too important in the comparison of Germany to Italy, since both are eurozone countries (we are ignoring differences in the purchasing power of a euro within this zone). The second source of error should be of no significance, since national gross average earnings in PPPs do not vary much across countries (the range is about 2,000 to 2,900 euros a month; see Bradshaw and Finch, 2002, tabs. A.3 and A.4). Nevertheless, the differences are smaller if benefits are expressed as percentages of average earnings. Benefits for one child then range between less than 1 and about 8 (and, in a majority of cases, only between 4 and 6) percent of gross earnings.

9. Benefits may differ with the age of children because of special arrangements for families with very small children. For a survey, see *Bundesministerium für Familie, Senioren, Frauen und Jugend* (1998). Another explanation could be higher tax allowances, or special subsidies, for families with children still in school or in higher education. Such rules are implicitly taken into account when assessing benefits for children aged 7, 14, or, in the next subsection, 17 in the family types covered here.

10. Again, the sources used for the figure are Bradshaw and Finch (2002, ch. 3) and the auxiliary information provided on the Web site of their research group.

11. In France, the total amount of benefits accruing to a couple with three children is about 660 euros a month, or more than 30 percent of the national average earnings.

12. In most countries covered here, national revenue codes are not neutral with respect to how the income is shared between partners. Where this applies, we have to depend on the two-earner interpretation of the last two cases. The main exceptions are France and Germany, where income taxes are levied at the household level, implying that these cases can also be interpreted as one-earner couples with the employed spouse earning a correspondingly higher wage. For a brief description of the relvant features of national tax systems, see OECD (2002b, tabs. S.1 and S.2).

13. The source is, again, Bradshaw and Finch (2002, ch. 3).

14. For an in-depth discussion of the policies developed by the two Anglo-Saxon countries, see Battle and Mendelson (2001).

15. Since 2002 the WFTC has been split into a working tax credit and a child tax credit.

16. As can be seen from figure 3.3, in Germany, child-related cash benefits again increase with income where this is equal to average male plus average female earnings or even higher.

17. For information on housing-related fiscal measures, and how they affect different types of families in different countries, see Bradshaw and Finch (2002, ch. 4).

18. For information on this topic, see the OECD series of publications on "Higher Education Management and Policy" and OECD (2001b, ch. B).

19. These calculations refer to the baseline case of a couple with average male earnings plus half the average female earnings, or of a single parent with average female earnings.

20. The calculations reported in table 3.2 are based on 2000 data. More recent information regarding all cost components is not available.

21. Alternatively, one could interpret our results as "expected" values, taking the current proportions of children attending (public) schools to be the relevant probabilities.

22. In Germany and the United Kingdom, medical prescriptions for children are free of cost. See Bradshaw and Finch (2002, ch. 6).

23. That is true whether the cost is measured by the share of total (private and public) health expenditures in GDP, on a per-capita basis, per patient or per doctor (see OECD 2003b).

24. We are deliberately ignoring outliers and extreme results. Keep in mind that some of the more detailed information presented in section 3.1 refers to specific levels of parental income and to children's age.

Chapter 4

1. Our survey is based on an extensive Internet search of platforms providing institutional details of national pension systems. Background information is taken from *Bundesministerium für Familie, Senioren, Frauen und Jugend* (1998) and *Verband Deutscher Rentenversicherungsträger* (1999). Information on a larger number of countries is included, in condensed form, in Fenge et al. (2003, tab. 1.12).

2. The loss is limited to earnings *net* of pension contributions, and pension benefits *net* of implicit taxes.

3. As long as regular pension benefits do not exceed half the principal earner's pension claims, this marginal tax amounts to no less than 100 percent of all contributions made to the pension system. See Fenge et al. (2006) for an extended discussion of this "gender tax gap."

4. Three years of contributions are next to automatically credited (as "starting credits") for individuals aged 16 to 18. These credits can be extended by a longer period of formal training.

5. See *Verband Deutscher Rentenversicherungsträger* (1999, p. 66).

6. This was not only the result of political decisions. The German Court of Justice played a role in declaring more than once that the new rules were in violation of the German constitution because they were not generous enough.

7. Women earn on average 25 percent less than the working male population.

8. All qualifying *Rentenversicherung* contributions (no matter whether earnings or child-related) are still subject to an overall ceiling on annual increments, at about twice the average earnings.

9. In any case, this amounts to only one out of each couple of parents.

10. The qualification period for individual pension claims to become effective is 60 months of contributions. Consequently the 72 months of notional contributions imputable for rearing two children fulfill the legal requirement. Pensions are nevertheless not payable before the individual reaches the statutory retirement age.

11. When established in 1972, the rule applied only to mothers of at least two children and the *majoration* was one year per child.

12. The minimum is three children, and at least five years of employment during the last 15 years preceding retirement.

13. The French *Régime Général* moved even further in that direction with the 1993 reform (see Blanchet and Legros 2002).

14. For comparisons on an EU level, see http://europa.eu.int/comm/eurostat/datashop.

15. Similar rules apply in other countries covered in this book. The employer or the institutions that take care of earnings replacement in case of sickness and pregnancy are then usually responsible for making contributions on the mother's behalf.

16. The basis for fictitious lump-sum credits is 200 percent of the current minimum pension benefit (*assegno sociale*).

17. At the time of retirement they must have at least five years of regular contributions.

18. On the other hand, the statutory retirement age for women is scheduled to rise from 55 to 60.

19. According to the new, almost actuarially fair benefit formula, the conversion coefficients "punish" early withdrawal.

20. Until April 2000 the employer had to pay the worker's share of the contributions over the parental leave period. From that date both employers and employees are exempt from payment.

21. Wherever appropriate, we included spouse benefits and survivor benefits in our calculations of implicit tax rates but ignored any contributions and "nonderived" benefits accruing to the spouse.

22. We do not go into the question of how the differential fiscal treatment of earnings as opposed to pension benefits affects net lifetime household income in the different countries considered.

23. For females (males), the estimation is based on 8,400 (15,100) observations concerning individuals aged 20 to 59. Of these observations, 3,800 (10,800) are noncensored, representing women (men) in employment. The data are taken from a pooled time series collected through the 1988 to 1998 German Socio-Economic Panel. For a brief description of this data set, see Burkhauser, Kreyenfeld, and Wagner (1997). The estimation is part of a Heckman (1979) two-stage probit model of labor force participation, involving OLS estimates of the wage equation. The estimated equations are

$$w^m = 12.199 + 0.978 \; Edu\_1 + 3.214 \; Edu\_2 + 23.550 \; Edu\_3$$
$$\qquad \underset{(***)}{} \qquad \underset{(***)}{}$$
$$+ 1.662 \; J\_Exp - 0.054(J\_Exp)^2 + 0.0005(J\_Exp)^3,$$
$$\underset{(***)}{} \qquad \qquad \qquad \underset{(**)}{}$$
$$w^f = 1.490 + 3.531 \; Edu\_1 + 4.492 \; Edu\_2 + 12.188 \; Edu\_3$$
$$\qquad \underset{(**)}{} \qquad \underset{(***)}{} \qquad \underset{(***)}{}$$
$$+ 0.893 \; J\_Exp - 0.005(J\_Exp)^2 - 0.0002(J\_Exp)^3,$$
$$\underset{(***)}{}$$

where f denotes females and m males, w is gross hourly wages (in 1995 DM), Edu_1 to Edu_3 are dummy variables for educational attainments (respectively, completed secondary schooling, vocational training, and a university degree), and J_Exp measures job experience in the full-time equivalent of the years spent in employment. As usual, *, **, and *** denote significance at, respectively, the 10, 5, and 1 percent levels.

24. For simplicity, we assume that both partners are of the same age.

25. Virtually all these countries are moving in the direction of penalizing early retirement. Thus the observation that the actual age at retirement is often much lower than the statutory age may not persist. Furthermore, if benefits are actuarially fair—and many countries are moving in that direction—the present value of total pension benefits is not affected by the age of retirement.

26. In our sample of working age German women, 43.8 percent of mothers with at least one child under the age of 3 are not working. The median number of hours worked by this category, 18.5, is approximately half the full-time workload. If the youngest child is aged 4 to 6, the fraction of mothers not working goes down to 31.6 percent, but the median number of hours worked raises to 24.0. If the youngest child is aged 7 to 11, 28.8 percent of mothers do not work at all, and the median number of hours worked is 32.0. Even among women with children aged 12 to 16, there is a fraction (26.7 percent) who does not work, but the median number of hours worked is 35.0 (approaching the full-time workload of about 38 hours). Average numbers of hours worked range between 19.8 and 25.1 across all categories. Standard deviations range between 17.1 and 19.6, indicating that there is a lot of variation in individual work biographies. All in all, the stylized biographies adopted for our simulations are similar to those shown to be "typical" for German mothers in Beblo and Wolf (2002) using the same GSOEP data set.

27. We assume a 4 percent real interest rate.

28. In our calculations "spouse" and "survivor" benefits paid to women by US Social Security, UK State Basic Pensions, and the Japanese National Pension Scheme are included in the benefit records of their husbands. The benefit entitlements of married women are reduced accordingly to determine the extent to which own, "nonderived" pension entitlements really make a difference.

29. In the United States, the United Kingdom, and Japan, spouse benefits are paid if the woman is inactive. If the woman decides to work, she collects very little in the way of additional, "nonderived," pension entitlements.

30. This is true of France for both men and women, and of Italy only where women are concerned.

31. This applies especially to Japan and less so to France.

32. The absolute amount of pension benefits shown in table 4.2 is based on the assumption that starting in the year 2003, UK Basic Pensions will be indexed to earnings. Should

they be indexed to prices only, as they have been over the last two decades, the simulated benefits could be much smaller. See section 2.3.2 and, for an extended discussion, Fenge and Werding (2004).

33. Child-related pension entitlements exceed the reduction in earnings-related benefits by close to 0.05 percentage points (this detail is invisible in figure 4.2).

34. In the United Kingdom, the result that there is no loss at all in the baseline scenario is a by-product of a norm applicable to a broad class of cases, and not just to women who take parental leave.

35. In reality single mothers without substantial support from a former partner tend to keep parental leaves down to a minimum. That is our reason for dealing with single mothers in an aside, and not returning to the subject in the rest of the chapter.

36. Women with just five years of labor force participation are not entitled to receive a full Basic Pension (other than in the form of spouse benefits). However, because their "home responsibilities" increase the number of qualifying years, women in this situation receive at least half the regular benefits.

37. In most cases, a full pension is received even before applying the home responsibilities rule.

38. Strictly speaking, we should have adjusted the work biographies to account for the likelihood that women with higher education enter the labor market later than less educated ones. For simplicity, however, we have ignored these potential linkages between education level and length of employment.

39. If couples including women with "high earnings" and more complete work records were used as a term of comparison, table 4.4 would show a reduction of net household wealth also for the last scenario.

40. Remember that the Japanese public pension scheme allows for only one year of leave (from a formally continuing job) per child. As we are assuming that a woman with two children stays away from work for six years, and a woman with three children stays away for nine years, we must also assume that the condition imposed by the Japanese system is met only for the first birth.

41. As in the case of Japan, this has to do with the way our biographies are constructed. Having assumed that mothers of two leave work for six years, and mothers of three for nine years, we can impute fictitious contributions for *assenza obbligatoria* or *assenza facoltativa* only to the first child. What makes a difference here is that mothers with three children can take advantage of a higher "conversion coefficient," or retire earlier, than women with fewer children.

42. See the "no leave" case of a mother with one child.

Chapter 5

1. Following a long-established tradition, we are reasoning *as if* a woman (hence the feminine gender) could reproduce herself without male intervention, and could deterministically choose how many children to have. We will drop the first of these assumptions later in this chapter, and the second toward the end of chapter 7. Except where we explicitly say the contrary, we assume that the physiological ceiling is never binding.

2. If she could not have that number of children, she would have the maximum that nature permits.

3. Were she pressing against the physiological fertility ceiling, the agent could not procure as many children (acquire as many entitlements to future transfers) as she would like, and would thus find it optimal to top-up her stock of domestic credits with market assets. In other words, she would save. Allowing for this possibility complicates the analysis without bringing many additional insights.

4. The analysis that follows draws heavily on Cigno (2006).

5. This selection criterion is akin to the renegotiation-proofness concept developed by Bernheim and Ray (1989) and Maskin and Farrell (1989). The difference is in that the latter examine a situation where the players are always the same. In an overlapping generations model like the present one, by contrast, the players change at each round.

6. Anderberg and Balestrino take n to be exogenous, and thus apply the ordinary Pareto criterion.

7. See, for example, Feldstein and Pellechio (1979) and Feldstein (1980).

8. An agent is not credit-rationed if she does not want to borrow or if she can borrow the amount she wants.

9. See the estimates and background discussion reported in chapter 2.

10. Something similar can arise in the early years of a Beveridgean scheme if the early generations of pensioners are granted the full pension benefit despite having paid less than the full contribution. See chapter 2 for evidence of such "inaugural gains."

11. If d' lies to the right of e, plan e implies borrowing the amount θ. If the agent can do that, her saving is again reduced by the amount of the pension contribution. If her credit ration is smaller than θ, then e is unattainable. So the agent's utility is maximized at a point on the same budget line, but to the left of e (d' itself if the credit ration is zero). Utility is consequently lower. This illustrates the well known result that in the presence of credit rationing, the introduction of a "large" pension scheme generates inefficiency.

12. To assume the contrary would imply that the implicit subsidy, $-\vartheta$, exceeds the contribution, θ. The legislator would then be giving back with one hand *more* than he takes with the other. However plausible, this is only an assumption. As no such assumption was necessary to sign the effect on an implicit pension tax, there is thus a small asymmetry between the effect on an implicit tax and the effect of an implicit subsidy.

13. With national variations reflecting cultural differences, but also the effects of different tax treatments of married couples, fathers still contribute relatively little to child care. See, for example, Davies and Joshi (1992, 1995) and Joshi (1998). For an analysis of the effects of different tax rules on the domestic division of labor, see Gustafsson (1985).

14. Rosati (1996) examines the particular case where a child's survival into adulthood is uncertain (a matter of great concern in developing countries).

15. Unless the physiological ceiling prevents them from having as many children as they would like, in which case they will do some saving to top-up the transfers they expect to receive in old age from their grown-up children.

16. A woman in career will hire a nanny for her young children, and a personal nurse for her elderly parents. A low-wage woman will give her children and parents mostly her own time.

17. They may do this by making bequests in excess of the money equivalent of the utility of the personal services that they received from their grown-up children.

Chapter 6

1. They are, in chronological order, Feldstein and Pellecchio (1979), Kotlikoff (1979), King and Dicks-Mireaux (1982), Feldstein (1983), Blinder et al. (1983), Dicks-Mireaux and King (1984), Diamond and Hausman (1984), David and Menchik (1985), Avery et al. (1986), Hubbard (1986), Bernheim (1987), Novos (1989), Gullason et al. (1993), and Gale (1998).

2. In two cases the mean estimate is virtually zero. Two other studies (David and Menchik 1985; Gullason et al. 1993) find a positive elasticity between 0.1 and 0.5.

3. These are King and Dicks-Mireaux (1982), Dicks-Mireaux and King (1984), and Hubbard (1986). For two further studies, the relevant band cannot be reconstructed from the results that have been published.

4. These are Feldstein and Pellecchio (1979), Feldstein (1983), Blinder et al. (1983), Bernheim (1987), and Gale (1998).

5. See Genosko and Weber (1992) or Althammer (2000) for Germany, Tasiran (1995) for the United States and Sweden, and Laroque and Salanié (2004, 2005) for France.

6. Child care subsidies may prove ineffective here because these policy measures reduce the marginal cost of providing a child with a given level of lifetime utility, rather than the marginal cost of children (the quantity–quality trade-off). It may also reflect an incomplete specification of simultaneous decisions regarding the number and timing of births.

7. See, for example, Heckmann and Walker (1990) based on Swedish data, or Laroque and Salanié (2004) based on French ones.

8. See Altonji, Hayashi, and Kotlikoff (2000).

9. See Ermisch (2004).

10. See Attias-Donfut and Wolff (2000).

11. See ISTAT (1993). The results of a second wave was becoming available at the time of writing.

12. Assuming, as we did in chapter 5, that time and personal services received from a close relative are not perfectly substitutable with time and personal services received from a perfect stranger, the money value (to the giver or the receiver) of this time or personal services should be calculated as either an equivalent or a compensating variation.

13. The figure is reproduced from Cigno and Rosati (2000).

14. The questionnaire asks about a list of different forms of help given or received, including "economic help," "help with health matters," "help with domestic chores," "help with bureaucratic matters," and so on. We have classified as money intensive not only what the questionnaire calls "economic help" but also "help with health matters,"

which involves direct expenditure on medicines, private nurses, and the like. We classify everything else as time intensive.

15. This proposition is known as the "rotten kid" theorem; see Becker (1974). In a dynamic context, it coincides with the "operative bequests" assumption; see Becker and Murphy (1988).

16. We may interpret y_2 as a pension, or think of y_1 and y_2 as income at two points of the pre-retirement period.

17. There remains the possibility that transfer behavior is governed by other considerations, such as "fairness" (Akerlof 1982; Fehr and Schmidt 1999). The difference between being "fair" and complying with a family constitution is, however, like the difference between being good and acting good for fear of hell. If we want to discriminate empirically between the two hypotheses, we must find an instance (e.g., killing infidels) where being bad does not entail going to hell. Finding such an example in the present context is not very easy.

18. The justification for using homeownership is that real estate is less risky than other assets, and thus most acceptable as collateral by lending institutions. The justification for using the area of residence is that, for historical and structural reasons, credit is notoriously more difficult to obtain, and more expensive, in the southern than in the northern regions of Italy.

19. Since the information about access to credit could refer to any household member, the rationed person could, in principle, be a coresident adult rather than the household head or the head's partner. It was thus important to know whether the effect of the ration remains positive if the possibility that rationing might apply to some of the couple's grown-up children or elderly parents living in is ruled out. Restricting the subsample with head working to households where there are neither children over the age of 18, nor parents of either the household head, or the head's partner, living in does not change the sign of the effect of credit rationing. The effect remains positive and significant.

20. These results are confirmed when they use the aggregate panel data available for a subsample of countries.

21. After 1995 no separate statistics are collected for the two parts of re-united Germany.

22. In the light of chapter 3, it thus leaves out important in-kind forms of support for children and their parents. However, the microeconometric evidence reported earlier does not find a significant fertility effect of these forms of support.

23. An LR test on the restriction that the male and female wage rates have opposite sign, but the same absolute value (i.e., that what matters is their ratio, not their levels) does not reject the null hypothesis of identical absolute effects on fertility; rejects it with regard to the effect on saving. The two wage rates are thus kept as separate explanatory variables.

24. The mis-specification tests performed for each equation, and for the system as a whole, include a version of the Portmanteau Ljung-Box statistic, the LM test for autocorrelation of order higher than one, and the Engle test for the existence of an ARCH structure of the residuals. In order to get rid of autocorrelation in the residuals, the authors include two lags in each equation. They also carry out the c2 test for normality of the residuals, and a multivariate versions of the Portmanteau and c2 normality tests to detect mis-specifications in the system as a whole. Except for a slight problem with the normality of the real interest rate, the model is shown to be correctly specified, and there does

not appear to be any problem with the distribution of the residuals in the model as a whole.

25. See, in particular, the very high estimates of the opportunity-cost of the mother's time in Joshi (1998).

Chapter 7

1. It is not possible to say, in general, whether an extra child should raise or lower the household's net tax bill. Balestrino, Cigno, and Pettini (2002, 2003) show that the sign of this effect depends on a number of circumstances, including the range of instruments available to the policy maker.

2. This is often ignored, on the assumption that we are dealing with an autarchic economy or with the world economy as a whole.

3. For the original contributions, see Bentham (1823, p. 12) and Mill (1848, pp. 191–92).

4. It does not go much better if the interest rate is endogenous. Then $\delta = 1$ means that the domestic rate of interest, hence the marginal product of capital, must be driven to zero.

5. It does affect utility, however, because it redistributes consumption over the saver's life cycle.

6. Essentially this is a *fiscal* externality, artificially created by the way public pension schemes are usually designed (Werding 1998, secs. 3.2 and 5.2). As demonstrated for the case of Germany in Sinn (2001), the effect of this externality can be huge.

7. The expression comes from the principal-agent literature, and applies to any situation where the agent's actions are observable by the principal. Applied to the number of childen, such a "contract" has an unpleasant totalitarian ring about it, but this is purely a consequence of the simplifying assumption that parents have perfect control of their fertility. If it is realistically recognized that parents can only choose the probability distribution of getting $0, 1, 2, \dots$, children, the policy takes the more palatable form of a fertility subsidy.

8. Sinn (2004) proposes reducing the pension benefit in proportion to the difference between the socially optimal and the actual number of children that a person has. That does not take care of the child's consumption.

9. In order to induce the agent to have the socially optimal number of children, Groezen et al. (2003) suggest that φ^t should be set equal to the present value, at t, of the contributions that the agent's children will make at $t + 1$. Later in this chapter we will see that something like this is optimal in a second-best setting with asymmetric information. In a first-best setting with full information, there is no need for the government to pay the parent anything in order to get her to behave optimally. It is enough to threaten her with a large enough penalty if she does not. The child benefit should be used, as we have indicated, to refund the agent of the optimal cost of having and maintaing a child over the first period of life. (Groezen et al. are not concerned with the child's consumption.)

10. This deficit must be debt financed. Were it covered by general taxation, current workers would be paying in the form of taxes what they are not paying in the form of pension contributions. The outcome would then violate the modified golden rule.

11. For the baseline case without uncertainty and asymmetric information, this is discussed in Werding (1998, ch. 6, 2003).

12. The former will include taxing different categories of goods at different rates as, for example, in Cigno and Pettini (2003). The latter will be some kind of nonlinear tax-benefit scheme, such as the one in Balestrino, Cigno, and Pettini (2002).

13. Think of the unhappy elderly parked in nursing homes all over the world.

14. Even a Pareto optimum is not possible from this population profile. Anderberg and Balestrino (2003) analyze education in a family constitution context with exogenous fertility, and show that parental investment in the human capital of the next generation may be inefficiently low. They also derive the properties of a second-best policy in the event of self-enforcing family constitutions.

15. School fees are imputable to children, but many other items are not. Similarly labor time is generally observable, but the way in which parents allocate their nonlabor time between leisure and helping their children through the learning process is not.

16. Broome (1992, pp. 128–29) defines a potential person as any "pair of an egg and a sperm ..., if the pair could possibly get together."

17. See the comments at the beginning of section 7.1.

18. It could reasonably be argued that the optimal φ is contingent on n. We will show in the next subsection, however, that this is not the case if agents can borrow. To simplify the presentation, we will assume that the optimal φ is constant.

19. Reproductive behavior has an expected future cost because of its effect on the probability distribution of births.

20. We may assume it to have been chosen on the basis of intragenerational equity subject to some fixed revenue requirement.

21. Furthermore, since $\psi(.)$ is adjusted to take account of the number of children that have been born, it is unnecessary to condition φ on n (see note 18, this chapter).

22. Since φ^{**} and ψ^{**} are per-child transfers, however, the agent is not insured against the risk of having more or less children than she would like. The reason is simply that because φ^{**} fully reimburses parents of the costs incurred in having a child, and because reproductive behavior is supposedly costless, there can be no question of anyone having "too many" or "too few" children.

23. The moral hazard problem can be reduced using *indirect taxation*. If the action e involves the purchase of goods (e.g., children's books, which are not consumed to the same extent by adults), welfare can be raised by distorting prices in favor of these goods (Cigno and Pettini 2003). If the direct subsidy is very costly to administer, it may in fact be optimal to use only indirect taxation. The opposite is never true, however, because an unconditional subsidy via the price system is always more effective than a conditional subsidy with the same expected monetary value (Cigno, Luporini, and Pettini 2003). Since agency problems arise only when the principal cannot observe, hence directly control, the agent's action, implicit in the foregoing considerations is that government can in any case set the visible side of education, formal schooling, at the desired level by either offering free *public education* or subsidizing private education.

24. The reader can easily check that the two schemes jointly satisfy (7.26).

25. Assuming that parents can deterministically choose how many children to have, and borrow from the market without limit, but not affect a child's future earning capacity, Kolmar (1997) finds that the optimal policy is *either* to offer agents a child benefit (and close down the pension system) *or* to offer them a pension conditional on the number of children (and no conventional child benefit). By these assumptions, a child benefit is a perfect substitute for a pension benefit conditional on number of children. Without these assumptions, two policy instruments are better than one. Fenge and Meier (2003) make assumptions similar to those of Kolmar but stipulate that rearing a child necessarily reduces the parent's labor supply (there is no leisure). The resulting trade-off between income and fertility leads to the conclusion that it is not socially optimal to make pensions entirely conditional on fertility (alternatively, to abolish pensions and pay only child benefits). The optimal policy is to have a fraction of the pension proportional to contributions paid, and the rest proportional to the number of children. This has some similarity to our result, though it is based on a completely different mechanism.

26. Even if the first generation in our story were perfectly homogeneous, the second could be heterogeneous as a result of chance.

27. Earning capacity is not the only possible differentiating characteristic. Another could be the minimum cost of rearing a child. Agents with lower p would then have a comparative advantage in parenting children over agents with the same w_0 but higher p.

28. As children are born sequentially, the realization of the final n does not come all at once.

Chapter 8

1. See also Orszag and Stiglitz (2000) or Barr (2001). The entire discussion on the illusory advantages of conversion to full funding is summarized in Sinn (2000).

2. See Werding (1998, 2003).

3. See section 2.2. In the short run the return can be raised above the growth rate of total income by increasing contribution rates or by allowing the scheme to make larger and larger deficits.

4. The state of knowledge is the fruit of research, not of education. Furthermore fundamental research (the real motor of progress) tends to take place in nonprofit-making institutions such as universities and science academies, and then the results are internationally disseminated through scholarly journals. Therefore the state of knowledge is to some extent an international public good. Although education and research are positively correlated, this link between parental expenditure on education and growth rate of domestic per-capita income is thus tenuous.

5. We say "may" instead of will because the positive scale effect (larger population) could counter the negative impact on human capital accumulation.

6. Also, in the second scheme, the benefits would have to re-distribute to some extent in favor of parents of children who choose worthwhile, but not highly paid professions (otherwise, parents could distort their children's comparative advantages by agreeing to pay only for certain types of education).

7. The contradiction between allowing, on the one hand, pension policy to affect the growth rate of real per-capita income and assuming, on the other, real wage rates to follow an exogenously determined path should not escape the perceptive reader.

8. See chapter 6.

9. See chapter 3.

10. See chapters 2 and 4.

11. This is the same model we used to make the projections presented in chapters 2 and 4.

12. The rules are stiffer, but not stiff enough to ensure actuarial fairness.

13. The 2001 reform was intended to cut annual pension entitlements by about 10 percent over the years 2002 to 2030.

14. In Germany the effective age of retirement has been lower than the statutory limit ever since the early 1970s (see chapter 2).

15. A more radical approach is that followed in the United Kingdom over the past two decades. There, consumer price indexation has been applied to *all* relevant thresholds and benefits, without any initial adjustment to reach a target replacement rate. Because it leads to a rapid erosion of the replacement level, the method has been corrected in the latest round of UK reforms (see chapter 2).

16. Under other circumstances the availability of more recent data would have been an invitation to run fresh estimates. In our case this is not possible. As already pointed out in chapter 6, 1960 to 1995 is the longest period for which data on West Germany are available. At the time of writing, the data available for the whole of Germany span no more than a little over ten years, and are thus of no use for time-series estimation purposes.

17. For the reasons indicated at the end of the last section, we should have shown the backward predictions of the econometric model as well as the actual data. Not to crowd the picture with too many "actuals", however, we only show the data.

18. Until 1991, pensions were indexed to gross wages. Between 1992 and 1999, indexation was to wages net of taxes, and all kinds of social security contributions. From 2001, pensions are indexed to wages net of pension contributions, and of "precautionary savings" (conventionally calculated using the rate "recommended" by the new bill of law). Child benefits are adjusted on a discretionary basis. Despite a remarkable expansion since 1986, these benefits have not kept pace with wage growth over the sample period.

19. In other words, the net replacement rate of the German pension system for a full working career would have to go down from a current 70 percent to less than 45 percent.

20. This is because even *CPI* guarantees a fixed replacement ratio in the first year of retirement. Hence pension expenditure is still driven by wage growth to some extent.

21. See chapter 4 for more details.

22. Of course, this does not imply that the use of additional child-related pensions should be limited to making up for losses in earnings-related benefits.

23. The work record of the hypothetical mother is that assumed in section 4.2. We suppose that the mother is 25 when the child is born and that she will go on working until retirement at age 65.

24. We did not explicitly deal with the distortionary effects of the tax used to finance the benefit, assuming the tax to be lump sum. But our estimates of the child-benefit

elasticities reflect the full range of tax instruments, some of which are distortionary, that are actually used to pay for public expenditure in Germany.

25. This does not mean that the pension deficit, or the deficit of the entire public administration, will rise. In any year the amount paid out to pensioners is equal to the amount paid in by their children. So no change occurs in the net flow of payments into the public coffers. The reason we can use the pension-deficit elasticites is that by applying the child-benefit elasticities to the present value of fertiliy-related pension benefits, we have implicitly assumed that the latter are financed (like child benefits) with the taxes paid by the beneficiaries themselves. Refunding the latter will then have the same effect as increasing the pension deficit by the same amount.

26. This is only true of Germany. Estimates for other countries show a negative effect of the pension deficit on the household saving rate; see Cigno and Rosati (1992, 1996, 1997).

27. Remember this is not true in other countries where the pension deficit is estimated to have a negative effect on fertility.

Conclusion

1. By contrast, if individual benefits increase with individual contributions, only the difference between the expected value of lifetime benefits and the capitalized value of the contributions made is a tax. See chapters 2 and 5.

References

Aaron, H. J. 1966. The social insurance paradox. *Canadian Journal of Economics and Political Science* 32: 371–74.

Aaron, H. J. 1982. *Economic Effects of Social Security*. Washington, DC: Brookings Institution.

Advisory Board of the German Federal Ministry of Economics (*Wissenschaftlicher Beirat beim Bundeswirtschaftsministerium*). 1998. Grundlegende Reform der gesetzlichen Rentenversicherung (Report). Mimeo. Bonn.

Akerlof, G. A. 1982. Labor contracts as partial gift exchange. *Quarterly Journal of Economics* 97: 543–69.

Alessie, R. J. M., A. Kapteyn, and F. Klijn. 1997. Mandatory pensions and personal savings in the Netherlands. *De Economist* 145: 291–324.

Alho, J. M. 1990. Stochastic methods in population forecasting. *International Journal of Forecasting* 6: 521–30.

Althammer, J. 2000. *Ökonomische Theorie der Familienpolitik*. Heidelberg: Physica.

Altonji, J. G., F. Hayashi, and L. Kotlikoff. 1992. Is the extended family altruistically linked? Direct tests using micro-data. *American Economic Review* 82: 1177–98.

Altonji, J. G., F. Hayashi, and L. Kotlikoff. 1997. Parental altruism and inter vivos transfers: Theory and evidence. *Journal of Political Economy* 105: 1121–66.

Anderberg, D., and A. Balestrino. 2003. Self-enforcing transfers and the provision of education. *Economica* 70: 55–71.

Attias-Donfut, C., and F. C. Wolff. 2000. Equity and solidarity across the generations. In S. Arber and C. Attias-Donfut, eds., *The Myth of Generational Conflict: The Family and State in Ageing Societies*. London: Routledge, pp. 1–21.

Avery, R. B., G. E. Elliehausen, and T. A. Gustafson. 1986. Pensions and social security in household portfolios: Evidence from the 1983 survey of consumer finances. In G. F. Adams and S. M. Wachter, eds., *Savings and Capital Formation: The Policy Options*. Lexington, MA: Lexington Books, pp. 127–60.

Baland, J. M., and A. Robinson. 2002. Rotten parents. *Journal of Public Economics* 84: 341–56.

Balestrino, A., A. Cigno, and A. Pettini. 2002. Endogenous fertility and the design of family taxation. *International Tax and Public Finance* 9: 175–93.

Balestrino, A., A. Cigno, and A. Pettini. 2003. Doing wonders with an egg: Optimal redistribution when households differ in market and non-market-abilities. *Journal of Public Economic Theory* 5: 479–98.

Barr, N. 2001. Reforming pensions: Myths, truths and policy choices. *International Social Security Review* 55 (2): 3–36.

Barro, R. J. 1974. Are government bonds net wealth? *Journal of Political Economy* 82: 1095–1118.

Battle, K., and M. Mendelson, eds. 2001. *Benefits for Children: A Four Country Study*. Ottawa: Caledon Institute of Social Policy.

Beblo, M., and E. Wolf. 2002. How much does a year off cost? Estimating the wage effects of employment breaks and part-time periods. *Cahiers Économique de Bruxelles* 45: 191–217.

Becker, G. S. 1974. A theory of social interactions. *Journal of Political Economy* 82: 1063–93.

Becker, G. S., and R. J. Barro. 1988. A reformulation of the economic theory of fertility. *Quarterly Journal of Economics* 103: 1–25.

Becker, G. S., and K. M. Murphy. 1988. The family and the state. *Journal of Law and Economics* 31: 1–18.

Ben-Porath, Y. 1980. The F-connection: Families, friends, and firms and the organization of exchange. *Population and Development Review* 6: 1–30.

Bentham, J. 1823. *An Introduction to the Principles of Morals and Legislation* (reprint 1970). London: Athlone Press.

Bernheim, B. D. 1987. The economic effects of social security. *Journal of Public Economics* 33: 273–304.

Bernheim, B. D., and D. Ray. 1989. Collective dynamic consistency in repeated games. *Games and Economic Behavior* 1: 295–326.

Beveridge, W. 1942. *Social Insurance and Allied Services*. London: Her Majesty's Stationery Office.

Binmore, K. 1994. *Game Theory and the Social Contract*. Vol. 1: *Playing Fair*. Cambridge: MIT Press.

Binmore, K. 1998. *Game Theory and the Social Contract*. Vol. 2: *Just Playing*. Cambridge: MIT Press.

Blake, D. 2002. The United Kingdom: Examining the switch from low public pensions to high-cost private pensions. In M. Feldstein and H. Siebert, eds., *Social Security Pension Reform in Europe*. Chicago: NBER/University of Chicago Press, pp. 317–41.

Blanchet, D., and F. Legros. 2002. France: The difficult path to consensual reforms. In M. Feldstein and H. Siebert, eds., *Social Security Pension Reform in Europe*. Chicago: NBER/University of Chicago Press, pp. 109–35.

Blinder, A. S., R. H. Gordon, and D. E. Wise. 1983. Social security, bequests and the life cycle theory of saving: Cross-sectional tests. In F. Modigliani and R. Hemming, eds., *The Determinants of National Saving and Wealth*. London: Macmillan, pp. 89–122.

Boldrin, M., and A. Rustichini. 2000. Equilibria with social security. *Review of Economic Dynamics* 4: 41–78.

Bosworth, B. P., and G. Burtless. 1998. *Aging Societies: The Global Dimension*. Washington, DC: Brookings Institution.

Bradshaw, J., ed. 2003. *Children and Social Security*. International Studies on Social Security, vol. 8. Aldershot: Ashgate.

Bradshaw, J., and N. Finch. 2002. *A comparison of child benefit packages in 22 countries.* DWP Research Report 174. Department for Work and Pensions, London.

Breyer, F. 1989. On the intergenerational Pareto efficiency of pay-as-you-go financed pension systems. *Journal of Institutional and Theoretical Economics* 145: 643–58.

Broome, J. 1992. The value of living. *Recherches Economiques de Louvain* 58: 125–42.

Bryant, R. C., and W. J. McKibbin. 1998. Issues in modeling the global dimensions of demographic change. *Brookings Discussion Papers in International Economics* 141. Washington, DC.

Buchanan, J. M. 1987. The constitution of economic policy. *American Economic Review* 77: 243–50.

Bundesministerium für Familie, Senioren, Frauen und Jugend, ed. 1998. *Übersicht über die gesetzlichen Maßnahmen in den EU-Ländern bei Erziehung von Kleinkindern*, Schriftenreihe des BMFSFJ, vol. 158. Stuttgart: Kohlhammer.

Burkhauser, R. V., M. Kreyenfeld, and G. G. Wagner. 1997. The German socio-economic panel: A representative sample of reunited Germany and its parts. *Vierteljahreshefte zur Wirtschaftsforschung* 66: 7–16.

Cannan, E. 1895. The probability of cessation of the population of England and Wales during the next century. *Economic Journal* 5: 505–15.

CBO. 1998. Social security and private saving: A review of the empirical evidence. Memo. Congressional Budget Office, Washington, DC.

CESifo. 2006. *Database for Institutional Comparisons in Europe* ⟨DICE; access via http:// www.cesifo.de⟩.

Cigno, A. 1986. Fertility and the tax-benefit system: A reconsideration of theory of family taxation. *Economic Journal* 96: 1035–51.

Cigno, A. 1991. *Economics of the Family*. Oxford: Oxford University Press and Clarendon Press.

Cigno, A. 1992. Children and pensions. *Journal of Population Economics* 5: 175–83.

Cigno, A. 1993. Intergenerational transfers without altruism: Family, market and state. *European Journal of Political Economy* 7: 505–18.

Cigno, A. 2002. Comparative advantage, observability, and the optimal tax treatment of families with children. *International Tax and Public Finance* 8: 455–70.

Cigno, A. 2006. A constitutional theory of the family. *Journal of Population Economics* 19: 259–83.

Cigno, A. 2007. Is there a social security tax wedge? *Labour Economics*, forthcoming.

Cigno, A., L. Casolaro, and F. C. Rosati. 2003. The impact of social security on saving and fertility in Germany. *FinanzArchiv* 59: 189–211.

Cigno, A., G. C. Giannelli, F. C. Rosati, and D. Vuri. 2006. Is there such a thing as a family constitution? A test based on credit rationing. *Review of Economics of the Household* 4: 183–204.

Cigno, A., and A. Luporini. 2003. Optimal policy towards families with different amounts of social capital, in the presence of asymmetric information and stochastic fertility. Paper presented at the 2003 CESifo Venice Summer Institute.

Cigno, A., A. Luporini, and A. Pettini. 2003. Transfers to families with children as a principal-agent problem. *Journal of Public Economics* 87: 1165–77.

Cigno, A., and A. Pettini. 2003. Taxing family size and subsidizing child-specific commodities? *Journal of Public Economics* 84: 75–90.

Cigno, A., and F. C. Rosati. 1992. The effects of financial markets and social security on saving and fertility behaviour in Italy. *Journal of Population Economics* 5: 319–41.

Cigno, A., and F. C. Rosati. 1996. Jointly determined saving and fertility behaviour: Theory, and estimates for Germany, Italy, UK, and USA. *European Economic Review* 40: 1561–89.

Cigno, A., and F. C. Rosati. 1997. Rise and fall of the Japanese saving rate: The role of social security and intra-family transfers. *Japan and the World Economy* 9: 81–92.

Cigno, A., and F. C. Rosati. 2000. Mutual interest, self-enforcing constitutions and apparent generosity. In L. A. Gérard-Varet, S. C. Kolm, and J. Mercier Ythier, eds., *The Economics of Reciprocity, Giving and Altruism*. London and New York: Macmillan and St. Martin's Press, pp. 226–47.

Cox, D. 1987. Motives for private income transfers. *Journal of Political Economy* 95: 508–46.

Cox, D., and G. Jakubson. 1995. The connection between public transfers and private interfamily transfers. *Journal of Public Economics* 57: 129–67.

Dasgupta, P. S. 1988. Lives and well-being. *Social Choice and Welfare* 5: 103–26.

David, M., and P. L. Menchik. 1985. The effect of social security on lifetime wealth accumulation and bequests. *Economica* 52: 421–34.

Davies, H. B., and H. E. Joshi. 1992. Daycare in Europe and mothers' foregone earnings. *International Labour Review* 131: 561–79.

Davies, H. B. 1995. Social and family security in the redress of unequal opportunities. In J. Humphries and J. Rubery, eds., *The Economics of Equal Opportunity*. Manchester: Equal Opportunities Commission, pp. 313–44.

Diamond, P. A. 1965. National debt in a neoclassical growth model. *American Economic Review* 55: 1126–50.

Diamond, P. A. 1977. A framework for social security analysis. *Journal of Public Economics* 8: 275–98.

Diamond, P. A. 2000. Administrative costs and equilibrium charges with individual accounts. In J. Shoven, ed., *Administrative Aspects of Investment-Based Social Security Reform*. Chicago: University of Chicago Press, pp. 137–72.

Diamond, P. A., and J. A. Hausman. 1984. Individual retirement and savings behavior. *Journal of Public Economics* 23: 81–114.

Dicks-Mireaux, L., and M. King. 1984. Pension wealth and household savings: Tests of robustness. *Journal of Public Economics* 23: 115–39.

Disney, R. 1996. *Can We Afford to Grow Older? A Perspective on the Economics of Aging.* Cambridge: MIT Press.

Disney, R. 1999. Notional accounts as a pension reform strategy: An evaluation. Social Protection Discussion Paper 9928. World Bank's Pension Reform Primer No. 1. Washington, DC: World Bank.

Di Tella, R., and R. MacCullogh. 2002. Informal family insurance and the design of the welfare state. *Economic Journal* 112: 481–503.

Ehrlich, I., and J.-G. Zhong. 1998. Social security and the real economy: An inquiry into some neglected issues. *American Economic Review* 88: 151–57.

Entwisle, B., and C. R. Winegarden. 1984. Fertility and pension programs in LDCs: A model of mutual reinforcement. *Economic Development and Cultural Change* 32: 331–54.

Ermisch, J. 2003. How do parents affect the life chances of their children as adults? An idiosyncratic review. Social and Economic Dimensions of an Aging Population Research Papers. McMaster University.

Ermisch, J. 2004. Fairness in the family: Implications for parent-adult child interactions. Mimeo. Institute for Social and Economic Research, University of Essex.

EU Economic Policy Committee. 2001. Budgetary challenges posed by ageing populations. Document EPC/ECFIN/655/01-EN final. Brussels.

European Observatory on National Family Policies. 1996. A Synthesis of National Family Policies. Social Policy Research Unit, University of York.

European Observatory on National Family Policies. 1998. *A Synthesis of National Family Policies.* Brussels: European Commission.

Eurostat. 2000. Revised long-term national population scenarios for the European Union. Mimeo. Prepared by Statistics Netherlands (*Centraal Bureau voor de Statistiek*). Luxembourg and Voorburg.

Faruqee, H. 2002. Population aging and its macroeconomic implications: A framework for analysis. IMF Working Paper 02/16. Washington, DC.

Fehr, E., and K. M. Schmidt. 1999. A theory of fairness, competition and cooperation. *Quarterly Journal of Economics* 114: 817–68.

Feldstein, M. 1980. International differences in social security and saving. *Journal of Public Economics* 14: 225–44.

Feldstein, M. 1982. Social security and private saving: Reply. *Journal of Political Economy* 90: 630–42.

Feldstein, M. 1983. Social security benefit and the accumulation of pre-retirement wealth. In F. Modigliani and R. Hemming, eds., *The Determinants of National Saving and Wealth.* London: Macmillan, pp. 3–23.

Feldstein, M., and A. Pellechio. 1979. Social security and household wealth accumulation: New microeconometric evidence. *Review of Economics and Statistics* 31: 361–68.

Fenge, R. 1995. Pareto-efficiency of the pay-as-you-go pension system with Intragenerational Fairness. *Finanzarchiv* 52: 357–64.

Fenge, R., A. Gebauer, C. Holzner, V. Meier, and M. Werding. 2003. *Alterssicherungssysteme im internationalen Vergleich: Finanzierung, Leistungen, Besteuerung.* Ifo Beiträge zur Wirtschaftsforschung, vol. 10. Munich: Ifo Institute.

Fenge, R., and V. Meier. 2003. Pensions and fertility incentives. CESifo Working Paper 879. Munich.

Fenge, R., S. Uebelmesser, and M. Werding. 2006. On the optimal timing of implicit social security taxes over the life cycle. *FinanzArchiv* 62: 68–107.

Fenge, R., and M. Werding. 2003. Ageing and inter-generational imbalances: Concepts of measurement. CESifo Working Paper 842. Munich.

Fenge, R., and M. Werding. 2004. Ageing and the tax implied in public pension schemes: Simulations for selected OECD countries. *Fiscal Studies* 25: 159–200.

Feyrer, J. 2002. Demographics and productivity. Mimeo. Dartmouth College, Hanover.

Gale, W. G. 1998. The effects of pensions on household wealth: A reevaluation of theory and evidence. *Journal of Political Economy* 106: 706–23.

Geanakoplos, J., O. S. Mitchell, and S. P. Zeldes. 1998. Would a privatized social security system really pay a higher rate of return? In R. D. Arnold, M. Graetz, and A. H. Munnell, eds., *Framing the Social Security Debate: Values, Politics, and Economics.* Washington, DC: Brookings Institution Press, pp. 137–57.

Genosko, J., and R. Weber. 1992. The impact of family allowances on demographic changes: A case study for Germany. *Diskussionsbeiträge der Wirtschaftswissenschaftlichen Fakultät der Katholischen Universität Eichstätt.* Discussion paper 18. Ingolstadt.

Graham, J. W. 1987. International differences in saving rates and the life cycle hypothesis. *European Economic Review* 31: 1509–29.

Granger, C. W. J. 1987. Cointegration and error correction: Representation, estimation, and testing. *Econometrica* 55: 251–76.

Greenwood, D., and E. N. Wolff. 1992. Changes in wealth in the United States, 1962–1983. *Journal of Population Economics* 5: 261–88.

Groezen, B. van, T. Leers, and L. Meijdam. 2003. Social security and endogenous fertility: Pensions and child allowances as Siamese twins. *Journal of Public Economics* 87: 233–51.

Gullason, E. T., B. R. Kolluri, and M. J. Panik. 1993. Social security and household wealth accumulation: Refined microeconometric evidence. *Review of Economics and Statistics* 75: 548–51.

Gustafsson, S. 1985. Institutional environment and the economics of female labor force participation and fertility: A comparison between Sweden and West Germany. Discussion Paper IIM/LMP 85-9. Wissenschaftszentrum, Berlin.

Hammond, P. J. 1975. Charity: Altruism or cooperative egoism. In E. S. Phelps, ed., *Altruism, Morality, and Economic Theory.* New York: Russell Sage Foundation, pp. 115–31.

Harsanyi, J. C. 1955. Cardinal welfare, individualistic ethics, and interpersonal comparisons of utility. *Journal of Political Economy* 63: 309–21.

Hayek, F. A. von. 1960. *The Constitution of Liberty*. London: Routledge and Kegan.

Heckman, J. J. 1979. Sample selection bias as a specification error. *Econometrica* 47: 153–61.

Heckman, J. J., and J. R. Walker. 1990. The relationship between wages and income and the timing and spacing of births: Evidence from Swedish longitudinal data. *Econometrica* 58: 1411–41.

Hobbes, T. 1651. *Leviathan, or the Matter, Form, and Power of a Commonwealth Ecclesiastical and Civil* (reprint 1966). Aalen: Scientia.

Hohm, C. H. 1975. Social security and fertility: An international perspective. *Demography* 12: 629–44.

Hubbard, R. G. 1986. Pension wealth and saving. *Journal of Money, Credit and Banking* 18: 167–78.

Hurd, M. D., and N. Yashiro, eds. 1997. *The Economic Effects of Aging in the United States and Japan*. Chicago: University of Chicago Press.

ISTAT. 1993. Sintesi dei Risultati dell'Indagine. *Indagine Multiscopo sulle Famiglie*. Vol. 8: *La Condizione degli Anziani*. Roma: Istituto Nazionale di Statistica.

Joshi, H. E. 1998. The opportunity costs of childbearing: More than mothers' business. *Journal of Population Economics* 11: 161–84.

Kant, I. 1785. *Grundlegung zur Metaphysik der Sitten*. Werkausgabe, vol. 7, ed. by W. Weischedel. Frankfurt/Main: Suhrkamp.

Kant, I. 1797. *Metaphysik der Sitten*. Werkausgabe, vol. 8, ed. by W. Weischedel. Frankfurt/Main: Suhrkamp.

King, M., and L. Dicks-Mireaux. 1982. Asset holdings and the life-cycle. *Economic Journal* 92: 247–67.

Kolmar, M. 1997. Intergenerational redistribution in a small open economy with endogenous fertility. *Journal of Population Economics* 10: 335–56.

Kotlikoff, L. 1979. Testing the theory of social security and life cycle accumulation. *American Economic Review* 69: 396–410.

Kotlikoff, L., and A. Spivak. 1981. The family as an incomplete annuities market. *Journal of Political Economy* 69: 372–91.

Laroque, G., and B. Salanié. 2004. Fertility and financial incentives in France. *CESifo Economic Studies* 50: 423–50.

Laroque, G. 2005. Does fertility respond to financial incentives? CEPR Discussion Paper 5007. London.

Lee, R. D., and S. Tuljapurkar. 1994. Stochastic population forecasts for the United States: Beyond high, medium, and low. *Journal of the American Statistical Association* 69: 607–17.

Leibenstein, H. 1957. *Economic Backwardness and Economic Growth*. New York: Wiley.

Leimer, D. R., and S. D. Lesnoy. 1982. Social security and private saving: New time series evidence. *Journal of Political Economy* 90: 606–29.

Lesnoy, S. D., and D. R. Leimer. 1985. Social security and private saving: Theory and historical evidence. *Social Security Bulletin* 48: 14–30.

Lindbeck, A., and M. Persson. 2003. The gains from pension reform. *Journal of Economic Literature* 41: 74–112.

Lüdeke, R. 1988. Staatsverschuldung, intragenerative Redistribution und umlagefinanzierte Rentenversicherung. In J. Klaus and P. Klemmer, eds., *Wirtschaftliche Strukturprobleme und soziale Fragen*. Berlin: Duncker and Humblot, pp. 167–81.

Maskin, E., and J. Farrell. 1989. Renegotiation in repeated games. *Games and Economic Behavior* 1: 327–60.

Mendelson, M. 2003. Cash benefits for children in four Anglo-American countries. In J. Bradshaw, ed., *Children and Social Security*. International Studies on Social Security, vol. 8. Aldershot: Ashgate, pp. 87–102.

Miles, D. 1999. Modelling the impact of demographic change upon the economy. *Economic Journal* 109: 1–36.

Mill, J. S. 1848. *Principles of Political Economy with Some Applications to Social Philosophy* (reprint 1976). Fairchild: Kelley Publishers.

Murphy, K., and F. Welch. 1998. Perspectives on the social security crisis and proposed solutions. *American Economic Review, Papers and Proceedings* 88: 142–50.

National Institute for Population and Social Security Research. 2002. *Population Projections for Japan 2001–2050*. Tokyo: IPSS.

Neher, P. A. 1971. Peasants, procreation and pensions. *American Economic Review* 61: 380–89.

Novos, I. E. 1989. Social security wealth and wealth accumulation. *Review of Economics and Statistics* 71: 167–71.

OECD. 2001a. *Economic Outlook*, no. 69 (June 2001). Paris: Organisation for Economic Co-operation and Development.

OECD. 2001b. *Education at a Glance: OECD Indicators* (2001 edition). Paris: Organisation for Economic Co-operation and Development.

OECD. 2002a. *OECD Revenue Statistics 1965–2001*. Paris: Organisation for Economic Co-operation and Development.

OECD. 2002b. *Taxing Wages 2000–2001*. Paris: Organisation for Economic Co-operation and Development.

OECD. 2003a. *Education at a Glance: OECD Indicators* (2003 edition). Paris: Organisation for Economic Co-operation and Development.

OECD. 2003b. *OECD Health Data 2003*. Paris: Organisation for Economic Co-operation and Development.

OECD. 2003c. *Economic Outlook*, no. 73 (June 2003). Paris: Organisation for Economic Co-operation and Development.

OECD. 2004. *Social Expenditure Database (SOCX)* ⟨http://www.oecd.org/els/social/expenditure⟩.

Oeppen, J., and J. W. Vaupel. 2002. Enhanced: Broken limits to life expectancy. *Science* 296 (5570): 1029–31.

Orszag, P., and J. E. Stiglitz. 2000. Rethinking pension reform: Ten myths about social security systems. In R. Holzmann and J. E. Stiglitz, eds., *New Ideas about Old Age Security: Toward Sustainable Systems*. Washington, DC: World Bank, pp. 17–56.

Palmer, E. 2000. The Swedish pension reform model: Framework and issues. Social Protection Discussion Paper 0012. World Bank's Pension Reform Primer No. 1. Washington, DC.

President's Commission to Strengthen Social Security. 2002. Strengthening Social Security and Creating Personal Wealth for All Americans. Final report of the President's Commission (Revised March 19, 2002). Washington, DC.

Robertson, D. H. 1956. What does the economist maximize? In D. H. Robertson, ed., *Economic Commentaries*. London: Staples, pp. 147–55.

Rosati, F. C. 1996. Social security in a non-altruistic model with uncertainty and endogenous fertility. *Journal of Public Economics* 60: 283–94.

Samuelson, P. A. 1958. An exact consumption-loan model of interest with or without the social contrivance of money. *Journal of Political Economy* 66: 467–82.

Sinn, H.-W. 1990. Korreferat zum Referat von K. Jaeger. In B. Gahlen, H. Hesse, and H. J. Ramser, eds., *Theorie und Politik der Sozialversicherung*. Tübingen: Mohr-Siebeck, pp. 99–101.

Sinn, H.-W. 2000. Why a funded pension system is useful and why it is not useful. *International Tax and Public Finance* 7: 389–410.

Sinn, H.-W. 2001. The value of children and immigrants in a pay-as-you-go pension system: A proposal for a transition to a funded system. *CESifo Economic Studies* 47: 77–94.

Sinn, H.-W. 2004. The pay-as-you-go pension system as a fertility insurance and enforcement device. *Journal of Public Economics* 88: 1335–57.

Tasiran, A. C. 1995. *Fertility Dynamics: Spacing and Timing of Births in Sweden and the United States*. Amsterdam: Elsevier.

Thum, M., and J. v. Weizsäcker. 2000. Implizite Einkommensteuer als Messlatte für die aktuellen Rentenreformvorschläge. *Perspektiven der Wirtschaftspolitik* 1: 453–68.

US Bureau of Census. 2000. *National Population Projections of the United States 1999 to 2100*. Washington, DC: GPO.

US Social Security Administration. 2002. *Social Security Programs Throughout the World 2002* ⟨access via http://www.ssa.gov⟩.

Verband Deutscher Rentenversicherungsträger, ed. 1999. *Rentenversicherung im internationalen Vergleich 1999*. Frankfurt/Main: VDR.

Werding, M. 1998. *Zur Rekonstruktion des Generationenvertrages*. Tübingen: Mohr-Siebeck.

Werding, M. 2003. Child expenditure and public pensions. In J. Bradshaw, ed., *Children and Social Security*. International Studies on Social Security, vol. 8. Aldershot: Ashgate, pp. 141–65.

World Bank. 2001. *Health, Nutrition, and Populations Statistics*. World Bank's Human Development Network ⟨http://devdata.worldbank.org/hnpstats⟩.

Zhang, J., and J. Zhang. 2004. How does social security affect economic growth? Evidence from cross-country data. *Journal of Population Economics* 17: 473–500.

Index